La Florida

Spanish Exploration & Settlement of
North America, 1500 to 1600

Solitude Press

La Florida
Spanish Exploration & Settlement of North America, 1500 to 1600

ISBN-13   978-1-928874-20-1 soft cover
ISBN-13   978-1-928874-21-8 hardcover

Printed in the United States of America

Published by:

Solitude Press
212 Brooks Street
Williamsburg VA 23185

To Kit
for her support, patience, and advice

To Annie
for her expert editing

And to Ann
for her love and unfailing encouragement

Table of Contents

Foreword

The study of history in the United States has traditionally proceeded from the perspective of British settlement in North America. Although modern social studies courses may mention Hernando de Soto's discovery of the Mississippi River or Juan Ponce de León's naming of Florida while on a quest for the "Fountain of Youth," our students (particularly in the eastern states) receive very little instruction regarding the important impact that the Spanish had on North America in the period before English adventurers began to settle along the East Coast.

These words spoken in 1932 by Herbert Eugene Bolton, president of the American Historical Society, still ring true:

> *In my own country the study of thirteen English colonies and the United States in isolation has obscured many of the larger factors in their development, and helped to raise up a nation of chauvinists." Bolton, in his presidential address, went on to say, "The universities of Mexico and Lima date from 1551, the Jesuit College of Quebec, ancestor of Laval University, from 1635, Harvard from 1636, William and Mary from 1695 [sic], and Yale from 1701. [Until] near the end of the eighteenth century, not Boston, not New York, not Charleston, not Quebec, but Mexico City was the metropolis of the entire Western Hemisphere.*

Bolton spent much of his career attempting to expand on our understanding of the Spanish influence in the Americas.

This book's nomenclature deviates from standard geographical terminology. In *La Florida*, North America generally refers to that portion of the continent above the Rio Grande. Mexico, or New Spain as it was called in the sixteenth century, is thus not included, primarily because of the marked difference in the success Spain had there versus in the rest of North America. Thus reference in this book to the

North American Indians or Native Americans excludes the Aztec and Maya Empires the Spaniards conquered in Mexico.

La Florida, the Spanish name for all of North America beyond the northern extent of New Spain, is somewhat of a moving target. As Spanish settlers pushed New Spain northward in the sixteenth century, La Florida was reduced, so that the territory included in La Florida varied as time progressed and as competing Spanish charters partitioned the land of North America under various conquistadors or governors. At the time of Ponce de León, La Florida represented nearly all of North America, and by the end of the sixteenth century La Florida designated approximately the eastern third of the continent. Modern-day place names, where known, are used without the customary "present-day" or "modern-day" to distinguish them from the sixteenth-century names. The reader will certainly recognize them as names originating long after the period covered in this book.

Accented and unaccented Spanish names appear in this book. Most Spanish and Portuguese names are as they should be written with accented letters, but some well-known historical figures such as Columbus and De Soto appear in their more familiar anglicized form.

This book provides a broad treatment of the Spanish exploration and settlement attempts in North America during the sixteenth century. With Hispanic citizens now making up the largest minority population in the United States, the time certainly has come to focus more on how and when Spain affected the Native American population of North America.

Of course, the Spanish attempts at settlement in North America had an effect on English and French settlement here as well. In the case of the French, harsh treatment by the Spanish put a decisive and chilling end to French settlement in what Spain termed La Florida. The English felt that same chill when they belatedly came to settle in North America, causing them to locate much farther north along the East Coast than they otherwise might have wished.

From the establishment of the first Spanish town on the American mainland, Santa Maria la Antigua at Darién in 1511, to Hernán Cortés' conquest of the Aztec empire, only ten years elapsed. Yet from Ponce de Léon's first landing in La Florida in 1513 until the end of the sixteenth century, Spain created only two fragile but continuously occupied settlements: Saint Augustine in Florida and Santo Domingo/Santa Fe in New Mexico.

One interesting question that arises when we consider Spain's failure to fully exploit the North American territory in the sixteenth century is how they could succeed so quickly and pervasively in Mexico, Central and South American and stumble so mightily in North America in spite of relatively massive expeditionary forces applied to their conquest attempts here.

The answer lies in the differences in the Indian cultures encountered in North America when compared to the Aztec, Maya, and Inca of Mexico, Central and South America. The political structure, the resources, and the diversity of the North American Indians meant that the Spanish techniques of conquest which proved so effective below the Rio Grande in the first few decades of the sixteenth century failed repeatedly in the territory to the north.

The Aztec and Inca cultures each dominated large geographic areas in which populations numbering in the hundreds of thousands came under the authority of centralized powers. These long-standing domineering authorities meant that there were complex political factions that the Spanish could exploit.

In the case of the Aztecs, Hernán Cortés eventually realized that he could enlist the support of a large and capable Indian polity that resented and opposed Aztec dominance in the central region of New Spain. Thus, with thousands of willing Indian allies, Cortés and his few hundred Spaniards, after first being ejected and suffering heavy casualties, were able to surround, lay siege to, and capture Tenochtitlán, the capital of the Aztec Empire. Cortés solidified Spanish dominance over New Spain relatively quickly. From that base, expeditions conquered other Indian polities in Central America.

In Peru, Francisco Pizarro took advantage of a civil war within the Inca Empire, backing a rival to Emperor (the Inca) Atahuallpa, to capture and dominate the Indian population. In Mexico and Peru, the presence of a strong, single Indian command structure allowed daring focused attacks to succeed.

The dispersion of the North American Indians into a wide diversity of cultures, language groups, and chiefdoms presented the Spanish with no central authority on which to focus their military efforts. Both Cortés and Pizarro also took advantage of Aztec and Incan mythology that predicted the return of a god, each conquistador assuming the god's identity to overthrow the power of Moctezuma and Atahuallpa.

Hernando de Soto participated in this successful campaign against the Inca. In North America, no similar mythology presented itself for exploitation. Although De Soto portrayed himself as the son of the sun god revered by North American Indians, he met skepticism. One doubting chief told De Soto he would believe that he was truly a god when he turned the Mississippi River dry. Consequently, techniques found highly successful in conquering the Aztec and Inca proved ineffective in North America.

Although it would seem that Spanish steel and firearms gave them an edge in weaponry, their European technology probably did not make much difference. Their two most important weapons were the horse and European diseases for which the American native population had no immunity.

The Indians had no experience with horses. Spaniards fighting with steel-tipped lances from horseback had a significant advantage over Indians on foot, lacking effective armor. Otherwise, Indian bows and arrows were about as deadly as Spanish harquebuses at any significant distance, and the Indians could fire six or more arrows in the time it took a

Spaniard to fire, reload and fire again. Surprisingly, a Native American bowman could shoot an arrow with sufficient force to penetrate Spanish armor. Also, nearly-naked Indian warriors were more nimble and effective in hand-to-hand combat against armor-clad Spaniards, who often were suffering from exhaustion, malnutrition, and sometimes illness.

Reflecting on the time when it appeared that they were doomed to become the next Aztec human sacrifices, one of Cortés' men said, "When the Christians were exhausted from war, God saw fit to send the Indians smallpox." The devastation that European diseases wrought on the Indian population certainly assisted the Spanish conquest in the Americas, and altered the balance of power among Indian cultures in North America. Conservatively, these diseases led to the reduction of Indian populations by at least one-third, and in some cases much more. Significant changes in the population of Indian cultures led to the coalescing of formerly hostile Indians into new alliances in North America.

In the empires of the Aztec and the Inca, Cortés and Pizarro found little difficulty maintaining the morale of their men in the face of incredible caches of gold and precious gems. Although North America would later provide gold and silver for those lucky enough to find and mine it, the Native Americans did not have gold or silver in any quantity. In the southeast, what the Indians did have came primarily from precious metals they had scavenged from wrecked Spanish treasure ships. The Spaniards found some quantities of copper and pearls, but those materials did not provide sufficient incentive to keep the men focused on the hard work of conquest and settlement when faced with long marches through difficult—sometimes impassable—terrain, starvation, and nearly continuous guerrilla attacks by hostile Indians.

Although the Spanish failed to establish an extensive network of settlements in North America prior to English settlement in Virginia at the beginning of the seventeenth century, Spain's assertion of dominion over North America and their presence in La Florida forced the English to look to the mid-Atlantic region for their first outpost. The Indians that the English first contacted were suspicious and wary of these other Europeans who came in search of gold, silver, and conquest; their suspicion resulted from years of sad experiences at the hands of the Spanish conquistadors and missionaries.

Regarding the organization of this book: Chapter 1 provides a short overview of the Native American cultures at the time of the Spanish incursion into the territory north of the Rio Grande; Chapter 2 provides a summary of the earliest Spanish expeditions into the Caribbean, Mexico, and Central America, ending with Cortés conquering the Aztec empire and establishing New Spain. Subsequent chapters develop the story of the Spanish exploration and settlement of North America more or less chronologically, focusing on that area that would become the United States of America more than a century later.

Chapter 1
The Native Americans

Paquinquineo had reached his breaking point. At age twenty-four he was ready to assume his place as a leading member of his tribe in the area his Spanish overlords called Bahia de Santa Maria and the English soon would call the Chesapeake Bay.

When he was fourteen, Spaniards had plucked him from an Atlantic shore and had taken him on a ten-year odyssey; first to Cuba, then to New Spain, and finally to Spain. Along the way they had baptized him, given him a new Spanish name, and subjected him to what they called education, depriving him of his opportunity to hone his skills as a warrior.

After tricking Jesuit priests into letting him lead them back to his homeland so that they could "convert" his countrymen, he had finally returned to his longed-for Indian way of life. Now the troublesome priests criticized him for marrying more than one woman, and their incessant demands for food finally became intolerable.

Paquinquineo and some other Indian warriors followed three of the Jesuits into the forest and put a quick end to them with their war clubs. They would do the same to the rest of the Spanish priests very soon. Perhaps elimination of these priests would deter more Spaniards from invading his domain.

This relatively obscure incident in the history of Spanish exploration and settlement of North America typifies the clash between Christian cultures from Europe and Native American cultures that had equally valid and successful beliefs in the sixteenth century. Since the Native Americans were here first, we take up their story first in this account of the Spanish in North America.

In 1921, historian Herbert Bolton wrote:

> *The conquest of the Aztecs, living in permanent towns, proved comparatively easy for Cortés, with his superior means of waging war; but the subjection of the northern tribes, who had no fixed abodes, who wandered over hundreds of miles in hunting and war, was another task. Europeans began the conquest of America by seizing Indians and selling them into slavery. It is an oft-repeated boast that tyranny has never thrived on American soil, but it is seldom remembered that the first battles for freedom in this land were fought by the red natives.*

Today we refer to these first warriors for freedom as Native Americans or Indians. Both terms appear in this book in reference to the people who occupied North America when the Spanish arrived in the early sixteenth century.

It might help to know a little bit more about these people incorrectly called Indians by Christopher Columbus and later European invaders. Until the end of the twentieth century, we felt certain that Native Americans descended from a relatively small population of Asiatic hunter gatherers who followed migrating herds of prey animals across the Bering land bridge and into the Americas about 13,000 years ago. However, finds of human artifacts such as worked-stone projectile points buried at Cactus Hill in Virginia, dating to 17,000 years ago, have led to new theories proposing who the first Americans were.

For humans to have arrived in the Americas at that time, they could not have come overland from Asia because a mile-high glacier blocked their way. Consequently, several theories have now gained adherents arguing that the first Americans arrived from Asia, Europe, or some other region, by boat. These theories receive some additional support from nearly 9,000-year-old human remains that appear markedly different from other more-typically Asiatic Native American remains (Kennewick Man) and from DNA analysis that shows European haplogroup markers in some Indian genetic material—a European genetic infusion dating back approximately 15,000 years. Although these issues are far from resolved, it appears that the Native Americans of the sixteenth century were descended from ancestors who arrived in the Americas over a broad period of time and from a variety of origins in Europe, Africa, and Asia.

When the Spanish arrived in North America in the early 1500s, the continent contained hundreds of separate cultures, relatively small populations speaking distinct dialects in perhaps a dozen or so major language groups, banded into chiefdoms overseeing small numbers of towns or villages, sometimes owing allegiance and paying tribute to regional paramount chiefs.

Frequently, people living in settlements separated by as little as fifty miles could not communicate using spoken language. In those situations, they had to rely on a universal sign language to move safely through outlying regions, to bargain for trade goods, or to treat for peace. Language barriers greatly complicated the movement of the Spanish through the North American countryside. They used a series of Indian interpreters to learn what lay beyond, to determine whether the Indians in neighboring settlements were friendly or hostile, and what food they would find along the way. Their constant question posed to these Native American interpreters sought the location of the most powerful nation, hopefully one with a hoard of gold or silver—another Aztec-type empire. The Indian interpreters, sometimes in collusion with others, quickly learned that the way to get rid of the Spanish interlopers before they exhausted the local food supply was to send them far away to an imaginary source of gold, ideally a region occupied by the local Indians' enemies.

Indian village in North Carolina in 1586

Some of the chiefdoms encountered by the early Spanish explorers were as described above by Bolton, people who lived as hunter gatherers wandering hundreds of miles across the Great Plains, living in temporary shelters that they carried with them. However, in much of North America, the Indians lived in permanent settlements that had existed for hundreds if not thousands of years.

These settlements varied in size from less than twenty houses to hundreds of houses. Many settlements had major religious and ceremonial structures such as earthen mounds seventy feet high, often with houses and temples atop the mound.

Indian communities contained mausoleums where their high-ranking dead reposed along with community treasures. Some villages were undefended, others stood within stout palisade walls covered with reinforced clay mortar and equipped with flanking towers from which bowmen could provide an effective field of crossfire.

Depending on the climate, Native American houses consisted of round huts built of saplings, with walls covered by woven mats and palm thatched roofs, or more substantial wooden structures of timber wall joists and a number of stout center posts supporting peaked roofs. These latter buildings often had walls made of wattle and daub quite similar to the medieval houses in Europe, lacking only a chimney to make the comparison complete. Instead, the Indian houses had central fire pits that provided heat in the winter as well as a

Zuni Pueblo ca. 1903

place for cooking. In warm weather, cooking often took place outside the house. Still other houses, in the temperate mid-Atlantic settlements, consisted of longhouses made of bent saplings forming curved arches over which woven mats or bark provided a waterproof covering. In colder climates the timber framed houses were set into the ground, and soil mounded around the base prevented water from flooding the interior and sealed out the cold drafts. In the Southwest, the Indian pueblos of adobe and stone construction provided multi-level housing that lasted for thousands of years.

In addition to their weapons and boats, the Indians made useful household craft items including woven baskets for storage, transport, and cooking; ceramic pottery vessels and platters made using the coiled-clay method; and carved wooden chests for storage. The latter, found in Indian mortuary houses, contained human remains, according to the Spanish chronicles. Indians also made effigies depicting various deities. In one report, carved life-sized images of animals and human warriors confronted Spanish explorers when they entered a village mausoleum.

Although we tend to think of the Indians as going about either naked, except for a loin cloth for modesty, or draped in an animal hide cape, American Indians wore a wide variety of clothing well-adapted to their environment and lifestyle. In the tropical regions, the Indians wore little if any clothing; however, in the temperate and colder climates they wore capes, leggings, and a type of shift or dress. These garments were stitched together from worked hides of deer and bear, as well as pelts of martin, sable, and the like that the Spanish treasured perhaps more than the Indians did. They also wore clothing made from fabrics woven from various plant fibers. Their clothes, whether of skin or cloth, were dyed in a variety of bright colors and decorated with painted designs.

Indians decorated their bodies with permanent tattoos or with painted designs using vegetable and mineral dyes. They wore various adornments in their pierced ears, lips, and breasts, wore chains around their necks, and decorations in their hair. The Indians highly prized pearls and shells for jewelry and decoration. The Spanish also considered the pearls quite valuable and were astounded at the great quantity and size of pearls found in some locations. However, the value of the pearls did not come close to offsetting the Spanish desire for gold and silver, both of which they found lacking among the North American Indians. High ranking Indians wore emblems of authority suspended around their necks including copper or shell gorgets. They decorated these devices of power with mythological designs or totemic symbols.

These Indian chiefdoms were often at war with adjoining communities. During times of war, they fought and killed their opponents with clubs, lances, and bows and arrows, using fire to flush out their enemies, destroying their settlements and returning home with trophies that included severed heads or scalps. Some of these battles included thousands of warriors arrayed in formations, but more commonly, the engagements consisted of ambushes or guerrilla attacks. In addition to heads and scalps, the victors returned to their settlements with women and children captured from their enemy as well as food, baskets, skins, and other booty. The Indians in various parts of North America highly valued copper, pearls, turquoise, shells, and animal pelts.

Native Americans had the ability to employ naval forces and tactics in battle. De Soto's expedition encountered a flotilla of Indian canoes on the Mississippi River that proved formidable, engaging in flanking tactics, cutting off Spanish boats and overwhelming them. The Indian battle line divided into squadrons that attacked in coordinated assaults from different directions with about seventy warriors in each canoe. Clearly, some Indian chiefdoms had military capability equal to the Spanish in the early sixteenth century.

Scalps and other trophies of war

North American Indians had highly developed mythology and religious beliefs, generally including a belief in the spirit's existence after death, a supreme deity as well as lesser gods, friendly and malevolent spirits, heaven, and hell. They made images of some of their gods and maintained them in temple structures.

A common creation concept runs through most North American mythology. They divided the world into three realms: the sky; the Earth with its land and waters; and the underworld. The sky was the realm of benevolent gods—the sun and moon—who created the world and gave it bountiful resources. All life began in the waters before some creatures moved to the land. The underworld harbored malevolent spirits that brought misery, famine, disease, and discord to humanity.

People had to deal properly with the benevolent and malevolent forces to achieve a balanced existence on Earth.

They revered the sun and moon, while propitiating the malevolent spirits as well. When the good and evil forces of nature were out of balance, droughts would come or other natural disasters would occur.

American Indian art often depicts these opposing forces of nature embodied in creatures such as a bird symbolizing the benevolent realm of the sky and a water serpent representing the underworld. In Indian art, these mythical creatures are depicted in a deadly struggle between good and evil.

Although all people took part in helping to maintain a positive balance within the natural world, the shaman served his community as the principal intermediary between the world of humans and the realms of the spirits. The shaman held ceremonies to placate these spirits to ensure prosperity and health for the community. Under his direction, the whole community participated in harvest festivals, such as the Green Corn ceremony, and other rites to ensure peace, plenty, and harmony within the community. The shaman interceded with the spirit world not only to end droughts, to bring forth a bounteous harvest, or to make the hunters successful, but also to heal the injured or the sick.

The shaman's ability to treat common medical problems and injuries was about as effective as European medicine at the time—in some cases more effective. For instance, the shaman didn't resort to bloodletting as European doctors did; consequently, he didn't introduce infection or further weaken an already sick or injured patient. On the other hand, the shaman had a variety of herbal remedies that proved effective, and he excelled at the psychological element of healing.

Álvar Núñez Cabeza de Vaca learned the power of shamanism from the Indians on his long trek across the American Southwest in the early 1500s. He survived, and at the end of his travels, led a huge following of Indians due to his reputation as a healer. He emulated the Indian shamans he met but substituted Christian prayers for the shamanic incantations. Many of the cures that he took credit for had a strong psychological component, although he attributed his success to divine intervention.

The Native Americans had well-developed civic ceremonies and protocols. Chiefs often appeared carried on litters covered by a canopy or traveled in special canoes also fitted with canopies. They staged entertainments in the plazas of their settlements complete with dancers and musicians playing flutes as well as drums. They carried distinctive banners into battle, and on the Mississippi, an attacking armada that followed the Spaniards down river paddled in multiple squadrons of canoes, each squadron composed of canoes painted in a distinct color. Tascaluza, chief of thousands of Indians in Alabama, had an emblem resembling a Maltese cross of white on a black background.

Indians engaged in slavery and traded slaves as chattel between chiefdoms. In some cases they hobbled the slaves by severing a tendon in one foot to make it harder for the slave to escape captivity. The Indians equaled the Europeans in torture and brutality when dealing with their opponents. Sometimes they killed women and children; they burned people alive in their dwellings; and they tied up captives and flayed them alive. They returned from skirmishes with their enemies' scalps or severed heads to display and prove their prowess as warriors.

In one reported case, the Indians of Florida erected a barbeque and began grilling a captured Spaniard, then relented, unfortunately not before the man had received serious burns that permanently disfigured him. In assessing brutality, it is probably impossible to conclude whether the Spaniards who cut off Indians' noses, hands and feet were more barbarous than the Indians. Both cultures carried out punishments that we cannot sanction today, but in the sixteenth century, they did not appear particularly extreme in Europe or among the Native Americans.

A barbacoa in Florida

Women as well as men led chiefdoms among the North American Indians. In fact, tribal leadership or authority passed through the matrilineal line. The Spanish and later the English encountered Indian women who led powerful chiefdoms in the Mid-Atlantic region. Generally, leadership of an Indian community employed a council, headed by the chief and composed of elders selected for their wisdom and accomplishments. Decisions came about from deliberation within the council, not from autocratic rule by the chief.

North American Indians generally approached the first Spanish they encountered in an open, non-threatening way. Their natural curiosity and their interest in trade shaped their conduct in these first meetings. Once the Indians had had protracted experience with the Spanish, hostility and mistrust developed.

In Florida, Spanish slave traders made the first contacts with the native population. Clearly, these interactions left the Indian population wary of the foreigners who came by sea. Thus, when Ponce de León and others made landfall in Florida, they met Indian hostility at the outset. But in other areas removed from the coast, the initial contacts between

Spaniards and Indians proceeded with curiosity and openness. Spanish conduct, however, soon drove the Indians to open warfare or passive resistance.

During De Soto's expedition through America, the Spanish captured an estimated 300 to 600 Indian women. Often they captured more women than men. They captured men to serve as porters and guides. The women served to satisfy the sexual desires of the Spaniards. This may not have been the case in the capture of the "Lady of Cofitachequi."

De Soto routinely captured the chief of each region he entered, holding that leader hostage until his expedition reached the next center of authority. He used this technique to minimize hostile attacks by the followers of each chief.

The female Indian leader in the region of Cofitachequi (South Carolina) received the same treatment in spite of the initial hospitality and cooperation she offered the Spanish, but she escaped and avoided recapture. This woman, whose name we don't know, ruled over a broad area of the Carolinas as a paramount chief. We can only wonder what treatment she received from De Soto and what her fate would have been had she not escaped.

We can imagine the fate of most of the captured Indian women. The liaisons between Spaniards and Indian women in North America must have resulted in a large number of children of mixed heritage left behind along the routes of the Spanish conquistadors. These children might have carried a beneficial legacy from their fathers—a greater resistance to European diseases.

Although many Indians died in combat with the Spanish invaders, a great many more died of diseases brought to them from Europe—diseases for which they had no defense. In North America, whole communities succumbed to small pox, measles and other diseases that did not exist on the continent before the Spanish came. Estimates of this devastation run up to ninety percent of the indigenous population.

The huge loss of life due to combat and disease caused major shifts in the centers of power in sixteenth-century North America. Indian communities that suffered most had no choice but to align with or become assimilated within other communities—at times with former enemies—to survive. Thus, Indians such as the Cherokee, who feature prominently during the eighteenth and nineteenth centuries, represent one such coalescing of a number of precursor communities. This process played out in various regions of North America in which Spanish contact led to severe population decline among the Native American settlements.

Other changes in Indian culture occurred as contact with the Spanish, and later other European colonists, forced the Indians into new political alliances and caused them to adapt to new technologies, new agriculture, and new beliefs.

Consequently, the Indian cultures of the early sixteenth century soon faced modification or extinction. The American Indians encountered and written about by later colonizers certainly differed from their ancestors of a century before. Aside from Spanish accounts dating to their earliest incursions into North America, we must depend on oral history of the successor Indian cultures, accounts of later explorers, anthropologists, and the work of archaeologists to know what the population of North America was like before European contact.

Valladolid Debate

In the mid-sixteenth century, the Spanish church authorities were divided over how to treat the Indians. Bishop of Chiapas Bartolomé de las Casas documented the cruelty suffered by the Indians at the hands of the conquistadors. He argued that American Indians deserved their freedom and humane treatment like any other citizens of Spain.

In a protracted formal debate held in Valladolid, Las Casas argued from first-hand experience that the Indians were fully rational human beings deserving of equal treatment under Spanish law. He believed that they could be converted to the Christian faith through kindness, respect and education.

Juan Ginés de Sepúlveda, a fellow Dominican, opposed Las Casas in the debate. Sepúlveda argued, partially on the philosophy of Aristotle, that Indians lived as barbarians and by their nature deserved to be enslaved. He supported the encomienda system instituted in the New World by Spain.

Under that system Spanish land owners in the Americas received grants of specified numbers of Indians from whom they could extract tribute in the form of gold, silver, corn, hides or other products. In exchange for the tribute, the holder of the encomienda had the obligation to care for the Indians, see to their physical welfare and convert them to the Christian faith. In practice, the Indians under the encomienda system lived as slaves, exploited and worked to an early death. The Spanish overlords placed little emphasis on education or conversion of the Indians to the Christian faith.

At Valladolid both sides claimed victory in the debate. Las Casas had some influence on the Spanish crown and later royal decrees called for humane treatment of the Indians, but little changed in the New World.

Chapter 2
First Contact

This chapter presents the gradual expansion of Spanish
exploration and settlement from the first colony at
Hispaniola to the initial settlement of the mainland at
Darién, presents Ponce de León's establishment of La
Florida, Balboa's expedition to the South Sea, and concludes
with the conquest of New Spain by Cortés.

Christopher Columbus sailed out from Palos de la Frontera
on August 3, 1492 aboard a carrack named *Santa Maria*
capping a seven-year lobbying effort. His brother Bartolomeo
had attempted to gain English sponsorship for a voyage west
from King Henry VII, and Columbus had made two
unsuccessful attempts to sell his idea to King João II of
Portugal in 1485 and 1488. He also traveled to Genoa and
Venice in an attempt to gain support from venture capitalists
in those two republics. All those attempts failed.

His plan—to establish a sea route to Asia by sailing
west—was controversial. Columbus argued that his proposed
route would be no longer than the traditional eastern route
that had fallen under the control of the Ottoman Empire.
Portugal planned to circumvent the bottlenecked land route
by sailing around Africa and up to the Asian silk and spice

ports. King João decided to follow that more conservative approach and Bartolomeu Dias returned in 1488 with the encouraging news that he had rounded the southern tip of Africa.

Sensing that the Portuguese crown was not likely to give him the support he wanted, Columbus also approached the recently (1479) combined monarchies of Aragon and Castile. On May 1, 1486, Columbus met with King Ferdinand II of Aragon and Queen Isabella of Castile. He proposed that he could pioneer a new route across the western ocean to the Indies and that the route would take no longer than the eastern journey. Ferdinand and Isabella listened attentively and told Columbus they would have a committee consider his proposal. You can imagine Columbus's reaction—death by committee. After a great deal of deliberation, the royal advisers judged Columbus's plan to be impractical. They concluded, correctly, that he had greatly underestimated the distance to Asia.

But Ferdinand and Isabella decided to hedge their bets. Since they didn't want Portugal or some other power to undertake the Columbus plan, they awarded him a substantial annual stipend of 12,000 maravedis (worth about $40,000 to $50,000 today) and gave him a royal letter ordering all towns and cities in their realms to give him food and lodging for free. That stipend provided Columbus with financial support for the several years it took him to finally convince the monarchs to back his expedition west.

Although Columbus had miscalculated the distance to the Indies, he felt certain that land could be reached by sailing west across the Atlantic Ocean. Norse sailors had found land beyond Greenland in the north, as had Portuguese João Vaz Corte-Reale only a decade or so before Columbus hatched his plan. Those voyages had discovered Newfoundland and the rich fisheries located there. English fishermen from Bristol also knew that route, and they had rejected Columbus's plan when his brother, Bartolomeo, presented it.

Christopher Columbus had most likely visited Iceland, where he would have learned about prior voyages to the west. When Columbus visited Galway, Ireland, he probably heard the stories of Brendan the Navigator's sixth-century voyage to a rich land across the western sea and his successful return. He certainly had heard the stories of the expeditions of Welsh Prince Madoc. He made a marginal note of Madoc's passage through the West Indies on one of the maps that he took on his pioneering voyage. Columbus clearly had reason to believe that land would be found before his crew ran out of food and water while traversing the western sea.

In 1481/1482, Columbus had sailed down the western coast of Africa to Ghana. On that voyage he learned of the westerly winds that could carry vessels across the ocean. Those offshore breezes between the Canaries and the Cape Verde Islands provide a conveyor that sweeps ships out to sea; experienced mariners traveling along the African coast would have talked about those westerly winds.

Columbus misjudged the distance to Asia, but his plan to sail south and pick up the westerly breezes ensured that his ships would not sail off into a vast unbounded sea. He had good reason to believe that he could reach a land beyond the western horizon and return to tell about it. He also had hope that the land would provide resources to make him a wealthy man.

In 1492, Ferdinand and Isabella finally authorized the expedition, providing some funding from the royal treasuries, but not before further drama. Isabella told Columbus that she would not support his venture on advice of her confessor. Then, as Columbus rode down the dusty trail out of Córdoba in defeat, Ferdinand convinced Isabella to relent. A royal guard found the dejected mariner and brought him back for another audience. In addition to support from Ferdinand and

Isabella, Columbus used funds he had secured in Genoa and Venice.

At last having the necessary financial backing and royal authority, Columbus assembled his fleet of three ships. In addition to the seventy-foot-long carrack *Santa Maria*, his flag ship, with a crew of about forty men, two smaller caravels, *Nina* and *Pinta* carried about twenty-four men each. The Pinzón brothers, Vicente Yáñez and Martin Alonso, captained the caravels.

Within a month, Columbus's small fleet reached the Canaries where they replenished their stores of water and food. They sailed away from La Gomera on September 6th and ventured into unknown territory for about five nerve-wracking weeks. On October 12th they spotted land, a tiny island in the Bahamas called Guanahani by its inhabitants and San Salvador by Columbus. The natives of the Caribbean called themselves Lucayan, Arawak, Taino, or Carib. Columbus called them "Indians," insisting that he had reached the fringes of the Indies in Asia. He also had this to say about these island occupants:

> *They ought to make good and skilled servants, for they repeat very quickly whatever we say to them. I think they can very easily be made Christians, for they seem to have no religion. If it pleases our Lord, I will take six of them to Your Highnesses when I depart, in order that they may learn our language. I could conquer the whole of them with 50 men, and govern them as I pleased.*

And Columbus did exactly that. His initial demeaning assessment of the Indians defined the Spanish attitude toward the indigenous people of the Americas at the end of the fifteenth and beginning of the sixteenth century.

Columbus went on to reconnoiter the northern coasts of Hispaniola and Cuba before leaving thirty-nine men to secure La Navidad, his first city in the New World, located in Haiti. On March 15, 1493, he arrived back in Palos with seven or eight natives of Hispaniola—all that remained from approximately twenty he kidnapped there. The rest died during the voyage. Columbus made three more voyages to the New World, returning from his last voyage November 7, 1504.

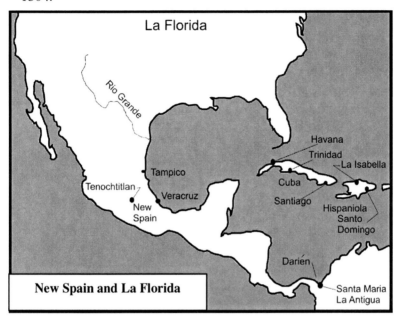

New Spain and La Florida

In his later voyages, Columbus sailed west until he encountered the coast of South America and Central America but found no passage beyond those lands. Nonetheless, the Spanish explorers who followed Columbus would consider all the lands they had found islands. Balboa would "discover" the South Sea (Pacific Ocean) and that would spur more exploration along the coasts of the Americas in quest of a passage connecting the Atlantic or the Caribbean to the Pacific. Throughout the sixteenth century, Spain sought this nonexistent passage to establish the commercially viable route to the Indies that Columbus had promised.

In 1493, La Isabella, Hispaniola (the island comprising Haiti and the Dominican Republic today), became Spain's first permanent settlement in America. By 1502, Hispaniola came under the authority of Governor Nicolás de Ovando. The

Spanish had discovered gold there and established mining villages and ports to exploit that resource. They raised cattle and exported hides as well as gold, but it was the gold that brought men from Spain to that island. The quest for gold quickly became Spain's top priority in the Americas, and subsequent settlement patterns around the Caribbean related directly to either finding gold or securing the safe transport of gold (and later silver) back to Spain. All other activities such as sugar cane production were secondary to the accumulation of gold. The Spanish also exploited the Indians of Hispaniola, employing them in the mines, as servants, and as laborers on sugar cane farms.

East of Hispaniola, Puerto Rico offered additional land for development with gold in the streams flowing down from the highlands. In 1506, Juan Ponce de León explored Puerto Rico, or Boriquen, as the Taino Indians called it. This was his second glimpse of the island, and one he had to keep secret. He had first seen the island of Boriquen when he sailed to the Caribbean in 1493 aboard one of Columbus's ships in his second voyage.

Spanish Goals in North America

Spanish explorers of North America had several goals:
1. First the discovery of gold, silver, precious gems
2. Location of the mythical passage between the Atlantic and Pacific
3. Establishment of fortified coastal ports to increase security for the annual treasure shipment from New Spain to Spain
4. Annexation and settlement of fertile lands for farming and cattle production.

That last goal appears to have been a very low priority based on the decisions made and the actions taken by the conquistadors in North America.

The crown had granted Vicente Yáñez Pinzón the right to settle the Puerto Rico, but he had not moved quickly enough, and his grant expired the year after Ponce de León made his secret trip there. Ponce de León moved quickly to secure the right to settle Boriquen.

Ponce de León came from a prominent family in Valladolid. He was born in 1474 in the village of Santervás de Campos, and as a young man, he was squire to Pedro Núñez de Guzmán, an important Spanish knight. By age eighteen, Ponce de León had gained valuable experience as a soldier fighting against the last Moorish forces in Spain.

Ponce de León.

He took part in the campaigns that drove the Moors from Granada in 1492. The next year he made his first voyage to the New World with Columbus. He traveled as one of 200 gentlemen on that second expedition and landed in Hispaniola where he eventually served as lieutenant to Governor Ovando.

In 1504, Ponce de León led Spanish forces against Taino Indians, putting down their rebellion. Ovando rewarded Ponce de León with the governorship of the new province of Higüey at the eastern end of Hispaniola. He married Leonora, an innkeeper's daughter, and they lived in a stone house in Higüey where they had three daughters and a son.

Following Ponce de León's secret trip to Boriquen where he found clear evidence of gold, he sought and received royal permission to conduct an official expedition to explore that island. In 1508, with fifty men, he sailed to San Juan Bay. Near there he built a storehouse and a small fort—the first Spanish settlement on San Juan Bautista, as Puerto Rico was called then.

After finding a significant amount of gold, Ponce de León and his men returned to Hispaniola. Ovando named Ponce de León governor of San Juan Bautista, and King Ferdinand confirmed the appointment on August 14, 1509.

Ponce de León had become wealthy in his first years in Hispaniola; he would add greatly to that wealth during his time in Puerto Rico, in spite of some political setbacks when Diego Colón, son of Christopher Columbus, took over control of Hispaniola. By 1511, Diego Colón achieved control of Puerto Rico and installed his own man there. That same year, the Spanish began the settlement of Cuba.

Soon after the Spanish began settlement of Hispaniola, slavers sailed to other islands and to the mainland of North America in search of Indian captives. They brought these unfortunate Indians to Hispaniola to work in the mines and on the plantations, replenishing the indigenous population that had succumbed to disease and harsh working conditions. A few African slaves had also been brought to Hispaniola from Spain. In 1518, the first shipment of African slaves coming directly from Guinea would arrive in the Caribbean. Eventually, African slaves would take the place of the Indian slaves, but that was yet to come.

Ponce de León had heard rumors of land to the north of Hispaniola and Puerto Rico from these slave traders. How long they had been bringing Indian captives from the north we don't know, since they didn't document those voyages. In 1511, King Ferdinand encouraged Ponce de León to seek out these new lands to the north. Juan Ponce readily agreed since he had lost his governorship of Puerto Rico.

The rumored land, believed to be an island, was called Bimini. King Ferdinand awarded Ponce de León a contract for the exclusive right to seek and settle Bimini and the adjoining islands for a period of three years. The contract began in February 1512. In addition, Juan Ponce would have the title of governor of those new lands for life. Ferdinand made no royal funds available for this venture—Ponce de León had to fund the entire enterprise. This royal policy would apply to most of the Spanish ventures into North America.

The small fleet of three ships—*Santiago, San Cristobal,* and *Santa Maria del Consolacion*—sailed from Puerto Rico on March 4, 1513, under guidance of pilot Anton de Alaminos. They coasted northwest along the Bahamas and reached Great Abaco Island on Easter Sunday, March 27th. Continuing to sail with the Bahamas astern, they crossed the open waters and sighted land on April 2nd. Ponce de León thought they had found another island, but they had reached the southern peninsula of North America. He named this land La Florida in honor of the Easter season (Pascua Florida in Spanish).

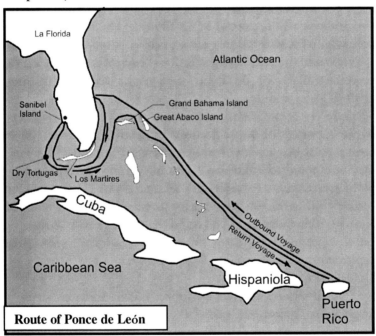

Route of Ponce de León

We can't be sure exactly where they made landfall, but the spot was somewhere in the middle portion of the east coast of Florida. They stayed at that first landfall for five days before heading south. Sailing out into the Florida passage between the mainland and the Bahamas, they discovered the Gulf Stream. The strong northerly current forced them backwards and carried the *San Cristobal* off into the distance.

It took that ship two days to make its way back to the other two.

In order to avoid the strongest flow of the Gulf Stream, they hugged the coast and continued their explorations down the east side of the peninsula, around the tip at Biscayne Bay, and along the Florida Keys, which they reached in mid-May. Ponce de León named the Keys Los Martires (The Martyrs), because he said, at a distance, they looked like suffering men. Sailing through a passage in the Keys, they headed toward the west coast of Florida, making a landfall on May 23, probably at the Charlotte Harbor/Sanibel Island area.

They anchored there for several days and had their first encounter with the people of La Florida. The wary Indians at first seemed interested in trading, but as soon as the Spanish approached, the Indians attacked and men were wounded on both sides. Ponce de León took eight Indians prisoner. Spanish slave traders may have already visited this area.

June 14, they sailed southwest for the Dry Tortugas, having learned of those islands from their captives. They found giant sea turtles (tortugas) there. From the Tortugas, they attempted to sail below Cuba but strong currents carried them too far east to sail south of the island. They changed course and retraced their path eastward along the Florida Keys to the Bahamas. At Grand Bahama Island, Ponce de León ordered the *Santa Maria* to continue with their explorations, and he sailed back to Puerto Rico, arriving on October 19th.

Puerto Rico was in turmoil. Carib Indians from a neighboring island had raided the settlement of Caparra and Ponce de León's family had narrowly escaped with their lives. Viceroy Diego Colón was continuing to make trouble as well. So Ponce de León sailed back to Spain to report to the royal court in Valladolid and to the La Casa y Audiencia de Indias (also known as the Casa de Contratación).

Ponce de León used his time at the royal court to negotiate a new contract ensuring his control over La Florida and Bimini. As part of his contract, the king charged him with a requirement to read a legal document to the natives of these new lands before he conquered them. This document, in Castilian, notified the Indians that the Spanish king claimed dominion over them and that the Catholic Church would be their new religion. They could either subject themselves voluntarily to the king and church or they would be forced to submit through military force. Inclusion of this "Requerimeinto" in Ponce de León's contract may be the first instance of its use in the New World.

The Casa de Contratación levied a tax on all goods coming into Spain from the Indies (ten to forty percent) and used some of those revenues to provide armed escorts for the merchant vessels sailing to and from the West Indies. The Casa also served as the repository for all the navigational data accumulated during the voyages of exploration.

They compiled that information into the Padrón Real— the secret map that reflected the latest information on the geography of the New World. The bureaucrats at the Casa kept notes of all that Ponce de León had discovered on his voyage to La Florida.

He also received orders to assemble an armada to wage war on the Carib Indians and bring them into submission. His small fleet of three ships set sail on May 14, 1515. He apparently had some success against the Caribs but details are lacking in the Spanish records.

Ponce de León spent the next six years in the Caribbean pursuing his business interests. By 1521, he felt ready to begin colonizing La Florida under the terms of his royal contract. With 200 men (farmers, artisans, priests), fifty horses and other animals, plows and other farm equipment, he departed for La Florida to create his first settlement.

They went ashore near where he had made landfall in 1513, on the west coast of Florida near Charlotte Harbor or the Caloosahatchee River at Sanibel Island. Quickly, Indians came out of the forest and attacked them. These Calusa Indians either remembered the capture of eight of their people by Ponce de León nearly a decade before, or perhaps

Spanish slavers had attacked them. In any case, they were hostile to the idea of Spanish living among them.

The Governor of La Florida felt an arrow slam into his shoulder. The arrowhead, penetrating deeply into his flesh, carried the poisonous sap of the manchineel tree, one of the most poisonous trees growing in Florida. Ponce de León had little time left. He and his settlers withdrew from La Florida and hurried to Cuba. He made it to Havana but died soon after. His men took the body of their governor back to Puerto Rico where he was buried. His memorial stone flanks the nave of the Catedral de San Juan Bautista in Old San Juan. Construction of the cathedral began in 1521. It is the second oldest cathedral in the western hemisphere. Catedral Santa Maria la Menor in Santo Domingo begun in 1514 is the oldest.

Ponce de León Memorial at Catedral de San Juan Bautista San Juan, Puerto Rico

This first attempt at settlement in North America came to naught in an instant due to the hostility of the Native Americans there. The Indians undoubtedly had provocation, not only from Ponce de León's first visit eight years before but also more likely from the depredation of Spanish slave traders. The slavers continued to visit the North American mainland during the next decade, and future conquistadors would experience the logical result of these attacks on the Indians of La Florida.

At this time La Florida referred to nearly all of Central and North America from above the recently conquered Darién coastal territory up to Tierra de los Bacalaos—what today we call Newfoundland. No one knew the full extent of North America, but Spain claimed sovereignty over the continent, basing their claim on the Papal Bulls of Donation of Pope Alexander VI and the Treaty of Tordesillas between Castile and Portugal. The treaty meant that all of North America, Central America, and all but the easternmost bulge of South America belonged to Spain.

Papal Bulls of Donation

Pope Alexander VI, born in Valencia, Spain, led a most interesting life for a man of the cloth. He had three sons and a daughter by his mistress, and one of them, Cesare, he made Archbishop of Valencia while still a seventeen-year-old student at Pisa.

In 1493, at the request of Ferdinand and Isabella, Pope Alexander conferred title to the Americas to the Spanish sovereigns. The next year, Spain and Portugal (or more precisely Castile and Aragon with Portugal) concluded a treaty that ceded ownership of lands to the west of a line of longitude 370 leagues (about 1,100 miles) west of the Cape Verde Islands to Spain. Lands to the east belonged to Portugal. This treaty applied to lands not already under the dominion of a Christian ruler.

Obviously, the Papal Bulls and the bi-lateral treaty signed in Spain carried little weight in the rest of Europe, particularly after England separated from the Roman Catholic Church and France began to exercise its own expansionist tendencies. However, in the early sixteenth century, Spain had no significant rivals for the land in North America other than those native people who already lived there. They would prove much more difficult to deal with than the would-be Spanish conquistadors reckoned.

Vasco Núñez de Balboa

After the settlement of Hispaniola, Puerto Rico, and Cuba, two years before Juan Ponce first discovered La Florida, Spain established its first town on the mainland, Santa Maria la Antigua del Darién on the Isthmus of Panama (in Colombia) founded by Vasco Núñez de Balboa. Balboa first came to this region in 1500 as a member of an exploratory crew sent out by Rodrigo de Bastidas to look for treasure. He returned with sufficient money to establish himself in Hispaniola as a pig farmer and planter, but not a very prosperous one.

In 1509, to escape his debts, Balboa stowed away aboard a ship bound for Darién by hiding in a barrel with his dog. When the ship's master discovered Balboa, he threatened to maroon him on the first uninhabited island they found. But he relented and Balboa joined forces with Francisco Pizarro when he landed in Colombia.

Since Balboa had knowledge of this region from his voyage nine years earlier, he suggested they establish their settlement at a location on the Gulf of Mexico that he knew to be suitable. As they neared that site, they came up against a force of 500 Indians under the command of Cémaco, casique (chief) of that tribe. The greatly outnumbered Spanish made a vow to the Virgin of Antigua that if they were victorious over the Indians, they would name their settlement in her honor. A fierce battle ensued, but the Spaniards won the day. After the Indians fled from their village, the Spanish collected a large quantity of gold ornaments. This Indian village became the first Spanish town on the continent, and after some political turmoil, Balboa became governor of the region.

Balboa then began a series of exploratory voyages and treks across land, looking for treasure. He accumulated a great deal of gold that he seized from the Indians he encountered. In 1513, Balboa and his men arrived at the Quarequa Indian settlement. Apparently, in this village the Indians practiced homosexuality in an open and accepted way. Balboa, scandalized by the Indians' behavior, set his dogs upon them. Here is how contemporary Spanish historian, Peter Martyr (an Italian), recorded the event:

Vasco discovered that the village of Quarequa was stained by the foulest vice. The king's brothers and a number of other courtiers were dressed as women, and according to the accounts of the neighbors shared the same passion. Vasco ordered forty of them to be torn to pieces by dogs. The Spaniards commonly used

Balboa's war dogs attack the Quarequa

their dogs in fighting against naked people, and the dogs threw themselves upon them as though they were wild boars or timid deer.

While among the Quarequa, Balboa first heard of "the other sea" to the west. He learned that great hoards of gold could be had there, although his Indian informant advised him that he would need at least 1,000 men to conquer the powerful Indian nation that held the gold. So he returned to Santa Maria la Antigua to assemble the necessary force and supplies for a march to the other sea. He could only muster 190 men and a pack of dogs. They set out on September 1, 1513 in their quest for the new sea. Along the way, more than 1,000 Indians joined Balboa's army, and by September 25th they had reached the summit of the mountain chain that runs along the spine of the Isthmus of Panama. From the summit, Balboa could see the Pacific, which he called the South Sea.

Balboa claims the South Sea

From the mountain top, Balboa sent three groups of men to scout the countryside for a suitable route to the sea. Alonso Martín's group arrived first on the shores of the Pacific and commandeered an Indian canoe for the first Spanish voyage on the South Sea.

On September 29, 1513, Martín led Balboa and a couple of dozen men back to the seaside, where Balboa waded into the water with a sword in one hand and a flag of the Virgin in the other and theatrically claimed the sea and, even more preposterous, all the adjoining lands for the rulers of Spain. Such was Spanish hubris in the sixteenth century.

Following that event, Spanish occupation of Central America proceeded quickly. The mines in Hispaniola had given up most of their gold by 1515. Attention turned to the newly discovered opportunities in the Isthmus of Panama and the unexplored land to the north. Hernán Cortés had the good fortune to lead the expedition to that northern territory of Mexico.

Cortés arrived on the Mexican Gulf shore in 1519 with 600 men, seventeen horses and a dozen cannon. He found that the Indians of the region were in constant conflict, and he participated in their wars, gaining Indian allies and increasing the strength of his forces. His support of the Indian factions won him many gifts, perhaps the most important being a nineteen-year-old Indian woman, Malinche, who became his interpreter, and later, mother of his son, Martín. On the coast he established his first town, Vera Cruz (today Veracruz).

Hernán Cortés

With the help of his Indian allies, Cortés defeated the Tlaxcala, a powerful Indian state that opposed the Aztecs at Tenoch-titlán. Within two years, Cortés had conquered the mighty Aztec empire. In spite of superiority in numbers, Moctezuma had allowed Cortés and his force entry into the royal city. One reason, perhaps, is that Cortés arrived on a date fraught with significance in the Aztec religion. Their god, Quetzal-coatl, had promised to return to them in that very year in their cyclical calendar. Moctezuma may have thought the bearded visitor arriving from the east could be the reincarnation of Quetzalcoatl. When he hesitated, Cortés took advantage of the situation.

Although greatly outnumbered, in a bold move the Spanish seized Moctezuma and held him hostage in his own temple. Armed conflict followed, Moctezuma died at the hands of his own people, and Cortés retreated from Tenochtitlán, losing half of his force. But in the end, Cortés won the day, gathering additional forces from Tlaxcala and laying siege to the royal city. A combination of Spanish weapons and smallpox tipped the scales in favor of the Spanish. By 1521, Hernán Cortés ruled New Spain and the golden treasures of America flowed back to Spain aboard an annual fleet of ships.

New Spain in a few years would be ruled by a Viceroy or agent of the king, thus assuring that Cortés would not set up an autonomous state and cut off Spain from the wealth of the Americas. New Spain included the Caribbean, Central America (except Panama) and Mexico; eventually California and the American Southwest would be included in the Viceroyalty of New Spain.

La Florida would continue to shrink as royal charters carved out portions of North America for new settlement attempts. While Cortés and his rivals contended for control in New Spain, many would-be conquistadors competed for the opportunity to explore and settle North America.

First, Spain required further exploration to determine the extent of North America. The Gulf of Mexico was still relatively unexplored. Perhaps a passage to the South Sea from the Gulf of Mexico existed—a much hoped for prospect in Spain.

Chapter 3
Conquistadors in La Florida

In 1519, the same year that Hernán Cortés entered Mexico, exploration of the northern Gulf of Mexico began. In 1517 and 1518 Antonio de Alaminos had mapped the Mexican coast from the Yucatan Peninsula up to the mouth of the Río Pánuco (at Tampico). That left the rest of the gulf coastline north to the mouth of the yet undiscovered Rio Grande and east to Florida still to be explored. The Spanish continued in their quest for that elusive passage into the South Sea.

In 1519, Alonso Álvarez de Pineda took up the challenge of this coastal exploration. With sponsorship by Francisco de Garay, the governor of Jamaica, Pineda set sail with four ships. From the Florida Keys he followed the west coast of Florida up to the panhandle and then sailed west still hugging the coast. He observed the mouth of the Mississippi River in June and named the river Río de Espíritu Santo. Continuing on, Pineda reached Veracruz where he landed. Cortés quickly returned to Veracruz when he heard that Pineda had landed, fearing interference by a competing claimant.

For his part, Pineda attempted to bargain with Cortés to establish a boundary between the land that Cortés had yet to conquer and the land that Garay intended to claim to the north. The negotiations failed and Pineda put out to sea while Cortés went on to eventual fame, wealth, and glory.

Pineda sailed up the Mexican coast and entered a river he named Las Palmas—today the Río Pánuco. There he repaired his ships and apparently decided to build a settlement to solidify his patron Garay's claim on the land. Pineda sent the fleet back to Jamaica with the map of the Gulf Coast he had prepared. He remained at the Río Pánuco settlement with a sizeable portion of the 270 men who had sailed with him.

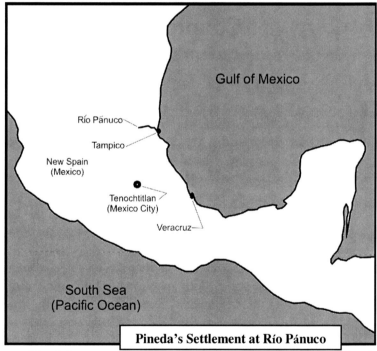

Pineda's Settlement at Río Pánuco

Pineda's map delineated the Gulf Coast of North America for the first time, establishing that there was no passage to the South Sea and also showing that Florida was a peninsula, not an island as Ponce de León had thought. A year later, a ship carrying relief supplies to Pineda and his settlers found only 60 men. The settlement was under attack by the Huastec Indians; Pineda, the horses, and all of his soldiers were dead. The exhausted colonists sailed to Veracruz on the relief ship, happy to avoid the fate of their leader.

At least as early as 1514, slavers such as Pedro de Salazar had coursed along the Atlantic coast capturing Indians for the mines and plantations in Hispaniola. Soon after Pineda completed his mapping of the Gulf Coast and at the time when Juan Ponce de León met his end on the west coast of Florida, Pedro de Quexos and Francisco Gordilla sailed north along the Atlantic Coast, exploring and abducting Indians. Francisco de Chicora (an Indian given a Spanish name) was seized along with seventy other Indians at or near Winyah Bay in South Carolina where four rivers enter the sea.

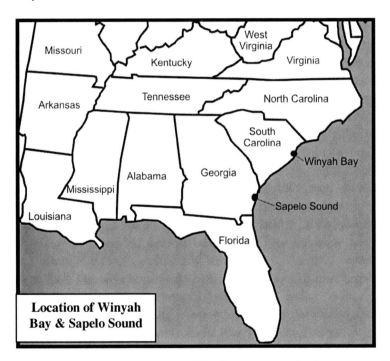

Location of Winyah Bay & Sapelo Sound

When Quexos and Gordilla first approached the mouth of the Pee Dee River at Winyah Bay, the Indians massed on the shore to observe the ships. But they soon departed when the Spaniards approached in small boats. Quexos and Gordilla managed to catch two of Indians and took them aboard their ship where they gave them clothes and treated them well, then released them. The two Indians then served as ambassadors to bring their countrymen back to the shore. Their chief sent many men with food for the Spanish. Quexos and Gordilla greeted the Indians, toured their land for a couple of days, and lulled them into a feeling of security. They invited the Indians to come aboard their ships for a visit. Then abruptly they raised anchor and sailed away with seventy captives destined for a life of slavery.

Gordilla was sailing under orders of Lucas Vázquez de Ayllón, a wealthy sugar planter in Hispaniola. He had ordered Gordilla to reconnoiter the Atlantic coast to find a place suitable for settlement. Gordilla's orders included the charge to treat the native inhabitants of the coast with respect. However, Gordilla had fallen in with Quexos in the Bahamas where Quexos was looking for Indians he could enslave. At Winyah Bay, Quexos had persuaded Gordilla to collaborate on the capture of the slaves.

When these men returned to Hispaniola, Ayllón was justifiably outraged at their behavior. He had them prosecuted before Diego Colón, Admiral of the Indies. Colón ordered the Indians set free and returned to their home at Winyah Bay. Only one of them, Francisco, would return home, and his return would happen only after he first sailed to Spain with Ayllón to see the king. With Francisco's help, Ayllón received in 1523 a royal license to settle, at his own expense, the vast expanse of the Atlantic coast. Charles V ordered him to evaluate the land and the people of Chicora— as Ayllón called the land—to determine how the Indians could be converted to Christianity, and to look for a passage to the South Sea. In return, Ayllón would have a temporary monopoly for trading into and out of his new land.

Estevâo Gomes
Portuguese pilot sailing for Spain

While Ayllón lobbied the Spanish court, in 1524 Estevâo Gomes explored the Atlantic coast, discovering Cape Cod and charting the coast all the way to Cape Breton, Nova Scotia.

He failed to complete his primary mission: to find a passage to the South Sea. On his return to Spain, he sent word ahead that he had captured some Indian slaves (esclavos), but the garbled message arrived at court saying that Gomes had brought cloves (clavos)—they thought he had found a route to the spice islands of the orient.

Gomes sailed in the wake of Giovanni da Verrazano, who sailed under the flag of the French king just ahead of Gomes. History has forgotten Gomes, and Verrazano gets the credit for exploration of the Atlantic coast <u>and</u> a bridge named after him.

It took Ayllón two years to prepare his expedition for Chicora. In 1525, he sent Pedro de Quexos back up the Atlantic with two caravels manned with a combined crew of sixty to explore farther north. Quexos sailed as far as Delaware Bay to chart the coast and record the depth of the waters to determine the most favorable place to colonize. Ultimately, Ayllón determined to settle at Francisco de Chicora's home. Francisco had told tales of regions upriver in the interior he named Duhare and Xapira, where powerful Indian rulers had great riches including pearls and gemstones. He probably referred to the domain of Cofitachequi that would play an important role in the story of De Soto.

Ayllón sailed from Santo Domingo in July, 1526, with six ships and 600 settlers along with stocks of supplies, cattle, horses, and the equipment to establish a permanent settlement at Winyah Bay. They reached their destination on September 29, 1526—a long time for a relatively short journey assisted by the Gulf Stream.

Francisco de Chicora and a few other captured Indians had made the trip with Ayllón to Winyah Bay. They quickly faded into the forest, never to be seen again. Since Ayllón had brought them to serve as guides and interpreters, he started off at a great disadvantage. Nonetheless, he pushed on. He also had with him some African slaves and three Dominican priests.

After some exploration to the north, Ayllón decided to move the settlement site to the south and established his colony, which he named San Miguel de Gualdape (at or near Sapelo Sound, Georgia), 175 miles southwest of Winyah Bay, and thirty-five miles south of Savannah.

Some of his colonists traveled by ship, but others apparently had to make the trek on foot through the forests and swamps that lay along the coast. They endured an arduous journey that must have put them in a low state of morale as well as poor physical condition by the time they arrived at San Miguel de Gualdape. The trip would have taken them at least ten days, and finding food during the trek must have added to their difficulty.

San Miguel de Gualdape represents the first Spanish settlement in what would become the United States of America. Ayllón and his colonists established their colony on October 8, 1526. Although they set to work building houses and other structures, it would not last long. They arrived there too late to plant crops, and the Guale Indians (as the Spanish called the local inhabitants) could not possibly support an additional 600 people. Not unlike the English at Jamestown in the seventeenth century, Ayllón and his colonists suffered from contaminated water, cold, and malnutrition that led inevitably to disease and death.

As soon as Ayllón—their leader—died, the rest of the colonists began to squabble. Finally, they decided to abandon San Miguel de Gualdape in the middle of the winter. By the time they arrived back in Hispaniola, only about 150 of the original 600 remained alive. Father Montesinos, one of the Dominican priests—a man of principles who had spoken out against the cruelty to the Indian slaves in Hispaniola—was among the survivors. He would die a few years later in Venezuela, ministering to the Indians there.

Aside from acquiring some detailed knowledge of the mid-Atlantic coastal area, the Indian settlements, and the weather conditions, Ayllón's sad attempt at settlement accomplished little, leaving his widow in Hispaniola with huge debts and a family to raise alone.

Spain had many would-be conquistadors waiting for the opportunity to colonize North America. One of these contestants, Pánfilo de Narváez, asserted his interest in conquering La Florida two years after Ayllón's failure.

Pánfilo de Narváez

Narváez was born in 1478 in Valladolid, Spain, to a noble family. He was part of the force that captured Jamaica in 1509. In Cuba during the initial conquest of that island in 1512, Narváez led his men in the extermination of 2,500 Indians who had brought food to the Spaniards. Fray Bartolomé de Las Casas observed his atrocities. Narváez's treatment of the Indians of La Florida would follow that pattern.

In 1520 Narváez led an army to Mexico in competition with Hernán Cortés where the two conquistadors fought and Narváez came away with one less eye. His fiery temperament matched his fiery red beard. However, his leadership skills didn't match his ambition. In his conflict in Mexico, most of his 900 men deserted him and went over to the side of Cortés.

After a successful appeal to Charles V, Narváez received the title of Adelantado (Governor) of Florida and a one-year term to establish two settlements on the Gulf Coast along with military garrisons to ensure their security. The expedition would be at Narváez's expense, augmented by whatever investors he could attract with the lure of riches anticipated to rival those of New Spain. The king granted this license on December 11, 1526, about the same time Ayllón's colonists decided to abandon their Atlantic coast settlement.

Narváez sailed with five ships and 600 men and women from San Lúcar de Barrameda on June 17, 1527 bound for the Canaries then Cuba to complete the outfitting of the expedition before pushing on to La Florida. The King's Treasurer and Provost Marshall was Álvar Núñez Cabeza de Vaca. His account of this expedition provides most of the information we have on the Narváez settlement attempt. Cabeza de Vaca was second in command to Narváez.

Because of his importance in this expedition, a bit more biographical information on Cabeza de Vaca is in order. His peculiar last name—meaning cow's head—came from his mother, who descended from a peasant, Martin Alhaja, credited with aiding in the Christian war against the Moors in the year 1212, by marking a secret mountain pass with the head of a cow. King Sancho of Navarre honored Alhaja by naming him Cabeza de Vaca. Álvar Núñez's paternal grandfather participated in the conquest of the Canary Islands and enslaved the Guanche natives there. Born in 1490, Cabeza de Vaca grew up near Cádiz, Spain's principal port for expeditions to the New World. He entered the army as a teenager and saw action in the devastating Battle of Ravenna in April 1512. Later, fighting in the service of the Duke of Medina Sidonia, he took part in the Comuneros civil war and in battles against the French at Navarre in 1520. His exemplary military record earned him the position of lieutenant to the Adelantado as well as his royal commission as Treasurer for the Narváez expedition.

Alonso Enríquez served as Comptroller. Alonso de Solís was the King's Inspector; and Franciscan Fray Juan Suárez led four more Franciscans on the expedition. The presence of the king's officials on the voyage points to the royal expectation of treasure from La Florida. The king had his officials on board to ensure that the crown received its customary twenty percent. The friars were there to see to the conversion of the Native Americans they would encounter.

Of the 600 who sailed from Spain, 450 were soldiers and slaves, the rest were sailors, some wives of the men aboard, and their servants. The number of women is not known, but probably did not exceed twenty.

After a stop in the Canaries where they topped off their water casks, took on more food and firewood, they headed west into the Atlantic. They reached Santo Domingo by mid-September, about three months after their departure from Spain. As soon as they made port, troops began to desert the expedition, more interested in trying their luck on the island of Hispaniola than risking the unknown in Florida. By the time they landed, the bedraggled settlers who had abandoned San Miguel de Gualdape had arrived in Santo Domingo. and their stories influenced 140 of the Narváez men to abandon the expedition while they had the chance. Later, they would congratulate themselves for their good sense.

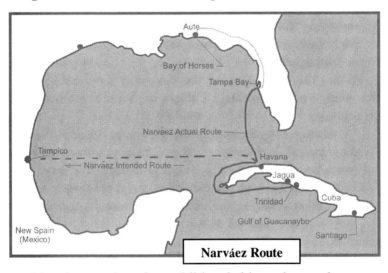

Narváez Route

Narváez purchased an additional ship and some horses at Santo Domingo, and then set sail for Cuba. At Santiago on the southeastern coast of Cuba, the governor recruited more men and purchased arms and horses. There he met Vasco Porcallo, a wealthy planter and miner residing at Trinidad (a city in Cuba), who joined the expedition and provided horses, arms and other supplies. Narváez divided his forces, sending some overland and the rest aboard the ships, two to Trinidad to load on the horses and supplies promised by Porcallo, and four to the Gulf of Guacanayabo.

After the two ships in Trinidad had loaded on the horses and supplies, a hurricane struck Cuba. Cabeza de Vaca described their experience at Trinidad as follows:

...the sea began to rise ominously and the north wind blow so violently that the two boats would not have dared come near land even if the head wind had not already made landing impossible. All hands labored severely under a heavy fall of water that entire day and until dark on Sunday. By then the rain and tempest had stepped up until there was much agitation in the town as at sea. All the houses and churches went down. We had to walk seven or eight together, locking arms, to keep from being blown away. Walking in the woods gave us as much fear as the tumbling houses, for the trees were falling, too, and could have killed us. We wandered all night in this raging tempest without finding any place we could linger as long as half an hour in safety.

When the storm cleared the next day, they saw that the two ships had disappeared. Cabeza de Vaca continued with his account:

Hiking along the shore looking for signs of [the ships], we found nothing for a quarter of a league and came upon the little boat of one of the ships lodged in some treetops. Ten leagues farther, along the coast, two bodies were found, belonging to my ship, but they had been so disfigured by beating against the rocks that they could not be recognized. Some lids of boxes, a cloak, and a quilt rent in pieces were also found, but nothing more.

Sixty persons had been lost in the ships and twenty horses. Those who had gone ashore the day of our arrival—they may have numbered as many as thirty—were all who survived of both ships.

Narváez saw that departure for Florida after those losses would be unwise. He regrouped his remaining ships and forces at Cienfuegos on the south coast of Cuba and made arrangements to replace his losses. By February, 1528, he had two replacement ships and on hand about 400 men and eighty horses. He planned to sail to Havana to replenish his stores and make his departure for La Florida.

His license from Charles V authorized him to settle anywhere along the Gulf coast from the Soto de la Marina River in Tamaulipas province in Northern Mexico to the southern tip of Florida. His license did not cover the Atlantic coast of La Florida since, at the time King Charles issued it, Ayllón had sent his expedition there under his own license. Narváez may have intended to settle in Tamaulipas to renew his rivalry with Cortés, but the weather, that had already caused havoc with his expedition, would dictate a much different destination.

Governor Narváez arrived at Jagua on the bay of Cienfuegos on February 20, 1528. He was aboard a new brig he had purchased at Trinidad and had a new pilot named Miruello, supposedly born on the northern Mexican coast and familiar with the whole stretch of the Gulf Coast. Two days later, under the guidance of the new pilot, the Narváez fleet of five ships, 400 men, eighty horses, and an unknown number of war dogs (mastiffs or a similar type of dog, bred for attacking Indians in battle) departed. They promptly ran aground off the southwestern coast of Cuba.

To add to their difficulties, a series of storms beset them for about two weeks and grounded the ships again. Finally, a fortuitous combination of breezes from the south and a high tide allowed them to sail off the shoals and continue on toward Havana. Within sight of Havana, the winds conspired against them and the fleet had no alternative but to sail before the winds to a landfall in Florida—not the western end of La Florida (i.e. northern Mexico) that Narváez intended, but Florida.

They sighted the west coast of Florida on April 12th. Narváez had lost more than a month attempting to sail to Mexico before he finally gave up and went where the weather directed him. The fleet had arrived at a point slightly north of Tampa Bay, the port their pilot had in mind. However, they could not immediately find it. No matter, they went ashore, erected a cross and Narváez claimed the land for King Charles and himself. The Indians who came down to the shore made it clear that the Spaniards should leave their land, but the Indians withdrew without hostility.

Over the next few days, Narváez led a small force of forty men, including Cabeza de Vaca and Fray Suárez, inland to explore. They found the entrance to Tampa Bay and relocated the fleet there. One of the five ships had foundered somewhere along the coast. The governor ordered the brig to explore the coast and then to return to Cuba to arrange for more supplies to support his expedition.

Continuing their exploration on land, the Spaniards captured four Indians. Not having an interpreter, they showed the Indians some corn and the Indians took them to a field where some was growing but was not yet ripe. At the Indian settlement, they saw some wooden boxes that contained the remains of Indian ancestors covered with painted deerskins. Here is what Cabeza de Vaca says they did:

[Fray Suárez] took this for some form of idolatry and burned the crates and corpses. We also found pieces of linen and woolen cloth and bunches of feathers like those of New Spain [Mexico]. And we saw some nuggets of gold. We inquired of the Indians by signs where these things came from. They gave us to understand that very far from here was a province called Apalachee, where was much gold and plenty of everything we wanted.

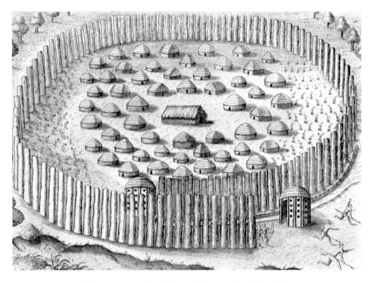

Timucuan Indian village in Florida

The Indians of Florida probably had found the gold on wrecked Spanish treasure ships. They clearly knew how to get rid of these unwanted intruders—send them off as far away as possible in quest of other Indians who possessed gold. This pattern of Indian behavior would repeat many times and the Spanish fell for it each time.

Continuing to hold the four Indians captive, they marched another ten or twelve leagues (about thirty miles) and came to a village of fifteen houses and a cornfield ready to harvest. They remained in the village two days before returning to the encampment on Tampa Bay.

An unexplained incident occurred in this village or one nearby controlled by a chief called Ozita. Someone in the Narváez expedition set their dogs on the chief's wife; the dogs killed and devoured her. Then the Spaniards turned on Ozita and cut off his nose. These atrocities would lead to the capture of a Spaniard from a later exploration party and would have an impact on the expedition of De Soto in the future.

When Narváez heard about the gold nuggets and the story of Apalachee, he decided to march overland to that location with 300 men while the ships and his other 100 men would sail up the coast to a port near the River of Palms (the Río Pánuco at Tampico). The pilots and the governor had no idea how far they were from Mexico.

The home of the Apalachee Indians was near Tallahassee in northwest Florida. Narváez's decision to march with 300 men into the unknown interior, separating his force from the supply link represented by his ships, proved a disastrous error.

Cabeza de Vaca must have sensed that Narváez was making a mistake because he strenuously objected to the plan. He pointed out that the pilots couldn't agree among themselves on where they were, they didn't know how far away Mexico was, they had no Indian interpreters so couldn't communicate with the Indians they would meet, and they lacked sufficient supplies to embark on a long march.

The Indians they had captured implied that Apalachee was a long distance from where they were. Cabeza de Vaca advised that they all continue in the ships until they came to a location with soils better suited for settlement in a secure location; their current location he described as "the most desert and poor that had been discovered in that region." He insisted that the notary should document his objection.

Fray Suárez proposed that they should remain ashore and march along the coast to the Río Pánuco (at Tampico). The pilots claimed that the river only lay about fifteen leagues (forty miles) from where they were. In fact, the distance from Tampa Bay to Tampico by water is about 1,000 miles and along the coast much more than 1,500 miles.

Narváez told Cabeza de Vaca that, since he obviously feared the overland march, he could sail in command of the three ships to establish a settlement at the port near the Río Pánuco. Cabeza de Vaca refused—that was his first mistake since joining the Narváez expedition.

The women remained aboard the ships. One of them predicted that the men ashore would never survive. She advised the other women that their husbands were "the same as dead and that they might as well be looking after whom they would marry next; she was going to." Cabeza de Vaca later wrote, "And she did presently 'marry.' So did the other wives 'marry' with men who remained in the ships."

Narváez began the march into the interior of Florida on May 1, 1528. Forty of the 300 men rode on horseback. This army marched northward paralleling the coast for fifteen days on rations of two pounds of biscuits and a half pound of bacon; soon they were starving. They found little along the route to augment the rations and met no Indians during their march, although the Timucuan people must have observed them from the cover of the forest.

Starvation of the Explorers

It is a curiosity that the Spaniards during this time and later the English in Virginia starved to death while surrounded with relatively abundant food resources. The situation seems inexplicable, but we must remember that these European adventurers often came from urban areas and had no experience foraging in the forests for game or plants to eat. Those who were of noble birth, the hidalgos, also expected their servants to cater to them.

Also, in the case of the Spaniards, large forces of men on horseback would have found little wild game while moving noisily through the forest. The Spaniards, French, and English depended on the generosity of the Indians when they could. When the Indians couldn't, or wouldn't, feed them, the European invaders were unprepared to find, catch, or grow their own food.

Consequently we read time and again of the starving explorers reduced to eating their leather shoes and belts, and also occasionally dying from eating poisonous plants. Of course, the Indians also struggled at times with periods of insufficient food, even when not faced with hundreds of hungry invaders at their gates.

It took a day for the army to cross the Suwannee River on rafts and by swimming. Once across, 200 Timucuan Indians stood in their path. The Spanish captured five or six and forced them to lead them to their town, about a mile away. To their relief, they found a great quantity of corn that satisfied their hunger.

While in the Timucuan town, Cabeza de Vaca tried to convince Narváez that they should move to the coast. The governor refused, but he allowed Cabeza de Vaca to take forty foot soldiers and scout ahead to find the sea. The army had covered about 140 miles in their march to this first Timucuan town. They must have realized already that the land was more extensive than the pilots had indicated.

On May 18th, Cabeza de Vaca, Captain Alonso del Castillo and forty men marched about four hours and came to the mouth of the Suwannee River where it enters the Gulf of Mexico. They returned to the Timucuan town and reported to Narváez that they had found the sea but could not tell whether it afforded a safe harbor. A second expedition to the mouth of the Suwannee established that it would not make a suitable anchorage for ships.

About May 21st or 22nd, the Narváez expedition resumed their march, rested and restored by the food the Timucuan Indians provided. Using their captured Indian guides, they marched about two weeks, seeing other Indians but failing to capture any. Then, on June 17th, they saw a strange spectacle. Out of the cover of the forest came a chief carried on another Indian's back, flanked by musicians playing flutes, and followed by a large contingent of the chief's subjects.

Using sign language, they learned that this chief, Dulchanchellin, was an enemy of the Apalachee. He agreed to march with them against the Apalachee. Narváez gave Dulchanchellin "beads, little bells and other trinkets." In return, the chief gave Narváez his own deerskin mantle.

The chief led the Spanish to the Apalachicola River; it took them another day to ford the river using a canoe that they built for the purpose. While fording the river, one of the

Spaniards and his horse drowned attempting to swim across the swift current. They mourned this first casualty, but had the horse for supper that night.

A day later they reached Dulchanchellin's village where, during the night, the Indians shot one of the Spaniards with an arrow, but he survived his wound. Next morning, Narváez found that the Indians had abandoned the town. As the governor led his army out of the town, Dulchanchellin's warriors followed the Spaniards along the trail. They managed to capture three or four of the Indians and used them as guides to lead them to Apalachee.

Their route took them through much more appealing country of tall trees and fertile soil. They continued through the forests until June 24th when they located Apalachee. Cabeza de Vaca wrote:

> We gave many thanks to God to be near this destination, believing everything we had been told about it and expecting an immediate end of our hardships. In addition to the distance we had come over bad trails, we suffered terribly from hunger. Once in a while we did find corn, but usually had to travel seven and eight leagues without any. Also, many men developed raw wounds from the weight of their armor and other things they had to carry. But having virtually accomplished our objective, with its assurance of plentiful gold and food, we seemed almost ready to feel our pain and fatigue lifting.

The area around the town consisted of mixed hardwood and conifer forests with many deep lakes. They spotted a wide variety of game including deer, bear, rabbits, and panthers.

Narváez ordered Cabeza de Vaca and Solís to invade the Apalachee village situated on the west bank of the Apalachicola River. Under their command, nine horsemen and fifty foot soldiers entered the village. At first they found forty small "thatch" houses, women and children. Soon, the Apalachee men returned and shot arrows at Cabeza de Vaca's men. Solís's horse was killed by arrows, although the Indians failed to harm any of the Spaniards. The Apalachee warriors fled from the village, leaving the women and children.

After a couple of hours, the Apalachee men returned and indicated they wanted peace and the release of their women and children. Narváez complied, but he held the chief hostage. His army moved into the village and occupied the houses, dining on the Indian corn they found there.

Early the next morning, the Apalachee attacked, surprising the Spaniards who were still asleep. The Indians set fire to the houses, rousing the army. Once the Spanish soldiers emerged from the fires, they chased the Apalachee warriors into a nearby swamp and cornfield, killing one Indian.

Narváez and his army remained at that location for nearly a month, making several forays into the countryside looking in vain for the major Indian city replete with gold and other treasures they had expected to find. The few Indians they captured on these raids told them that the village the Spanish already occupied was the largest in the territory of the Apalachee. They now knew that the story of golden treasure held by the powerful Apalachee was untrue.

Still, they learned from their captives that nine days to the south, Aute, a village on the sea, could provide them with plenty of food including corn, melons, and fish. During their forays in search of a golden Apalachee center, the Spanish had suffered additional casualties from guerilla attacks. One of those casualties was an Aztec prince, Tezcuco, who had accompanied Fray Suárez on the expedition.

The Spanish army marched to Aute, the journey taking nine days. During the march through most difficult terrain including swamps and thickets, the Indians continually harassed the Spaniards, picking off men and horses with well placed arrow shots. Cabeza de Vaca observed that the Florida Indians shot with incredible power and accuracy. He mentioned instances where the arrows completely penetrated red oak trees as thick as a man's thigh. He said, "Their bows were as thick as an arm, six or seven feet long, accurate at 200 paces." An hidalgo named Avellaneda died instantly when an arrow transfixed his neck just above his cuirass (breastplate portion of his armor). They buried Avellaneda at Aute.

Finding Aute, a village just above the mouth of the Apalachicola, deserted and the houses burned, Narváez and his men feasted on the food they found there, remaining two days. Then, Narváez sent Cabeza de Vaca and a small party consisting of Fray Suárez, Captain Castillo, Andrés Dorantes, seven other horsemen and fifty infantrymen to search for the sea.

Although they couldn't know it, they had come to the mouth of the river that flows into an almost completely enclosed bay (Apalachicola Bay) protected from the sea by barrier islands about seven miles off shore. Cabeza de Vaca and his men couldn't reconnoiter such an extensive body of water. It took them all day to reach the shore, and they recognized that what lay beyond was not the Gulf of Mexico but an extensive inlet. They feasted on oysters they found there.

The next morning, August 1st, Cabeza de Vaca sent out twenty men to search along the coast to find the passage to the sea. After two full days the men returned and reported that they had not found the passage and that it would take many more days to explore so vast an area of bays, islands and coves. Cabeza de Vaca decided to abandon the search, and he and his men marched back to Aute.

They found Narváez and his men sick in camp. To compound their problem, the Indians had attacked them, and had wounded many who could not fight effectively because of their illness.

On August 3rd, the army abandoned Aute and marched with great difficulty back to Apalachicola Bay. They had so many suffering from malaria and dysentery that they didn't have sufficient horses to carry the disabled men. By the time they reached Cabeza de Vaca's campsite on the bay, the men decided they could go no further on this adventure. The governor was too ill to argue.

At that point, some of the cavalry conspired to abandon the rest of the army and to seek their own salvation. But word reached the officers, and the horsemen abandoned their desertion plan, agreeing to share the common fate of the rest of the army. The next day, the officers decided that they would build boats to take them to Mexico, believed by most to lie only a short voyage to the west. From Apalachicola bay to the Río Pánuco they would actually need to sail at least 780 miles, assuming they sailed in a straight line.

Now, Narváez' army undertook an ambitious and remarkable effort. They sent men back to Aute where they collected about 100 bushels of corn and other foodstuffs. That corn and the horses they still had would sustain them while they built their boats.

Others built a forge and melted down iron stirrups, spurs, crossbow parts, iron kettles, and other bits of metal to make saws, hammers, and nails with which to construct the boats. They used the local palmetto frond fibers to make caulking cordage. Don Teodoro, a Greek, knew how to make pitch for waterproofing from pine resin. Work began on August 4th with their one carpenter directing the others cutting timbers, sawing planks, and assembling five barges in sixteen days—an incredible feat.

The barges were about thirty feet long and capable of carrying about fifty men each. That was sufficient since forty had died and a significant number more had fallen in Indian attacks. The barges could be propelled with oars and also had sails made by stitching together the men's shirts.

On September 22nd, only one horse remained. The army dined on the last horse, loaded their water skins, some remaining corn, and their weapons into the five barges and made their way out into what they called the Bay of Horses in honor of their main source of food for the last two weeks. The five boats sailed slowly across the broad expanse of Apalachicola Bay and searched along the barrier islands for an outlet to the sea; they searched for nearly seven full days before locating an outlet into the gulf, probably passing between Sand Island and Saint Vincent Island.

Before they exited the bay, they spotted five canoes. The Indians abandoned the canoes when the Spanish barges drew near, and the men in the barges recovered the canoes to tow behind. On the island the Spaniards found a village, and within the village, they found fish and dried fish roe that they ate. After that feast, the five barges exited the bay and sailed out into the gulf, but soon they rowed to shore. Apparently the barges had settled deeper in the water when fully loaded with fifty men aboard, causing them some concern when they reached the unprotected waters of the gulf. They sawed boards from the Indian canoes to raise the sides of their barges, providing more freeboard and a safety margin.

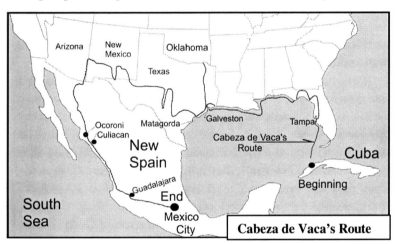

Cabeza de Vaca's Route

Lacking any charts or compass, they hugged the coast, rounding Cape San Blas and proceeding northwest and then west. They continued on this course for thirty days, weaving in and out of each bay. They soon found their greatest need was drinking water and had to make excursions ashore to search for it. Some men drank sea water and five died.

They rowed, or sailed when the wind was favorable, both day and night, and in the thirty days apparently only covered about 140 miles, placing them somewhere east of Pensacola,

Florida. On the evening of the thirtieth day, they heard a canoe pass nearby, but in spite of their shouts, the Indian continued on his way. When day broke, they found themselves near a small island where they took shelter as a storm broke over them. They stayed ashore, taking refuge from the storm for six days.

Before the storm had abated completely, the five barges rowed in the direction of the canoe that had passed them days before, the wind and seas nearly claiming the five boats. At sunset they passed a cape and spied a sheltered bay. Indians in canoes paddled out to greet them and, with signs of peace, invited them onto the shore.

When they reached the beach, they saw that the Indians had brought down clay jars of water and cooked fish. The chief conducted the governor and his officers up to his own lodge to banquet and spend the night. The rest of the men received similar hospitality from the other Indians of the settlement.

Around midnight, without warning the Indians attacked the men in their sleep. Narváez received a blow to his face with a rock. Cabeza de Vaca also was hit in his face; three Spaniards died. The officers grabbed the chief, but he managed to slip out of his robe and escaped. All but fifty men, including Narváez, made it to their barges. Cabeza de Vaca and the remaining men stayed ashore and fought off three assaults by the Indians before daybreak.

In the morning, Cabeza de Vaca destroyed thirty Indian canoes and set them alight to ward off the chill of the late October wind. The stormy weather continued for a few more days, keeping them on the shore.

Finally they set out and continued west for four days, until their limited supply of drinking water caused them to chance another landing. This time they had reached Mobile Bay where they met more Indians in canoes. Teodoro the Greek and an African man went with the Indians to get fresh water. Two of the Indians remained with the Spaniards as hostages.

With night falling, the Indians returned without the two men and without water. The Greek and his servant may have decided to trust their luck with the Native Americans of the Alabama River rather than continue on with the ill-fated Narváez expedition. From information learned years later by De Soto, it seems that these two men lived among the Indians for about ten years.

As the confrontation with the Indians escalated, more canoes appeared and it became clear they planned to encircle the five barges and keep them from escaping. Before that happened, Narváez ordered the barges to head for open waters. The Indians followed them out into the gulf, attacking with stones thrown from slings, but withdrew when the wind came up. Two days later Cabeza de Vaca in the lead barge came to a cape beyond which flowed the Mississippi River, about fifty miles from Mobile Bay.

It appears that the barges must have ducked between the barrier islands and the mainland after they eluded the Indians and continued west along the shore, passing Pascagoula. That would explain how they covered nearly fifty miles in two days when it had taken them about a month to go 140 miles in the open waters of the gulf, and would also square with Cabeza de Vaca's statement that he "discovered a promontory, on the other side of which flowed a vast river. Off a little island at the point, I anchored and awaited the other barges."

Today, Cat Island and Ship Island are in that vicinity; however, nearly 500 years ago the barrier islands could have been considerably different.

The barges joined together in a little bay and, to their delight, the men found that the water flowing out of the land was fresh; they replenished their supply of drinking water without having to go ashore and risk another hostile Indian attack.

When they rowed out into the river channel, the strong current carried them inexorably out to sea. They tried in vain for a couple of days to reach the shore, but the barges became separated and the men began to fear for their lives.

Cabeza de Vaca and his men finally spotted two other barges. He urged his men to row to the nearest one that carried Narváez.

The governor asked Cabeza de Vaca for his opinion on what they should do. His advice: row to the lead barge and join together for the good of all. Narváez opposed this, indicating that the other barge was too far away. He told Cabeza de Vaca that if he wished he could row behind his barge; and so they set out.

But the governor's barge soon pulled away. Cabeza de Vaca shouted to the governor to throw them a rope so that they could stay together. Narváez replied, "Each must do as he [thinks] best to save himself." That clearly was what Narváez had in mind. Cabeza de Vaca then directed his men to row toward the other barge farther out at sea.

That was the last sighting of Narváez and his men. They never returned to live among the Spanish of the West Indies, and were presumed lost at sea. Cabeza de Vaca learned much later that the governor and his men made landfall near the Lower Colorado River in Texas, and most of them succumbed to the cold and starvation—a few descending into cannibalism, then dying. One died at the hands of one of his crewmates. The governor and two others put out to sea in a boat and apparently died at sea.

For five or six days the remaining two barges rowed on together, the men feeble and ineffective. Finally near dawn, they heard the sound of breakers on a shore, and too weak to avoid it, the men in the barges rode the breakers up onto the coast where the boats quickly became swamped and filled with sand. The men barely had the strength to crawl up out of the surf. Cabeza de Vaca said the date was November 6th. They had fetched ashore at Galveston Island and had covered a distance of at least 400 miles rowing and sailing when the wind permitted it.

Although they didn't have the strength to dig out the boats, the men did regain some strength and hope from having survived the landing. They ate parched corn and drank what water they had. Cabeza de Vaca ordered one of his men to climb a tree to survey the area. He reported that they had come ashore on an island. Then the man went off on foot to see what he could find. Some time later he returned with a jug of water, a dog, and some fish he had found in a deserted Indian village. As he returned to the shore, three Indians with bows and arrows followed him at a distance.

Later, 100 bowmen appeared. Cabeza de Vaca and Solís walked out to greet the Indians and make peace. They offered them some glass beads and bells, and the Indians gave them each an arrow in return as a sign of friendship. Night falling, the Indians signed that they would return in the morning with food for the Spaniards. True to their word, the Indians came bearing gifts of fish and "certain roots which taste like nuts, some bigger than walnuts … mostly grubbed from the water with great labor." They returned again in the evening with more food, bringing their women and children with them, and the Spaniards distributed more of the trinkets they had. This went on for several days.

Finally, Cabeza de Vaca decided they should dig out their barge and depart for Río Pánuco. The work went slowly due to lack of tools. When they tried to launch the barge, they first stripped off their clothes and put them aboard the boat. The naked men pushed the boat out into the surf, then clambered aboard and grabbed the oars.

They managed to row a few hundred yards offshore before a wave swamped the boat, threw the men into the cold surf, drowned Solís and two other men, and fetched the survivors up onto the beach. All their possessions were gone. They stood naked, shivering on the shore, and hope of Mexico faded quickly. Cabeza de Vaca said, "Our bodies [were] so emaciated we could easily count every bone and looked the very picture of death." They had eaten very little in the last two months since leaving the Bay of Horses.

The disconsolate Spaniards found some embers from a fire and, with difficulty, stoked a fire that helped them avoid succumbing to the cold wind. Their Indian saviors returned again that evening with food. The Indians wept at the pitiful sight of the nearly-drowned Spaniards. At this point, Cabeza de Vaca seems to have begun to view the "savages" in a more favorable light. In time, he came to admire the natives of North America and deplored the treatment they received from his countrymen.

The Spaniards reached a consensus that their best hope was to go and live among the Indians. With that decision, they followed the sympathetic Native Americans to their village where they found a lodge newly erected for their use with a warm fire inside. Cabeza de Vaca and his men entered the house and spent a worried night as the jubilant Indians sang and danced until late into the evening.

In the morning, the Indians provided more food, reassuring the Spaniards that they had no malicious plans for their new guests. That day Cabeza de Vaca spotted an Indian wearing a Spanish trinket that had not come from him or his men. He learned that the Indians knew of another group of Spaniards who had wrecked not far away on the coast. Soon, those survivors of one of the other barges joined Cabeza de Vaca's company.

The other Spanish crew of forty-eight men was under the leadership of Captain Andrés Dorantes and Captain Alonso del Castillo. This crew still had all of their clothing and other equipment. After the officers conferred, they decided to repair the barge of Dorantes and Castillo for a select group of fit men to continue on to Mexico and bring relief for those who would remain among the Indians on the Texas coast.

This plan proved fruitless, for when they dug out the barge—with one man dying in the process—the unseaworthy barge sank. Finally, they selected four of the fittest men to walk to Río Pánuco to get help. Those four men had no idea that their destination was at least 600 miles away. They failed in their mission, dying on the way due to starvation, misadventure or, on at least one occasion, Indian attack.

Cabeza de Vaca and the roughly eighty remaining men from the three barges resigned themselves to spend the winter among the Indians of Auia—the name of their location on Galveston Island. He referred to the Indians tribes living there as Capoques and Han. Apparently the large number of Spaniards did not all live in one location. Five men living apart on the coast turned to cannibalism for want of food. Only one of those five survived, but not for long. His was the only body found.

The Capoques and Han were horrified by this barbaric act of cannibalism. Cabeza de Vaca feared they would turn on the Spaniards. He and his men were suffering from dysentery and they soon numbered only fifteen or sixteen. Then, when the Indians began to die from the same disease, the rest blamed the Spaniards. Cabeza de Vaca called that place Malhado—Island of Doom. Although the Indians at first came to kill the remaining Spanish, they thought better of it and generously let them live among them.

The Indians of Auia were tall and well-proportioned. The men wore a wooden lip plug and lengths of cane pierced through each nipple. The Capoques and Han lived on the barrier islands from October through February. The rest of the year they moved onto the mainland and foraged, fished and hunted to support themselves. Cabeza de Vaca and his few men lived among the Capoques, and Castillo and Dorantes with their crew lived among the Han. The Han spoke a different dialect than the Capoques; they apparently lived on opposite sides of Galveston Bay. The Indian men went about naked, so the sight of the naked Spaniards didn't elicit any concern. The women wore only some "wool that grows on trees" for modesty, according to Cabeza de Vaca.

The two groups of Spaniards passed the winter among the Capoques and Han without further incident. In April 1529, they took part in Indian springtime celebrations. While among the people of Auia, Cabeza de Vaca, Dorantes, and Castillo, along with a black servant named Esteván from North Africa, received training as healers. Cabeza de Vaca wrote:

> *The Islanders wanted to make physicians of us without examination or review of diplomas…. The medicine-man makes incisions over the point of pain, sucks the wound, and cauterizes it. This remedy enjoys high repute among the Indians…. The medicine-men blow on the spot they have treated, as a finishing touch, and the patient regards himself relieved.*

The Spaniards substituted recitation of the *Our Father* and *Hail Mary* prayers for the Indian incantations, but otherwise emulated the Indian healers. Their Indian hosts placed great store in the Spaniards' healing ability and treated them well.

That spring all the Spaniards, except for Cabeza de Vaca and two others on the island, left Auia and headed southwest. Cabeza de Vaca was ill and unable to join them. When he fell ill, the Capoques began to treat him badly. Similarly, Castillo, Estevár, and Dorantes, living among the Han, began to suffer abuse; one of their crewmen died there, and another, Lope de Oviedo, remained a prisoner of the Han.

Cabeza de Vaca eventually recovered his health and traveled inland great distances, trading materials among the various Indian communities he came across. He ranged north as far as Oklahoma on these trading expeditions, always returning to Auia. Over the next four years he pleaded with Oviedo to escape with him, but Oviedo put him off, saying, "Next year." Finally in November 1532, Cabeza de Vaca managed to get Oviedo off the island and over the next week apparently as far as Matagorda Island (about 130 miles).

Near Matagorda Island they met some Indians called Quevenes who told them that not far away lived three men like themselves—Spaniards. When asked about the other ten, the Indians said that they had died from cold, hunger and abuse at the hands of their captors. Oviedo became fearful as this story unfolded, and he insisted on returning to the Han at Auia with a party of Deaguanes Indian women who were traveling there. Oviedo disappeared at that point, never to be heard of again.

Cabeza de Vaca remained with the Quevenes. Two days later, at a gathering of various tribes of the Southwest during the pecan season, he reunited with Dorantes, Estevám, and Castillo. This region lay along the Lower Colorado River perhaps thirty or forty miles north of the Texas coast.

Dorantes, Estevám, and now Cabeza de Vaca lived as slaves of the Mariames tribe. Castillo was held by the Yguaces Indians. The Spaniards immediately began discussing how to escape and make their way to Mexico. Dorantes cautioned that they would have to wait at least six months until the season of the prickly-pear cactus fruit harvest when hundreds of Indians from various tribes would come together. Among that large number of people, the Spaniards would have a better opportunity to slip away; otherwise they would be discovered and murdered.

When six months had elapsed, the Indians and their Spanish captives went to the vicinity of San Antonio where the cactus fruit harvest took place. But an argument among the Indians resulted in Cabeza de Vaca and the other three being separated. This was August 1533. They met again in the prickly-pear season the next year and renewed their plan to escape. While waiting, Cabeza de Vaca learned the fate of the fifth barge. It also had been forced ashore and wrecked in a storm. The men stumbled onto the shore in feeble condition, where they died at the hands of an Indian tribe named Camones.

At the end of September or early October of 1534, Cabeza de Vaca, Dorantes, and Estevám came together in the Mariames camp with Castillo. As soon as possible they slipped away and headed into the wilderness. This began a year-and-a-half-long odyssey across the American Southwest, taking the four men through west Texas, into New Mexico near Pecos, across New Mexico and into Arizona and the Sonora Desert. As they traveled, they practiced and refined their craft as healers.

Eventually, they walked at the head of a large entourage of Indians. As news of their approach reached the next town,

Indians would come out to greet them with all manner of food and treasures. They claimed to have received emeralds—more likely turquoise. They observed how the Indian communities changed as they moved north and then west, seeing more permanent houses of wood and then long-standing dwellings of stone. The people's appearance also changed as they came among Indians who wore woven clothing.

Their Indian followers came to believe that the four strange men had come from heaven, and the Spaniards did nothing to dissuade them from that opinion. They used Estevan as their spokesperson to maintain their distinctness. During their time among the Indians, Cabeza de Vaca claimed that they had learned six languages and could also fall back on sign language when necessary.

Also during this long sojourn through the Southwest, Cabeza de Vaca developed a genuine admiration for the American Indians. He said, "They are a substantial people with a capacity for unlimited development." He owed his life and his fellow wayfarers' lives to the Indians and realized that they deserved treatment as equals by the Spanish, not the harsh slavery that still prevailed in the West Indies. Later he would write to the king, "Clearly, to bring all these people to Christianity and subjection to Your Imperial Majesty, they must be won by kindness, the only certain way."

By January 1536, Cabeza de Vaca and his companions found themselves among the Pima along the Sonora River. They encountered an Indian who had an amulet around his neck made of a Spanish harness buckle and a nail. He had gotten it from some bearded men who also came from heaven. Those men had come and then departed to the sea where they sailed away.

Setting their course in the same direction as those mysterious Spaniards, they marched across a vast area, seeing signs of Spanish presence such as horse tracks, abandoned camp sites, and hearing from the natives about other Christians having been there. They also saw unmistakable signs of gold and silver in the mountains. Among the Jumano Indians, they came to a recently abandoned camp site, and Cabeza de Vaca, Estevána, and eleven Indians traveled about thirty miles ahead where they finally encountered four Spaniards on horseback.

Near Ocoroni on the Sinaloa River, Cabeza de Vaca met Captain Diego de Alcaraz, who was in the region attempting to capture Indians for the slave trade. They were about ninety miles from Culiacán, the northern frontier town in New Spain at that time. When they joined Dorantes and Castillo, they found 600 Indians in their entourage. Alcaraz attempted to enslave the Indians, telling them that the four men they had been following were mere mortals and that the Indians must obey Christians like him. The Indians replied:

> ...*the Christians lied: We [Cabeza de Vaca, and his three companions] had come from the sunrise, they from the sunset; we healed the sick, they killed the sound; we came naked and barefoot, they clothed, horsed, and lanced; we coveted nothing but gave whatever we were given, while they robbed whomever they found and bestowed nothing on anyone.*

Only with great difficulty did Cabeza de Vaca convince his 600 followers to return to their homes and not follow him farther into New Spain.

When he learned that Alcaraz planned to round up and enslave those Indians in his absence, Cabeza de Vaca met with the Alcade Mayor Melchior Díaz (the senior official) of Culiacán. The two of them met with representatives of the local Indian tribes and, with the Indians' pledge to live as Christians, declared that they could safely reoccupy their villages and not fear enslavement. Alcaraz returned to Culiacán without captives, apparently having received orders from Díaz to abandon his expedition.

Cabeza de Vaca still had over 900 miles to go to reach Mexico City, but that part of his journey occurred without incident. After two months' recuperation in that city, he traveled to Veracruz and, in the early spring of 1537, sailed home to Spain on a voyage that was quite eventful. The ship leaked badly; he barely made it to Havana. Finally, he sailed for Santo Domingo; then, on the way home, a French privateer attacked his ship near the Azores, and he barely escaped capture. He arrived in Lisbon on August 9, 1537, ten years and two months after he had embarked with Adelantado Narváez on his ill-fated expedition.

Chapter 4
Seven Cities of Cibola

When Cabeza de Vaca, Dorantes, Castillo, and Estevan reached Mexico in 1536, the Spanish officials thought they had died eight years before. They had received no word from the 300 men and their Governor, Pánfilo de Narváez, since they went ashore at Tampa Bay, Florida. These four men created a sensation when they arrived in Mexico City.

The Viceroy, as well as all the other Spaniards in that town, wanted to know what the Narváez expedition had discovered in La Florida. Had they found gold or silver? Had they found the Seven Cities of Gold? Cabeza de Vaca and the others must have told of their experiences and they clearly came back empty-handed, but that didn't stop rumors from developing around their fantastic survival story.

Some speculated that these four survivors were not telling the whole story. Also, Cabeza de Vaca claimed that Indians they met along their journey told them of distant cities that had a wealth of gold, but he admitted that they had never seen those places. He had received "emeralds" from Indians in the southwest but he had lost them when he rushed to save his Indian followers from enslavement near Culiacán.

Antonio de Mendoza, appointed Viceroy of New Spain only a year before Cabeza de Vaca's arrival in Mexico, pressed that ranking member of the Narváez expedition for details of their eight years in the territories to the north. Cabeza de Vaca held back much information, insisting that he report directly to Charles V, his sovereign who had placed his trust in him. Undoubtedly, Cabeza de Vaca also wanted to return to La Florida, not as a lieutenant, but as Adelantado and successor to Narváez. He didn't want Mendoza or anyone else getting ahead of him. But he couldn't stop the rumors and speculation.

Unfortunately for Cabeza de Vaca, time worked against him. When he arrived at Veracruz to sail for Spain and his audience with the king, his ship capsized, delaying his departure by half a year. By the time he arrived in Spain, Charles V had appointed Hernando de Soto Governor of Cuba and Adelantado of La Florida, successor to Narváez, Ayllón, and Ponce de León, all three having died in their attempts to conquer La Florida. De Soto asked Cabeza de Vaca to accompany him to La Florida, but he refused. However, he encouraged others to participate in De Soto's expedition.

Cabeza de Vaca made his report to Charles V and, since his wished for position could not be granted, the king designated Cabeza de Vaca Adelantado of the South American provinces of Río de la Plata (Uruguay and Argentina). His first mission would be to relieve the settlement at Asunción on the Páraguai River and then move on to Buenos Aires to re-establish an abandoned settlement there. Cabeza de Vaca arrived at Santa Catarina Island (Brazil) and set out in November 1541 on foot through the jungle for Asunción, a journey of about 1,000 miles. He reached Asunción in March 1542.

In the summer of 1543, Cabeza de Vaca led his men up the Páraguai River in search of a fabled city of gold, but was forced back to Asunción by fatigue. There his men turned against him, deposed him, and returned him to Spain in chains. He languished in Spain for eight years awaiting his trial. The Council of the Indies concluded their investigation with a finding of fault and sentenced him to banishment to Africa. However, with the king's intervention, Cabeza de Vaca returned to favor and lived out his remaining few years on a pension. He died in 1557. His report to Charles V concerning the Narváez expedition and its aftermath was published in 1542 as *La Relación*, later as *Naufragios* (meaning shipwrecks).

Viceroy Mendoza of New Spain would not wait for royal direction with regard to the rumored cities of gold to the north. He failed to get Cabeza de Vaca, Dorantes, or Castillo to remain under his command and lead an expedition back to the territory north of the Rio Grande. Instead, he employed Estevan, Dorantes' slave, to assist him. In a seemingly unprecedented approach, Mendoza enlisted Fray Marcos de Niza (a French priest of the Franciscan order who came from Nice) to head the expedition with Estevan as his guide. Their company included Aztec porters and other Indians of New Spain as well as another priest, Fray Honorato. The total number varied depending on the number of Indian followers at any given time. Honorato soon fell ill and stayed behind, leaving Fray Marcos and Estevan to lead the expedition.

Marcos and his company left Culiacán in March 1539 and marched parallel to the Gulf of California for several hundred miles, then followed the Río Matapé to its intersection with the lower reaches of the Sonora River; they followed the Sonora River north.

Marcos found local Indians who had no contact with Christians. He sent a party of Indians to the west to explore the coast. At this time, the Spanish still thought that New Spain and the land to the north was an island and expected that the South Sea (Pacific Ocean) flowed east above this island. They hoped to find a northern port that would provide easy access by sea to the mythical cities of gold. From these Indians, Marcos learned that the coast veered west rather than turning east as had been expected. They probably explored the head of the Gulf of California that turns abruptly northwest.

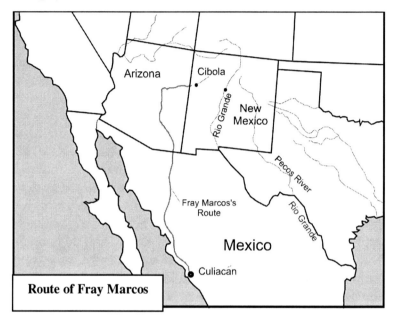

Route of Fray Marcos

In his cassock, Fray Marcos carried samples of gold, silver, copper, and iron. Now among Indians who had no prior contact with the Spanish, Marcos showed them his samples. He wanted to know where he could find gold. The Indians told him that great cities to the north used gold as the Spanish used commoner metals for everything from eating utensils to toothpicks. Marcos immediately sent Estevan north with some of the Indians to scout a route to the cities of gold.

Estevan traveled decked out as an Indian medicine man complete with bells on his wrists and ankles and a special gourd rattle he had picked up on his prior trip through the southwest. He also had two greyhounds with him. He made good speed with his traveling companions and soon crossed the border with Arizona near Naco and continued on a northerly route along established Indian trails.

Fray Marcos had instructed Estevàn to send a messenger back with a cross to indicate what he had found. The size of the cross would represent how important a city he had found: a small cross for a small city, a larger cross for a major city. Four days after his departure, Estevàn's Indian messenger returned with a cross almost as big as he was. Indians had told Estevàn that a fabulously wealthy city lay just thirty-days' march to the north. Estevàn, contrary to his orders, pressed on with Indian guides in his quest. Fray Marcos hurried behind him, never quite catching up. As the race continued, Indians continued to backtrack to the priest with large crosses, spurring him ever onward.

As Marcos pushed north along the Sonora River, the local Indians reassured him that fabulous cities lay to the north with multistoried houses of stone and great wealth. Perhaps the priest should have realized that to the relatively poor Indians of the Sonora, living in rude huts of brush and adobe, "great wealth" could be a highly subjective concept. Over a period of weeks, Marcos continued to follow Estevan's path, nearing his destination, the cities of gold.

One day as Fray Marcos neared the fabled cities, one of Estevàn's companions limped into camp. He reported that Estevàn had died, and he had barely escaped death at the hands of the warriors of the nearest of the Seven Cities of Cibola (as the land was supposedly called). Estevàn had entered the pueblo of Hawikuh, part of the Zuni Indian lands.

Estevàn had made many conquests during his trek across the southwest with Cabeza de Vaca—romantic conquests of Indian women. He was apparently a very charismatic man, exotic looking, dressed in his colorful medicine man costume. Among his possessions from his previous travels he had a special rattle made from a gourd. His practice was to send in his gourd with a messenger as a sign of his authority. The messenger would announce Estevàn's arrival outside the city. In the past, the Indians had invited Estevàn in, giving him many presents including young women.

When he tried that approach at Hawikuh, the leader of the pueblo smashed the rattle to the ground and averred that he knew whom Estevánrepresented. He warned the messenger that he would kill Estevánand his Aztec companions if they attempted to enter the city. Estevá, showing an incredible lack of caution, defied the pueblo leader and entered the city. As warned, the Indians seized him, bound him and confined him over night. The next day, Estevánand his Aztec followers were set loose on the plain outside the pueblo where they had to run a gauntlet of pueblo Indian warriors to escape. Estevánand most of his men died, shot full of arrows.

At least that is one version. Indian lore also provides variations on this story. In several, Estevánis the only one killed. His special gourd rattle may have been his downfall— he had gotten it from Indians who were enemies of the pueblo Indians. Thus he died for guilt by association. Another purported motive for killing Estevávcenters on his exotic good looks and charisma: the Indians killed him because their women found him so attractive.

Whatever the reason for Estevá's death at the hands of the warriors of Cibola, Fray Marcos halted in sight of this pueblo, looking across at it from the heights to the west of the Zuni River in a cover of desert scrub. Marcos wrote:

> *Cibola is situated on a plain at the skirt of a round hill. It has the appearance of a very beautiful town, the best I have seen in these parts. The houses are of the style that the Indians had described to me, all of stone, with stories and terraces, as well as I could see from a hill where I was able to view it. The city is bigger than Mexico City. At times, I was tempted to go on to the city itself, because I knew I risked only life, which I had offered to God on the day I started the journey. But in the end I was afraid to try it, realizing my danger and that if I died, I would not be able to make a report on this country, which to me appears the greatest and best of the discoveries I have made.*

The Indians told Marcos that this pueblo, Hawikuh, was the least impressive of the seven cities of Cibola. His report continues:

Viewing the geographic setting of the city, I thought it appropriate to name this country the new kingdom of Saint Francis. There, with the aid of the Indians, I made a great heap of stones, and on top of it I placed a cross, small and light because I lacked the equipment to make it larger. I announced that I was erecting this cross and monument in the name of Don Antonio de Mendoza, Viceroy of New Spain, for our lord the Emperor, in token of possession and conforming to the instructions. I proclaimed that in this act of possession I was taking all of the seven cities....

Zuni Pueblo ca. 1903

Having gotten as close to Cibola as he dared, the French priest and his Aztec companions made a prudent strategic withdrawal. On or about May 24, 1539, they made their way as quickly as possible through the difficult mountain and desert terrain back to New Spain. The marker he left behind signified, to the Spanish, that the land of Cibola now belonged to Spain, claimed by Marcos on behalf of Viceroy Mendoza and Charles V. Marcos was back in Mexico City in August and he delivered a written report to Viceroy Mendoza dated August 26, 1539.

Rumors again circulated wildly in New Spain that Marcos had found the cities of gold, now given the name the Seven Cities of Cibola. In fairness, his report refers to a "rich and populous" civilization called Cibola. He did not write about finding gold there. If he made that assertion privately, there is no record of it. But his expedition and report to the viceroy would soon lead to a full-blown invasion of Cibola and the rest of Southwest and Midwest America the next year, officially backed by Viceroy Mendoza, and financed by numerous wealthy investors.

One week before Fray Marcos gazed down from his hiding spot atop a hill onto one of the gleaming cities of Cibola, another expedition sailed to conquer La Florida. This invasion force sailed from Havana, Cuba, under the command of Hernando de Soto on May 18, 1539.

Hernando de Soto

De Soto was born in the Extremadura region of Spain near the Portuguese border in 1496 or 1497. His parents were hidalgos—Spanish gentry. In 1514, young Hernando sailed with Pedrarias Dávila, the first governor of Panama, in the conquest of Central America. He made his mark there by seizing native caciques (chiefs) and then holding them hostage to force capitulation by their Indian subjects. He gained fame as an excellent horseman and deadly lancer. The mounted Spaniard with a steel-tipped lance was a devastating weapon against the Indian warriors, much more so than Spain's relatively primitive firearms.

In 1530, De Soto held office in Nicaragua and also explored the Yucatan Peninsula looking unsuccessfully for a water passage to the South Sea. Although he was one of the richest men in Nicaragua at that time, having accumulated a great deal of Indian gold, he was not satisfied with his accomplishments or the size of his estate.

In December 1531, De Soto sailed with the expedition of Francisco Pizarro and took part in the invasion of the Inca Empire. As Pizarro's lieutenant, De Soto boldly rode into the camp of the Inca Emperor, Atahualpa, at the head of fifteen men to parlay with the powerful overlord of hundreds of thousands of Incan warriors.

At the Battle of Cajamarca the next day, November 16, 1532, De Soto captured Atahualpa and plundered his tents. Pizarro, with 168 Spaniards, took advantage of the civil war that destabilized the Inca Empire, murdered Atahualpa, and put a puppet ruler he could control at the head of the empire. For his role in this magnificent accomplishment, De Soto shared a major portion (fourth largest) of the Incan gold and silver, worth one hundred thousand ducats (approximately $10 million today) according to one report. That, added to his already sizeable wealth accumulated in Central America, meant that De Soto could return to Spain and live in luxury never dreamed of by his parents.

De Soto arrived in Spain in 1536 but clearly had no plans to settle down there. He longed for greater conquests. In November, he married the daughter of his first commander, Dávila. He and his bride, Isabel de Bobadilla, lived in luxury in Seville with a sumptuous household maintained by many servants. De Soto began to petition the court of Charles V for a governorship, first targeting Quito then Guatemala. Charles V looked favorably on De Soto not only because of his impressive accomplishments but also because he owed De Soto 50,000 ducats ($5 million today).

Charles V ultimately granted De Soto the title of Adelantado of La Florida in 1537. Perhaps he would succeed where Narváez, Ayllón, and Ponce de León had failed so miserably. The king gave De Soto many concessions including all but the royal one-fifth of gold and silver he would find, tax incentives on what wealth he would accumulate, the right to select thirty-six square miles of the best land as his personal estate, and the title of marquess of a colony that would extend about 600 miles along the coast of La Florida. He had four years to accomplish his conquest of this new territory. During that time he would also serve as Governor of Cuba, giving him specific advantages there to acquire the necessary ships, horses, supplies, and equipment not brought directly from Spain.

To assist him, De Soto selected several men with whom he had served in Central America and Peru. He appointed Luís de Moscoso y Alvarado to the positions of camp master and field marshal. He named Nuño de Tovar as captain general. Juan Rodríguez Lobillo, another of his former comrades in arms, served as captain of a company of foot soldiers.

The Royal Accountant, Juan de Añasco, came from Seville. He would play a major role in the expedition, serving as a captain of mounted soldiers, and De Soto would call on him frequently for particularly dangerous assignments. Another key person, Baltasar de Gallegos, a relative of Cabeza de Vaca, became highly regarded; he liquidated his Spanish estate to help finance De Soto's venture.

Three individuals who provided contemporary accounts of the De Soto expedition also deserve mention: Luís Hernández de Biedma served as Royal Factor (responsible for trading goods or materials for the crown); Rodrigo Rangel was De Soto's private secretary; and an anonymous "Gentleman of Elvas," a Portuguese citizen who took part in the De Soto expedition. These three men experienced the full scope of the expedition on land and at sea with all of the hardships, dangers, and privation. They lived to tell about it and, fortunately for us, wrote about their experiences.

A fourth account, in many ways the richest report of the expedition, was written in 1596 by a very interesting person. Author Gómez Suárez de Figueroa was born on April 16, 1539 to Spanish Captain Garcilaso de la Vega and Inca noblewoman Chimpu Occlo, granddaughter of Pizarro's puppet Inca Emperor Tupac Inca Yupanqui. This young man eventually adopted the name Garcilaso de la Vega, the Inca. He was educated in Cuzco and later made a career in Spain as a soldier and literary figure. His crowning achievement—his history of the De Soto expedition, that sailed for La Florida one month after his birth—he derived from lengthy interviews with an old veteran of the expedition, Gonzalo Silvestre. Consequently, Silvestre plays a major role in most significant adventures in Garcilaso de la Vega's account of the De Soto expedition.

Each of the four narratives of the De Soto expedition provides a different perspective, contains the author's personal bias, and none are complete; also, at times, they are contradictory. From them historians have attempted to establish the route De Soto and his men took as they crossed a great expanse of North America. This book synthesizes the most recent theories regarding the route into one consolidated account.

Most of the men recruited by De Soto came from his native region of Extremadura. That region was impoverished and many notable conquistadors including Cortés and Pizarro came from there. For the most part, the estimated 700 men came from a wide network of kinsmen and associates known to De Soto, Moscoso, or some of the other principals. Their average age was twenty-four, but some were as young as fifteen; De Soto was about forty at the time he assembled his expeditionary force in Spain.

There were at least six women in the force. The men had various skills in addition to their duties as soldiers; they included tailors, farmers, blacksmiths, carpenters, sword makers, and farriers. A number of priests also joined the expedition. All these professions would play a role if De Soto found a suitable place in La Florida to colonize. All of them risked their own fortunes as well as their personal safety. The only members of the De Soto expedition who could expect compensation for their service were personal servants, and some of them were slaves. Many of the principals invested their own fortunes in underwriting the venture, buying horses, equipment, and supplies for the expedition. De Soto must have spent a great deal of his wealth on the enterprise; Charles V, as usual, invested nothing and stood to gain his share at no risk.

On April 7, 1538, De Soto sailed from San Lúcar in his newly built flagship, *San Cristóbal* accompanied by his few other ships, bound for Cuba. Twenty ships of the treasure fleet bound for New Spain sailed under his command, in a measure meant to increase their security during the Atlantic crossing. Standing orders forbade any ship from overtaking the flagship—the penalty, imposed by De Soto, would be death for the ship's master who disobeyed that order.

The very night they sailed, a ship under the command of Gonzalo de Salazar, passed the flagship. Sentries on the flagship sounded the alarm, thinking they had been overtaken by a corsair. The men aboard *San Cristóbal* fired their cannon at the ship now ahead of them, the ball ripping through every square sail and striking the water ahead of the ship. The damage to the sails caused the ship to lose headway and *San Cristóbal* would have regained the lead. Unfortunately for all parties, the two ships passed so close that the rigging on both ships became entangled and the flagship nearly capsized.

De Soto, irate from his close encounter with disaster less than one day out of port, decided that Salazar had deliberately disobeyed orders and, at first, decided to behead him. Cooler heads still attached to senior officers talked Adelantado De Soto out of that vindictive act. However, Salazar carried his grudge all the way to New Spain, where he often boasted that he would settle his score with De Soto some day.

Isabelle de Bobadilla, De Soto's young wife, sailed with him. She traveled with her personal attendants, among whom were both white and black slaves. The fleet arrived at the Canary Islands on April 21ˢᵗ, where Isabelle's cousin served as governor. The governor placed one of his illegitimate daughters, a beautiful seventeen-year-old woman named Leonor, under the care of Isabelle and Hernando to serve Isabelle until they could arrange a proper marriage for her in La Florida.

The fleet reached Cuba on June 7, 1538 after an uneventful crossing—uneventful except for Leonor. Incredibly, young Leonor and Nuño de Tovar had spliced their main-brace, to use a nautical euphemism, and Leonor found herself pregnant soon after they landed. Tovar married Leonor, but De Soto demoted him from captain general anyway. Isabelle, Leonor, and the other members of the De Soto household would make their home, temporarily they thought, in Cuba until the Adelantado had erected a suitable settlement in La Florida.

At Santiago, Cuba, Vasco Porcallo, then fifty years old, joined De Soto's expedition, providing a wealth of horses, equipment, and supplies; but the most important element he contributed was a large herd of hogs, that would sustain the expedition on what would be their epic march across North America.

Porcallo had similarly contributed to the Narváez expedition and his brother had died during that debacle. Porcallo, who had a long history of slave capture, may have joined with that purpose in mind. He was the wealthiest man in Cuba and his mines and plantations consumed slaves quickly; he continually needed to replace them with new slaves. De Soto rewarded Porcallo with the title of lieutenant general of the expeditionary force.

During the winter, De Soto acquired additional ships, horses, and supplies. In anticipation of an early voyage in the spring, he sent out an advance party to scout the west coast of Florida for a suitable landing site. Juan de Añasco,

Francisco Maldonado, and fifty men in three ships sailed along the Gulf Coast of Florida searching for suitable landing sites and capturing Indians to serve as interpreters and guides for the expedition. Juan López served as their pilot. They returned after two months thankful that they had survived their ordeals, which included near-starvation.

De Soto showed the captured Indians gold, and they indicated that much of that metal could be had in Florida. De Soto's enthusiasm for an early departure became even more heightened when he learned that Viceroy Mendoza in New Spain had a second expedition preparing to enter into La Florida—following the favorable report by Fray Marcos regarding the Seven Cities of Cibola.

De Soto would brook no competition on his royal charter for settlement of La Florida. A messenger De Soto sent to Mendoza notifying him of De Soto's charter returned with the response that La Florida extended so great a distance that the Adelantado should not be concerned; their two expeditionary forces would not come into contact or conflict. As it turned out, the two expeditions would come close, but fail to make contact.

Mendoza was undeterred by what he heard from De Soto. He dispatched Francisco Vázquez de Coronado on his equally epic journey on February 23, 1540. By that time, De Soto would have spent his first winter in La Florida. We will take up the Coronado expedition in a later chapter.

Appointing Isabelle as acting Governor of Cuba, De Soto made his will on May 10th, and eight days later set sail from Havana for La Florida. His fleet consisted of nine ships. Five naos designed for deep water cargo operations carried men, horses, pigs, dogs, equipment, and supplies. Two caravels and two bergantines provided shallower draft capability to ferry men, horses, cattle, and supplies ashore and also served for exploration in shallow waters and restricted bays. The caravel was the fastest vessel of the fleet. The bergantines' large open interior contained two masts with sails and benches for oarsmen to row the boat. They could accommodate up to fifty passengers as well as their crew.

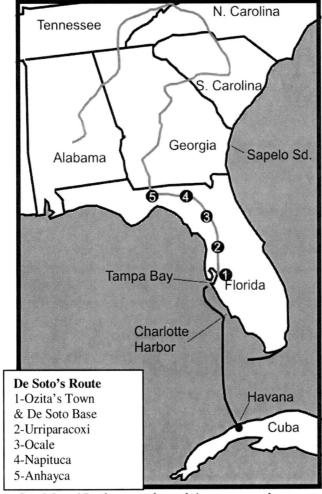

On May 25, they anchored in protected waters on the north side of the Florida Keys, at a position their pilot estimated as due west of the Bay of Juan Ponce, known today as Charlotte Harbor. Añasco couldn't recognize where they were with regard to his voyage of the winter, so he, De Soto and the fleet pilot, Martín, boarded one of the bergantines and rowed to shore, coasting along in a northerly direction looking for the deep bay they had found on their earlier voyage. When night fell, they still had not found the bay, and the wind kept them on the shore. They went ashore and made camp in an area where they saw clear signs of an Indian presence. This recklessness typified De Soto's career and he carried it into his exploration of La Florida.

The next day, they located Tampa Bay, the one Añasco had chosen during the winter, and began the difficult process of navigating the narrow inlet into the bay. They may have used the channel between Edgemont Key and Anna Maria Island, which provides a two-and-one-half mile wide passage today. The other passage between Edgemont key and Mullet Key is considerably narrower. In any case, they spent five days piloting their boats into the bay, stationing a ship on each side of the passage to prevent grounding as the other ships navigated the channel.

Unbeknownst to De Soto, they had chosen their base camp within the domain of Chief Ozita, who, as we know from the Narváez expedition, had already lost his mother and his nose to the Spanish. He thus had no intention of offering his support for De Soto's invasion of his homeland.

Oblivious to this situation, De Soto began unloading his 600 men and women, 223 horses, a large but unknown number of mastiffs, greyhounds and Irish wolfhounds, and a large herd of pigs, as well as all the other trappings of an expeditionary force that planned to stay ashore for a year or more. They occupied the former village of Ozita on the east side of Tampa Bay adjoining the north side of the Little Manatee River.

Now we need to go back twelve years to an earlier Spanish landing here—the Narváez expedition. After Narváez had marched off into the great unknown, his wife in Cuba had sent men to search for him along the Florida coast. In 1528 at the last known location of Narváez, Juan Ortiz and another man went ashore to talk with what he thought were friendly Indians to learn where the expedition had gone. The Indians promptly seized Ortiz and killed his companion who resisted. This began a twelve-year ordeal for Ortiz. His captors took him to Chief Ozita whose hatred for all Spaniards had reached a crescendo by this time.

Ozita had a large fire built in the center of his village and a barbacoa (a grill of green saplings) placed over the glowing coals. Four Indians seized Ortiz's arms and legs and threw him atop the grill, holding him there as he writhed in agony. When his flesh had seared on his back, they prepared to turn him over. At that point, Ozita's daughter pleaded with her father to spare the poor man any more punishment. The chief nodded to his men and they removed Ortiz. Ozita's wife and daughter cared for Ortiz until his burns healed; his back was a mass of scars. For several years Ortiz lived as a slave, abused by Ozita and forced to do the most menial labor.

Later a neighboring chief, Mocozo, waged war on Ozita, forcing him to temporarily abandon his village. Ozita, for no good reason, took out his wrath on Ortiz. Ozita's daughter learned that her father planned to kill Ortiz, and she arranged for Ortiz to reach the village of Mocozo. Mocozo took Ortiz in and treated him well for the remaining eight or nine years leading up to De Soto's landing in Florida. Ortiz would soon play a major role in the De Soto expedition.

Back to De Soto's expedition: When De Soto landed, he had with him the Indians captured by Añasco. When he took them ashore, he failed to restrain them in chains—a practice he generally used to keep all of his Indian captives from escaping. He soon found himself with no Indian guides or interpreters. This was a very big setback for his expedition; without guides and interpreters he would have to travel through the unknown territory with no idea which direction to take, what to expect from the people, or what resources lay ahead. Juan Ortiz would solve that problem.

In a maneuver that De Soto would often employ, he sent out several small scouting parties in different directions with orders to report back on what they found. One of those parties of forty men headed by Baltasar de Gallegos found Juan Ortiz. He was indistinguishable from the Indians who accompanied him. He was naked, tattooed, burned dark by the sun, and had nearly forgotten how to speak his native language. When one of Gallegos' men attempted to kill him with a lance, Ortiz knocked the lance aside and yelled, "Seville, Seville!" Eventually, he found his tongue and said, "Sirs, for the love of God and St. Mary, don't kill me. I am a Christian, a native of Seville. My name is Juan Ortiz." It took Ortiz many days to recover fully his fluency in Spanish.

Ortiz proved a godsend for De Soto—a Spaniard with a mastery of the local Indian language and familiarity with their customs. But he was ignorant of the lay of the land much beyond their current base camp. He had traveled as far as Mocozo's territory and about thirty miles farther. He told De Soto that a chief called Urriparacoxi lived about 100 miles away in the interior and that his land was fertile, producing much corn.

Urriparacoxi's land sounded much more appealing as a place for settlement since the land around Tampa Bay appeared "too barren." With his base camp established and a reliable interpreter, De Soto was now anxious to begin his march into La Florida. He sent Gallegos out with eighty horsemen and 100 foot soldiers to search for Urriparacoxi. They left base camp on June 20.

While the rest of the expedition waited in Ozita's village, they came under frequent attack by the Indians, suffering casualties and killing some Indians. Vasco Porcallo decided to take Indian slaves to ship back to Cuba. He rode out into the swampy area surrounding their camp with a small company of soldiers in pursuit of the Indians. After a short distance, his horse became mired in the mud and fell on its side, pinning Porcallo under him in his suit of armor.

Porcallo nearly drowned before his men could extricate him. When he was back astride his horse, he was in a foul mood. When they failed to capture more than a few Indian women, his temper rose further. By the time he returned to camp he had decided to abandon the expedition and return to Cuba. The richest man in Cuba made a wise decision. He agreed to leave all of his supplies including the herd of pigs for De Soto's use. He boarded one of the ships with his slaves and servants to return to Cuba. De Soto sent the large cargo vessels back to Cuba and kept the smaller ships for coastal exploration in Florida.

During this early period in the land of Ozita, the chroniclers report some disturbing incidents. In the first, Porcallo, led by one of the Indian guides, went in search of a village of Ozita. The Indian guide apparently led them off on a difficult route through mangrove swamps and thickets in an attempt to lose them. Porcallo decided that the Indian had disobeyed him and had him thrown to the dogs. In another case, De Soto sent an Indian messenger to the land of Urriparacoxi. Before the Indian left, one of the captive Indian women warned him not to return. De Soto learned of this and had the women thrown to the dogs. The Spanish used these brutal acts to intimidate the Indians several more times during their first three months in Florida.

Gallegos had reached the land of Urriparacoxi and found that the Indians had fled from their villages. Finally, thirty men approached the Spaniards and asked what they wanted. Gallegos, with the help of Ortiz, interrogated these men. He found that the territory they were in was not much different from the base camp area. Urriparacoxi's men told Gallegos that a much better land, Ocale, lay to the west. Their description seemed so fantastic to Gallegos that he suspected them of lying in order to get the Spanish to leave their province. Gallegos had his men seize the Indians, place them in chains, and send them back to De Soto under the control of eight of his men.

Along with the Indians, his men took two letters from Gallegos for De Soto. De Soto had conspired with Gallegos to send these two letters reporting on his discoveries: one letter to provide a truthful account, and the other to be a glowing report on the land to encourage the people of the expedition. The public letter from Gallegos indicated that wonderful things lay ahead, somewhere beyond the land of Urriparacoxi. He reported that the Indians of Urriparacoxi said the Ocale people had herds of deer and domesticated turkeys and they traded in gold, silver, and pearls. Of this report, the anonymous Portuguese Gentleman of Elvas wrote:

> ...that the people of that land were hostile to others living in other lands where it was summer most of the year. That land had gold in abundance and when those people came to make war ... they wore hats of gold resembling helmets.

De Soto's men had heard enough. They shared his desire to march for Ocale and to find the Indians who had helmets of gold. De Soto ordered Captain Pedro Calderón to remain at the base camp with forty horsemen and sixty foot soldiers to protect the landing site and await further orders. De Soto had also sent orders back to Cuba to have ships return to the landing with additional supplies.

On July 15, 1540, De Soto led 320 men, women, and enslaved Indian porters into the tangled swamps of Florida bound for the land of Urriparacoxi to join with Gallegos and his 180 men, then on to Ocale where he planned to establish his winter headquarters. Mounted soldiers led the way and another troop of mounted soldiers followed the force to protect their rear from Indian guerrilla attack. Swineherds drove the herd of pigs along with De Soto's army. They left a trail anyone could have followed through the wilderness as they traveled northeast first to the land of Mocozo and then north to the area of Ocale dotted with lakes.

Two days into the trek, a page named Prado, assigned to De Soto, died of the heat. A few days later, they entered the land of Chief Urriparacoxi. De Soto sent Gallegos to summon the chief to a meeting, but the chief never appeared. De Soto moved on. By July 23rd they had reached the vicinity of Nobleton, Florida—about seventy-three miles from their base camp on Tampa Bay. Their ability to cover only nine miles per day gives an indication of the difficulty of moving an expeditionary force of several hundred people and animals through Florida in the sixteenth century. De Soto must have come to realize that he would be in La Florida a very long time to fully explore it.

To maintain morale and fitness of his men for such a long campaign in so hostile an environment took a special talent. De Soto apparently possessed that ability because his men followed him for several years through incredible hardships over a vast area of North America. The lure of gold or other wealth certainly kept them motivated for much of the journey. Later, the fear of death in that foreign land would spur them on. Along the journey, De Soto allowed his men to plunder the Indian villages for whatever they needed, particularly food, but also they took advantage of the Indian women and seized whatever valuables they found. These incentives kept his force moving through difficult terrain in broiling heat and freezing cold in spite of heavy losses due to malnutrition, disease, and combat with the Indians.

In Ocale, the Spaniards met stiff resistance. The Indians of that region had already met the Spanish when Narváez and his men passed through twelve years before. Like Urriparacoxi, the chief of Ocale refused to meet with De Soto. Instead he sent the following message according to Garcilaso de la Vega, the Inca:

> *The cacique replied haughtily, saying that he had already had much information from other Castilians who had come to that country years before as to who they were, and he knew very well about their lives and customs, which consisted in occupying themselves like vagabonds in going from one land to another, living from robbing, pillaging, and murdering those who had not offended them in any way. He by no means desired friendship or peace with such people, but rather mortal and perpetual warfare, and even though they might be as brave as they boasted of being, he had no fear of them because he and his vassals considered themselves no less valiant.*

True to his word, the chief of Ocale captured a number of Spaniards, killed them, and sent their heads back to De Soto as a sign of what would come if he remained at Ocale.

Clearly, De Soto and his force were not welcome there. From a captured Indian, he learned that an Indian land farther away, called Apalachee, was rich with corn and other foodstuffs—the things the Spanish needed most urgently at this point. They had been nourished for most of their journey so far by corn stolen from Indian villages along the way. At Ocale they reckoned that they had enough for about three months. Soon they would need much more.

De Soto rode out of Ocale on August 11th at the head of fifty horsemen and 100 foot soldiers, bound for Apalachee, which he thought lay seven days away. He left Luis de Moscoso in charge of the rest of the force. During the next thirty days De Soto and his men slogged on through the forests, over rivers, and through swamps, encountering hostile Indians from several different polities. Along the way, he sent word for Moscoso to bring up the rest of the force, and they continued as one body toward Apalachee.

At the village of Napituca De Soto engaged in a very risky tactic. He had continued to capture chiefs of various tribes along the way and would hold them hostage as he passed through their lands. At Napituca, the Indians asked him to release one of their allies' chiefs. He agreed to come with the chief and a small number of men to meet with the chief of Napituca. Juan Ortiz was informed by his Indian interpreters— apparently more loyal to the Spanish than to the Indians of Napituca—that the proposed meeting with the chief was a trap. Ortiz warned De Soto that the Indians planned to kill him when he met with their chief.

The day De Soto had agreed to meet with the Napitucans, 400 Indian warriors concealed themselves in the woods around the clearing where the meeting would take place. De Soto and a small number of men went to the appointed spot for the meeting. He had arranged for Moscoso to stand ready with his forces to come to his aid when he had a trumpeter blow the signal. Even before the trumpet blast, Moscoso saw that the Indian warriors were streaming toward De Soto. He led his soldiers forward and the mounted lancers engaged the Indians, killing many.

De Soto mounted his horse and took up the fight, but his horse fell under a barrage of Indian arrows. Other horsemen surrounded De Soto, protecting him from the onslaught of arrows. The Indians fled from the mounted soldiers, many taking refuge in two lakes near the battle site. The Spaniards surrounded the lakes and prevented the Indians from escaping. They stayed in the lakes all day and through the night; gradually most came ashore. Finally the next day, the remaining Indians swam ashore. De Soto took about 300 prisoners, placing them in iron collars and chaining them together.

The chiefs, about a dozen in all, De Soto freed. He expected them to become his friends. Instead, one of them attacked De Soto, striking him in the face with his fist, knocking him unconscious. At that, all of the Indians rose in revolt, grabbing Spanish swords or anything else at hand, and began to attack their captors. Many Indians were killed as well as a few Spaniards in this exchange.

De Soto slumbered through most of the battle. When he awoke, he found he had several teeth missing, cut lips, and a bad temper. He ordered the young Indian boys to be kept in chains as porters, and then had the rest of the Indians taken to the plaza of the village. There they were tied to stakes, and the more docile Indians captured earlier in their journey obeyed De Soto's order to shoot them with arrows. De Soto had to exist on a liquid diet for a week or so until his throbbing mouth healed.

On September 23, De Soto resumed his march for Apalachee, soon arriving at the east side of the Suwannee River about thirty miles from the coast. Since leaving Tampa Bay on June 15th, they had covered a little over 200 miles. During that journey, the country and the Indians had taken their toll. De Soto had lost men and horses; the contemporary chroniclers rated the horses as important if not more important than the men.

At the Suwannee they had to stop and build a bridge to cross the river. By September 25th, they were across the river and arrived in the region of Apalachee on September 30th. There they captured some Indian women. As they pressed on into Apalachee, one Spaniard who had lingered behind with one of the captured women had to be rescued when she got the better of him after he tried to assault her. His comrades found her with a firm grip on the man's most tender anatomy, the man screaming for help. Clearly, if the warriors of Apalachee were as fierce as their women, De Soto's army was in for a fight.

De Soto and his force marched on toward Anhayca, the principal city of Apalachee. The approach to that city was through a jungle of trees, vine, cane, and swamp, the cover so thick and impenetrable that the Indians maintained a path through it. However, they cleverly kept the width of the path to about six feet—only wide enough for two men to walk abreast. That way, they could easily prevent a large raiding party from storming into the city. The defense was also effective against De Soto and his army. The vanguard widened the path using hatchets to allow a larger force to come behind them. They had to proceed slowly, fighting all the way. Their horses were useless in this confined wooded gauntlet.

When they broke out into more open territory, they found that the Apalachee had built defenses against horses by tying horizontal logs at a low height between trees. These Indians had learned of Spanish combat tactics from the Narváez expedition twelve years earlier and were more prepared to fight the Spanish than any others they would encounter. However, the hurdles didn't prevent the horsemen from entering the cornfields outside of the village beyond.

Horsemen rode about the fields killing with their lances every Indian who resisted or showed aggression. They bivouacked in a village named Calahuchi on October 5th. The next day, they proceeded to Anhayca (Tallahassee), which they found abandoned. De Soto decided to make this city their winter quarters. He had covered 320 miles since leaving Tampa Bay, arriving in Anhayca with nearly all of his force intact, most of his horses, all of his pigs, hundreds of Indian slaves in chains, and all but his most favorite dog, Bruto, that had died attacking the Indians during the crossing of the Suwannee River. In 1987, archaeologists uncovered artifacts of sixteenth-century Spanish origin in that city, identifying the winter quarters of De Soto's army.

The Spanish depended on Indians to carry their burdens while traveling, and also to do menial labor such as gathering and grinding corn, and bringing firewood to the camp. The Gentleman from Elvas described the capture of Indians near Napituca during the final push of the troops to Anhayca:

> ...the governor sent two captains, each one in a different direction, in search of the Indians. They captured a hundred head, among Indian men and women. Of the latter [women], there, as well as in any other part where forays were made, the captain selected one or two for the governor and the others were divided among themselves and those who went with them. These Indians they took along in chains with collars about their necks and they were used for carrying the baggage and grinding the maize and for other services which so fastened in this manner they could perform. Sometimes it happened that when they went with them for firewood or maize they would kill the Christian who was leading them and would escape with the chain. Others at night would file the chain off with a bit of stone.... Those who were caught at it paid for themselves and for those others, so that on another day they might not dare do likewise. As soon as the women and young children were a hundred leagues from their land, having become unmindful, they were taken along unbound, and served in that way, and in a very short time learned the language of the Christians.

From the foregoing we can see that De Soto had his pick of the female captives. He moved into the chief's house in Anhayca and set up his household with ample servants to cater to his needs through the winter. The store of food including maize, dried venison, melons, squash, nuts, and other goods found in Apalachee would provide ample supplies for their winter encampment. However, during his stay there the men would not be idle. De Soto sent out several scouting parties to explore the land of Apalachee. One party led by Juan de Añasco headed south to find the coast that Indians said was about ten leagues distant—a very accurate estimate. With Indian guides, he traveled over difficult terrain until he reached the village of Aute at the mouth of a river flowing into a large bay.

There is disagreement among historians regarding where on the coast Añasco arrived. Some argue that he came to the mouth of the St. Marks River in Apalachee Bay. Others have him arriving at Apalachicola Bay. This latter position corresponds much more favorably with the description given by Cabeza de Vaca as the departure point of the Narváez expedition, and Añasco reported that he found on the coast evidence of that expedition's boatbuilding and horse butchering. Further, the Indians indicated that they had taken him to the spot where the previous Spanish expedition had departed, obviously hoping Añasco and his associates would do the same. Thus, the Spanish dubbed this bay the Bay of Horses.

Añasco returned to De Soto at Anhayca and reported what he had found. De Soto rewarded him with an even more challenging assignment. He was to ride with a detachment of twenty-nine horsemen the 320 miles back to Tampa Bay to summon Calderón and his horsemen to join him at Anhayca. Añasco's orders were then to sail the boats with Calderón's foot soldiers back to the Bay of Horses. Añasco must have had some experience as a navigator for De Soto to entrust this mission to him.

On November 17th, Añasco left Anhayca on his perilous mission, often traveling at night to avoid Indian settlements, and when they could, traveling by day as well. Along the way, they foraged for food and raided Indian caches when given the opportunity. Amazingly, he made it back to Tampa Bay and Ozita's village in eleven days—a journey that had taken De Soto's army more than eighty days. The detachment arrived on November 27th with the loss of two men, both of whom died of some unknown illness along the way.

Captain Calderón's first words were, "Is there much gold in the land?" Añasco could only repeat rumors that he had heard at Apalachee that a rich tribe to the northeast had much gold, pearls, and other wealth. De Soto planned to go to that location as soon as winter was over.

Calderón's passage back to Apalachee proved much more difficult than Añasco's. He traveled with a combined force of horsemen and foot soldiers since the two bergantines available to sail to the Bay of Horses could not carry all the foot soldiers. Forced to travel cross-country more slowly, Calderón's force attracted more attention, and a pitched battle broke out at one of the river crossings in which the Indians inflicted some damage, wounding many. He arrived at Anhayca having lost two men and seven horses. Many of his men were wounded. He arrived before Añasco reached the Bay of Horses.

Añasco had difficulties that delayed his arrival until December 28th. At Tampa Bay, the bergantines needed repairs before they could safely put to sea. Then, if they sailed along the coast (and probably did for safety), they had a distance of 250 miles to cover. He had left flags in the tops of trees at the inlet to the bay so that he could locate it from the sea, but found he couldn't see them when he explored the coast. Consequently, the bergantines spent a great deal more time searching for the Bay of Horses and his men were exhausted by the time they reached Anhayca.

Nonetheless, De Soto had most of the men he had started with together in Apalachee, most of his horses, hundreds of Indian slaves, and planned to make a fresh start for a fabulously wealthy city somewhere to the northeast as soon as his men were rested and the weather permitted.

Chapter 5
De Soto's March to Death

The winter rest De Soto had counted on at Anhayca did not prove restorative. The Apalachee attacked his men whenever they ventured out of the stockade he had built around the Indian city. These guerrilla attacks took their toll on life and morale. Most troubling, the Apalachee set fire to the winter camp twice, succeeding in destroying most of the buildings less than two months after De Soto occupied the city. The Spanish couldn't go more than a few hundred yards beyond the stockade without grave risk. The Apalachee attacked the men when they went out to cut firewood; if they sent the slaves out to gather the firewood, the Apalachee released them from their chains and spirited them away. In spite of the food they found in Anhayca, they soon had to leave their fortified camp to raid outlying villages for corn. Those foraging parties also came under attack and suffered casualties.

De Soto ordered punishment for the Apalachee to deter their aggression, but it had no effect. When the Spaniards captured Apalachee warriors, they cut off their noses, cut off their hands or feet, and resorted to burning some of them alive. The Apalachee men took this punishment with incredible stoicism, proclaiming that they were men of Apalachee and would bow to no one.

The Apalachee taunted the Spaniards when they caught them outside the city. Garcilaso the Inca wrote of one such encounter:

A gentleman named Diego de Soto, the governor's nephew, who was one of the best soldiers in the army and a very good horseman, rode out to capture the Indian, more to show his skill and courage than from any need he had for him. When he saw the rider, the Indian ran with extreme swiftness to race with the horse to see whether he could escape by flight, for the natives of this great kingdom of La Florida are swift and famous runners and pride themselves on it. But seeing that the horse was gaining on him, he got under a tree close by, which is a cover that foot soldiers, lacking pikes, are always accustomed to take as a protection against horses. Placing an arrow in his bow—for as we have already said, they always go armed with these weapons—he waited until the Spaniard should come within range. The latter being unable to go under the tree, passed by on one side at a run and made a thrust at the enemy, the lance passing over the left arm, to see if he could reach him. Guarding himself from the blow of the lance, the Indian shot an arrow at the horse at the moment that he came abreast and struck him between the girth and the stirrup with such strength and skill that the horse stumbled on for fifteen or twenty paces and fell dead, not moving again. At this moment there came up at a canter another gentleman, named Diego Velázquez, the governor's groom, no less brave and skillful in horsemanship than the first one. He followed Diego de Soto to aid him if he should need it. Seeing then, the shot that the Indian had made at his companion, he urged his horse and, not being able to go under the tree, he passed to one side, throwing another lance as Diego de Soto had done. The Indian did the same as in the first case, for as the horse came abreast he gave him an arrow wound behind the stirrup, and as before the horse stumbled along until he fell dead at his companion's feet. The two Spanish comrades rose hastily with their lances in their hands and assailed the Indian to avenge the death of their horses, but the latter, content with two good shots he had made in such a short time and with such good fortune, went running to the woods, ridiculing and jeering at them, and turning around to make wry faces and gestures. Keeping pace with them, not running as fast as he could, he said to them: "Let us all fight on foot and we shall see who are the better." With these words and others that he said in vituperation of the Castilians he got away safely, leaving them sorely grieved at such a loss as that of the horses, for since these Indians felt that advantage the Spaniards had over them on horseback, they endeavored and were more pleased to kill one horse than four Christians, and thus they carefully and diligently shot at the horse rather than at the rider.

On another occasion, two Portuguese men went out of the city to pick fruit growing in a tree. After picking the fruit they could reach from the ground, they climbed into the tree. Apalachee warriors watching from the woods saw the two men in the tree and raced toward them with bows ready. One of the men saw the Indians coming and jumped down and ran toward his horse. An Apalachee bowman shot him from behind, and the arrow passed through the man's back with a quarter of the length of the arrow sticking out the front.

The Apalachee had the other Portuguese man trapped in the tree. They took their time and "pierced [him] from one side to the other with three arrows." When the dead man tumbled out of the tree, the Apalachee scalped him in front of Spanish rescuers who were racing to save him. Scalping enemy killed in battle brought prestige to the Apalachee warriors, and the Spanish recorded that warriors advanced in rank through three stages based on the number of scalps they had taken and the rank of their victims.

The power of the Apalachee bows and the nimbleness of their warriors gave them a distinct advantage over the Spaniards. Even the powerful advantage horses had given the Spanish over the Aztec and Inca warriors, who fought in formation, proved less daunting once the Indians of La Florida learned how to take them down with well-placed bow shots. When the Spanish examined some of the horses killed by the Indians, they found that the arrows could penetrate the heavy muscles of the horses and pass nearly through their bodies. The bows of the Indians in North America were rated as much more powerful than those encountered in Central and South America, and the bowmen stronger and more accurate shots.

De Soto had learned from captured Indians that the only wealth to be found in Apalachee was stockpiles of food. But two of the Indians captured, young men of about sixteen years old named Marcos and Pericos (aka Pedro), had experience in trading for goods far from Apalachee. They described the land of Cofitachequi as having "much gold and silver and many valuable pearls." This intelligence gave De Soto his next destination.

Prior to leaving Anhayca for Cofitachequi, De Soto dispatched Francisco Maldonado with fifty men to take the two bergantines from the Bay of Horses and explore the coast to the west to locate a suitable river inlet that had deep water and an Indian village nearby. This would serve as his port on the Gulf Coast for transferring men and goods into and out of La Florida. Maldonado returned in two months and reported that he had found such a place. He said the Indian village of Ochuse lay about sixty leagues west of the Bay of Horses. Historians place Ochuse at Pensacola, Florida, and the coast-wise distance from Apalachicola Bay to Pensacola is about sixty leagues—about 200 miles.

Maldonado received orders to sail to Cuba to take on supplies, brief Doña Isabelle on their progress, and then to rendezvous with De Soto at Pensacola late in the summer. If he failed to find De Soto there by the end of summer, he was to sail along the coast in search of him and his army. Maldonado set sail for Cuba on February 26, 1540.

Just before the Spanish were to leave Anhayca, a strange event occurred. Their principal guide to Cofitachequi,

Pericos, came under a "demonic possession" and nearly died from fear. Garcilaso the Inca tells us:

> It happened about midnight of the night before the departure [Pedro] shouted so loudly for help, saying that they were killing him. The whole army was aroused, believing that it was some treason of the Indians, and thus they sounded the alarm and very quickly got under arms, the cavalry and infantry drawn up in squadrons.... They went out to see where the alarms had come from, and they found that the Indian Pedro had caused it with his shouts. He was trembling with fear, terrified and half dead.... He said that the devil, with a horrible visage and accompanied by many servants, had come to him and told him not to guide the Spaniards where he had promised to guide them or he would kill him.... The devil had hissed at him and dragged him through the room, giving him many blows all over the body....He knew [the devil] would have ended by killing him if two Spaniards had not been able to come so quickly to his assistance.... He begged them for the love of God to baptize him at once so that the devil would not come back to kill him....The general ordered the priests, clerics, and friars to be summoned and told them to do what they considered best after inquiring into the case. Having heard the Indian, they baptized him immediately and remained with him all that night and following day....

On March 3, 1540, De Soto and his army left Anhayca following Pericos, their young convert, north for Cofita-chequi. De Soto and a small party rode out ahead of the main force, as was his wont, to scout ahead and search for trouble as well as possible sources of food. They had many rivers and swamps to cross before they would reach the region of Cofitachequi in South Carolina on the Wateree River. They would pass through barren areas where no Indians lived and also pass through various villages of distinct groups including Capachequi, Toa, Ichisi, Altamaha, Ocute, Cofaqui, and Hymahi.

The journey through these villages was without much combat once they left the area under the Apalachee behind them. One man was killed in a skirmish with Indians at Capachequi, and Beníto Fernández drowned crossing a river. As they progressed farther north into the interior, the houses built by the Indians changed from simple structures with a bent sapling frame and thatch covering to more substantial post-in-ground construction with wattle and daub walls, roofed with woven cane matting.

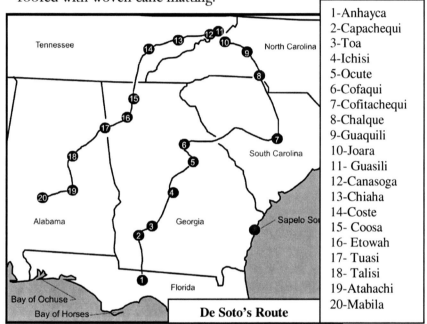

1-Anhayca
2-Capachequi
3-Toa
4-Ichisi
5-Ocute
6-Cofaqui
7-Cofitachequi
8-Chalque
9-Guaquili
10-Joara
11- Guasili
12-Canasoga
13-Chiaha
14-Coste
15- Coosa
16- Etowah
17- Tuasi
18- Talisi
19-Atahachi
20-Mabila

De Soto's Route

At most villages, the Indians treated them kindly and generously, offering not only food and water but also porters to carry the Spaniards' baggage. One village, Cofaqui, provided 700 porters; Ocute provide 400. By mid-April the Spaniards, and apparently their Indian guides, were lost somewhere in South Carolina between the Savannah and Congaree Rivers. The Savannah River carried off a significant number of De Soto's hogs. Their descendants are foraging in the Georgia forests to this day.

The army had to subsist on scant rations and, as a last resort, De Soto agreed to the slaughter of a few of the full-grown hogs to supplement the meager corn diet the army had left. The trail they had followed to the Savannah River had petered out, and neither Marcos, nor Pericos, nor any of the other Indian guides knew the route that would take them to what must have seemed an illusory Cofitachequi. Pericos said he thought that a four-day march to the east would take them there; the other guides disagreed, but none seemed credible to De Soto. He sent out scouting parties in four different directions to try to identify the proper trail. One brought back four Indian captives from an area south of their position. De Soto, through his interpreter, interrogated one of the men, demanding to know where he could find a major Indian village. The man refused to talk. De Soto had him burned alive in front of the other three. They also refused to talk and met the same fate.

On April 27, Captain Gallegos, leader of one of the scouting parties, returned to report that he had captured a woman who said there was a powerful city to the north. On April 30, De Soto rode at the head of some of his horsemen, guided by the woman Gallegos had found. They came to the Wateree River where they made camp. They had traveled a bit over 300 miles since leaving Anhayca nearly sixty days before.

Juan Añasco led a scouting party of thirty men ahead to see if he could locate the city of Cofitachequi and take some hostages. As he crept forward in the fading light, he and his men heard voices coming through the woods. At dusk, they came to a river bank and saw that a village lay on the other side of the river. The scouts returned to De Soto and told him what they had found.

The next morning, De Soto and his troop of horsemen went up to the west side of the river and Pericos called to men on the opposite shore. They could understand his Muskogean dialect; taking dugout canoes, the Cofitachequi men paddled across the river. Along with the men came a young woman of noble status. She told the Spaniards that they were welcome in her city and canoes would come to ferry them across the river.

As they awaited transport across the river, a grand show took place. A woman decked out in the finest clothing of the region arrived at the opposite side of the river carried on a litter covered with an awning. She stepped down from the litter and boarded a specially prepared dugout canoe with a cushioned seat and an awning. Once settled on her floating throne, Indians paddled her canoe across to De Soto. The Spaniards took this woman to be the paramount chief of the region of Cofitachequi; unfortunately, none of the chroniclers recorded her name. They called her the Lady of Cofitachequi.

The Lady approached De Soto who sat on a camp stool that his servants carried from site to site. The Lady of Cofitachequi also had a seat brought for her use placed in front of De Soto. She spoke these words to him according to the Gentleman from Elvas:

'O, Excellent Lord: May your Lordship's coming to these our lands be of very good augury, although my possibility does not equal my wishes and my services are not equal to what I desire and to the merits of so powerful a prince as your Lordship; for good will is more worthy of acceptance than all the treasures of the world which may be offered without it. With

very sincere and open good will I offer you my person, my lands, my vassals, and this poor service."

And she presented him a quantity of clothing of the country which she brought in the other canoes, namely, blankets and skins. And from her neck she drew a long string of pearl beads and threw it about the neck of the governor, exchanging with him many gracious words of affection and courtesy.

After De Soto and his men crossed the river in the Indian canoes, he received a gift of many hens (turkeys). The chroniclers say that the land was fertile and pleasant and De Soto's men believed they had found a good place to settle. Further, the Indians told them that the sea was only two days march to the east. That might have been true for Indians, but it would have taken De Soto's men perhaps a week to make the journey. They soon learned that these Indians knew of the failed settlement of Ayllón, and they showed the Spaniards a dagger and some trade beads that could only have come from Ayllón's expedition. They also knew that Ayllón had died and the rest of his colonists had abandoned their coastal settlement. The Gentleman of Elvas continued:

All the men were of the opinion that they should settle in that land as it was an excellent region; that if it were settled, all the ships from New Spain and those from Peru, Santa Marta, and Tierra Firme, on their way to Spain, would come to take advantage of the stop there, for their route passes by there; and as it is a good land and suitable for making profits.

All the men were correct; De Soto should have settled there, but he had more grandiose plans, which the anonymous Portuguese chronicler recorded as:

Since the governor's purpose was to seek another treasure like that of Atahualpa, the lord of Peru, he had no wish to content himself with good land or with pearls, even though many of them were worth their weight in gold and, if the land were to be allotted in repartimiento, those pearls which the Indians would get afterward would be worth more; for those they have, inasmuch as they are bored by fire, lose their color thereby. The governor replied to those who urged him to settle that there was

*not food in the whole land for the support of his men for a single
month; that it was necessary to hasten to the port of Ochuse
where Maldonado was to wait; that if another richer land were
not found they could always return to that one whenever they
wished....*

As he invariably did, the Governor of La Florida asked
the Cofitachequi whether a great ruler lived near them. This
was invariably also the Indians chance to send the Spaniards
on their way by directing them to a land far away or into the
perils of their enemies. The Cofitachequi told De Soto that
twelve-days' journey northwest lay the region of Chiaha
under the control of the Coosa—De Soto had heard of the
Coosa while at Apalachee. He had his new destination and
the army would have to forget settling down permanently in
the pleasant woodland of South Carolina.

Before the Spaniards left the hospitable village of the
Lady of the Cofitachequi, they robbed the Indian graves of all
the pearls they contained. In the village temple they took 200
pounds of pearls, but De Soto ordered them to leave most of
them there when the Lady of Cofitachequi told him he would
find so many pearls in the town of Talimeco that their horses
would not have the strength to carry them.

With the Lady of Cofitachequi as guide, they went to
Talimeco, a city of 500 houses situated about two miles from
the first village. At Talimeco they found the temple on a
mound adjacent to the chieftainess's house. The temple was
festooned with ropes of pearls. Garcilaso tells us that the
temple was one-hundred-paces long and forty-paces wide. As
they entered the darkened interior, the sight of twelve giant
figures startled them. Garcilaso continued:

*[These statues were] such faithful imitations of life and
with such fierce and bold posture that the Castilians stayed to
look at them for a long time without passing on, marveling to
find in such a barbarous country works that, if they had been in
the most famous temples of Rome in the most flourishing period
of its power and empire, would have been esteemed and valued
for their grandeur and perfection. The giants were placed as if to*

guard the door and oppose the entrance of those who might enter.

There were six on one side of the door and six on the other, one after the other, descending gradually in size from the largest to the smallest. The first was four varas high [about twelve feet], the second somewhat less, and so on to the last. They had various weapons in their hands made in proportion to the size of their bodies.

They found wooden chests containing the remains of buried nobles or chiefs of the Cofitachequi. Each chest had a carved image, presumably of the deceased. The chests held pearls and carved shell gorgets as well as the remains of the dead. In addition to large stores of weapons, they also found cloth shawls, feather mantles, painted deerskins, furs, leggings and moccasins. The Spaniards helped themselves to as much plunder as they could carry.

At this city, the Indians told them that whole villages had been abandoned after a pestilence swept through the region. The likely source of such a disease would have been the ill-fated settlement of Ayllón on the coast. Apparently it had taken a decade or so to spread this far into the interior of South Carolina.

De Soto may have been wrong to disagree with his men when they said he should settle in Cofitachequi. On the other hand he correctly stated that the Cofitachequi food supply could not sustain them for long. The winter had passed and the first harvest of the growing season was months away. It made sense from that standpoint to move on. In his typical fashion, he made a prisoner of the Lady of Cofitachequi to guarantee safe passage, food supplies along the way, assistance of Indian porters, and reliable guide services on their journey. They set out for Chiaha on May 14, 1540.

As they left the territory of the Cofitachequi behind, they entered a region dominated by the Cherokee. Near a mountain village the Spaniards called Joara, the Lady of Cofitachequi slipped away, saying she needed to relieve herself in the woods. Along with a slave woman who had accompanied her into the woods, she made her escape, and though De Soto sent men to apprehend her, they failed to find her. At Joara, she joined other slaves that had slipped away including a Cuban, a North African slave, and a black slave. Two Spaniards also may have attempted to slip away, but they were found and returned to the army. From them, De Soto learned that the Lady of Cofitachequi had entered into a liaison with the black slave. The Lady and her lover were headed back to Cofitachequi.

De Soto's route took them into North Carolina near Charlotte, then west and northwest across that state to Tennessee, probably crossing near Embreeville, Tennessee and proceeding to the Indian village of Guasili on May 30. The people of Guasili treated them well, providing what food they could, and also provided porters (whether they were provided voluntarily we don't know). While there, De Soto learned of mines of "yellow metal" in the vicinity. He sent two men, Juan de Villalobos and Francisco de Silvera, with Indian guides to examine the mines, said to be thirty leagues away. They returned in ten days, reporting that the mine appeared to be "brass" (probably copper) but they seemed convinced that the mountains well might also contain gold and silver.

The Spanish army left Guasili on May 31st headed for Chiaha and reached it on June 5th. Their journey from Cofitachequi to Chiaha covered at least 250 miles and it took them twenty-two days, a bit better than they had been averaging, but they had no opposition along the way from the Indians in the territories they traversed and they had sufficient food provided by those same people. That good luck would not continue for much longer.

Chiaha was a village on Zimmerman Island in the French Broad River, according to Charles Hudson. His exhaustive work has become generally accepted among historians, although local authorities anywhere near the purported De Soto route sometimes strongly disagree when Hudson's version of the route bypasses their town. I have relied on his analysis in this book.

The Coosa paramount chief held sway over Chiaha and other villages in this region. At Chiaha they rested and dined on corn, bear meat, honey, and hickory nuts. Initially they joined in games with the Indians of Chiaha, swam with them in the river, and fished there. The idyll was not to last. A dispute over women (what else?) caused hostility to erupt.

Sometime in the middle of June, De Soto told the chief he wanted women for himself and his men. Rodrigo Rangel, De Soto's secretary, said with regard to De Soto's demands for women, "…they wanted the women also in order to make use of them and for their lewdness and lust, and that they baptized them more for their carnal intercourse than to instruct them in the faith…"

On June 19th, the Indians took their women and children and deserted the Spaniards. De Soto caught the chief and forced him to take him to where the Indians were hiding. At the head of a column of thirty horsemen, De Soto rode after the Indians, along the way ordering his men to destroy the cornfields. He found the Indians on a small island. By the time he reached them he had decided not to press for women but he demanded porters. The chief provided 500 men to serve as porters with the condition that they not be restrained in iron collars and chains.

June 28th, the army left Chiaha headed on an arcing route that would take them to a rendezvous with Maldonado at Ochuse. By July 2nd they had reached the village of Coste on an island at the mouth of the Little Tennessee River. Spaniards foraging in the village for food took corn and other belongings from the Indians. This theft provoked the following response recorded in Rodrigo Rangel's first-hand account of the event:

> …the governor entered in the town carelessly and unarmed [that is without armor] with a few unarmed men, and when the soldiers did as was their custom and began to climb on the barbacoas, in the instant they began to do that, the Indians

began to beat them and take their bows and arrows and come forth to the plaza. The Governor commanded that all should suffer it and be tolerant, because of the evident danger in which they were, and that no one should put hand to his weapons; and he began to quarrel with the soldiers, and in order to dissimulate, he also thrashed some of them, and he flattered the cacique and told him that he did not wish that the Christians should anger them, and that he wished to leave to take lodging at the savannah of the island. And the cacique and his people went with him, and as they had withdrawn from the town, in the clear, he gave the command to lay hands on the cacique and ten or twelve principals, and they put them in chains with their collars, and he threatened them and said that he would burn all of them, because they had laid hands on the Christians.

De Soto and his companions spent eight days in that tense situation at Coste waiting for the rest of the army to catch up with him. On July 9th, the governor and his vanguard resumed their march and by July 16th they had reached the main town of the Coosa chiefdom. As they neared, Indian messengers met them on the trail and offered signs of peace. Within sight of the town, the chief came out to greet them borne on a litter carried on the shoulders of some of his men. He wore a robe of marten skins and a crown of feathers. Flanking him in procession were other tribal leaders wearing tall feather headdresses. Adding to the pomp, flute players and singers accompanied the chief, lending their music to the occasion.

The Gentleman from Elvas gives a flowery account of the address the chief made to De Soto. He humbled himself before De Soto and promised him all the support he could provide. He said, "Do not expect me to offer you what is yours, namely my person, lands and vassals. I wish only to occupy myself in commanding my people to welcome you with all diligence and due reverence ...."

This chief of Coosa ruled over many lesser chiefs along the Coosawattee River valley. He was young, in his mid-twenties, and held sway over a fertile and productive region with a population of about 5,000 people. His people spoke various dialects with Muskogean predominating. The Spanish enjoyed access to the corn, beans, grapes, and plums that the Coosa harvested.

In spite of the paramount chief's pledge of friendship, De Soto took him prisoner along with a large number of his men and placed them in chains. This prompted most of the people to evacuate the town, pursued by Spanish soldiers. The soldiers returned with hundreds of men and women in chains. Eventually, De Soto freed the principal men of the Coosa, but kept the chief, his sister, and some tribal leaders hostage.

He departed Coosa at the head of his army with a long train of Indian porters and Indian women in chains on August 20, 1540, headed south toward the Gulf Coast and his rendezvous with Maldonado. He was still several hundred miles from Pensacola.

A day later they had to remain at an Indian village due to the flood condition of the Etowah River. While there they received "the necessary tamemes [Indian porters] and thirty women as slaves." This town, like most that lay ahead on the De Soto route, was heavily fortified with a stout palisade wall made of logs. If De Soto needed a clue, and he probably didn't, the strong defenses meant he was entering a much more warlike region than he had seen since leaving Apalachee in the spring.

On August 30th, the army moved on. During the next two weeks, they passed through several Indian villages where they took more porters and at least sixty more women as slaves. Also during that period, a number of slaves and soldiers slipped away, intent on deserting De Soto and remaining among the Indians. They must have established friendly liaisons with the Indians or they wouldn't have remained behind. Their offspring probably greeted the next foreigners to pass through that region.

They arrived at the village of Talisi on September 18th; there De Soto released the paramount chief of the Coosa, but refused to release the chief's sister. This caused great consternation, the chief weeping for the loss of his sister, but De Soto was unmoved. More than just a sister, that woman could well have been the mother of the next chief of the Coosa, since the line of descent of rulers in their society passed through the female side.

At Talisi, De Soto met representatives from paramount chief Tascaluza, including the chief's son. Although still in his teens, this boy towered over the Spaniards and seemed unimpressed when they galloped about on their horses. De Soto decided to follow the Indian trails into the domain of Tascaluza and to his principal town of Atahachi. It was in the direction of the coast and seemed to be worth his time to investigate regarding its suitability for settlement and possible wealth. The trails paralleled the Coosa River to Atahachi on the Alabama River at Montgomery, Alabama.

The Gentleman from Elvas described the first sight of Tascaluza:

> [De Soto] *sent the maestre de campo, Luis de Moscoso, with fifteen horse to inform [Tascaluza] that he was coming. The cacique was in his dwelling under a balcony. Outside, in front of his dwelling, on an elevated place, was spread a mat for him and on it two cushions, one above the other, where he came to seat himself. His Indians gathered about him, separated somewhat, so that they formed a courtyard and an open space where he was—his most principal Indians being nearest him, and one holding a sort of fan of deerskins which kept the sun from him, round and the size of a shield, quartered with black and white, with a cross made in the middle. From a distance it looked like taffeta, for the colors were very perfect. It was set on a small and very long staff. This was the device he bore in his wars. He was a man, very tall of body, large limbed, lean, and well built. He was greatly feared by his neighbors and vassals. He was lord of many lands and many people. In his aspect he was very dignified.... [Moscoso] galloped their horses in front of him, turning them from one side to the other, and at times toward the cacique. He with great gravity and unconcern from*

*time to time raised his eyes and looked as if in disdain. The
governor arrived but [Tascaluza] made no move to rise.*

Tascaluza was no fawning lesser chief; he would not be
intimidated by the Spaniards. Other chronicles describe
Tascaluza wearing a full-length feather cape and a turban on
his head. De Soto and Tascaluza exchanged words of peace,
the paramount chief speaking in a Muskogean dialect and
Ortiz translating for both parties. Rodrigo Rangel wrote that
De Soto and his men slept in Atahachi that night and in the
morning, De Soto demanded Tascaluza give him porters and
one hundred Indian women. Tascaluza indicated he was not
accustomed to people demanding things from him, he made
demands and people complied. However, this great chief
provided De Soto 400 porters and said that if De Soto and
his army would come to Mabila, another of his towns, he
would provide the women and more porters. Rangel says that
what the Spaniards most desired were the women.

On October 12th, De Soto rode out of Atahachi with
Tascaluza seated on a horse beside him for the journey to the
town of Piachi, a stop on the way to Mabila. At Piachi,
Indians opposed the army's crossing of the river and two
Spaniards died in the conflict. They learned there that, "…
they had killed Don Teodoro, and the black man, who came
forth from the boats of Pánfilo Narváez." More clues that
De Soto needed to be alert for trouble.

Tascaluza had sent messengers ahead, supposedly to
arrange for the additional porters and women slaves, but in
reality to put the city on alert and prepare for battle. He
intended to make short work of this Spanish army in an
ambush there.

De Soto sent two soldiers, Gonzalo Quadrado Xaramillo
and Diego Vázquez, to Mabila (near Selma, Alabama) to
scout the city and report back to him. On October 16th,
Vázquez reported that the city was filled with armed Indians
and women and children were conspicuously absent. It
appeared the city stood ready for battle.

The final push to Mabila began on the morning of October 18, with De Soto, as usual, leading the way with forty horsemen, crossbowmen, footmen, a friar, a priest, a cook, porters, and other slaves. The army straggled along behind him, apparently not taking the warning of pending attack seriously. They had become complacent. Consequently, De Soto arrived at Mabila well ahead of much of the army. Rangel described their arrival:

> ... in order for the Governor not to show weakness, he entered in the town with the cacique, and all entered with him. The Indians then did an arieto, which is their kind of ball with [women] dancing and singing.
>
> While watching this, some soldiers saw them placing bundles of bows and arrows secretively in some palm leaves, another Christian saw that the huts were filled high and low with concealed people. The Governor was warned, and he placed his helmet on his head and commanded that all should mount their horses and warn all the soldiers who had arrived; and scarcely had they left, when the Indians took command of the gates of the wall of the town. And Luis de Moscoso and Baltasar de Gallegos and Espíndola, Captain of the guard, and seven or eight soldiers remained with the Governor.
>
> And the cacique plunged into a hut and refused to come out from it; and then they began to shot arrows at the Governor. Baltasar de Gallegos entered for the cacique, and he not wanting to leave, he [Gallegos] cut off the arm of a principal Indian with a slash. Luis de Moscoso, awaiting him at the door in order not to leave him alone, was fighting like a knight, and he did everything possible, until he could suffer no more, and said: "Señor Baltasar de Gallegos, come forth, or I will have to leave you, for I cannot wait for you any longer."

The city of Mabila was surrounded by a strong palisade of logs and sturdy gates. The Spanish had entered the city with their Indian porters who had deposited all the Spanish belongings on the ground within the walls. When the ambush erupted, Solis died immediately in a hail of arrows. De Soto barely made it out of the city; he had twenty arrows that had stuck in the thick quilted cotton armor he wore. Baltasar and Gallegos made their retreat through another gate. The Indians slammed the gates; in addition to the Spanish supplies, they had a number of their horses tied within the city. The full force of the army still had not arrived at Mabila.

De Soto arrayed his forty men in the plaza outside the city gates. Indian warriors came out to shoot at the Spaniards, but would not venture far from the city wall. Don Carlos Enríquez rode toward those warriors and his horse received an arrow in the chest. When Don Carlos dismounted to remove the arrow, an Indian shot him through the neck and he fell dead.

To draw the Indians out into the open plaza, the Spaniards pretended to retreat, and the trick worked. A large number of Tascaluza's men chased after the fleeing horsemen, who then turned and flanked the Indians, killing them with their lances. At that time the rest of the army arrived. They set fire to the palisade, chopped holes through with axes, and entered the town, setting alight the houses there. In the bitter fighting within the city, Diego de Soto dismounted and began hacking at Indians with his sword. An Indian shot an arrow into Diego's eye; the arrow passed through his skull and he died instantly.

The governor fought from horseback and received an arrow wound in his buttock. The arrow remained there during the rest of the battle and Adelantado De Soto had to stand in his stirrups for the rest of the engagement as it was too painful to sit on his saddle. The battle at Mabila lasted about eight hours.

When most of the warriors had been killed or had surrendered, three Indian men and some women dancers remained cornered by the Spaniards. The men stood behind the women who indicated to the Spaniards that they wished to surrender. As the soldiers came forward the three men shot at them with arrows. Two of the Indians died at the hands of the Spaniards and the third climbed to the top of the palisade wall and, while the soldiers looked on, tied his bowstring around his neck and hanged himself.

De Soto's army had won the battle, but nearly all their possessions that the Indian porters had carried into the city were destroyed in the fire. They lost all their spare clothing, and more than 200 pounds of pearls they had brought all the way from Cofitachequi. Twenty-two men died in the ambush (Garcilaso said forty-seven), and the Indians killed seven horses.

Rangel reported that 148 Spaniards had a total of 688 wounds, some quite serious. Garcilaso wrote that thirty-five soldiers died from their battle wounds later. Rangel also tallied the Indian dead as several thousand, Tascaluza's son among them. We don't know the fate of Tascaluza. The Spaniards did not find his body, spawning stories that he escaped. Others speculate he died in the fire, but no one knows the truth. As usual, the Indian women who survived the battle became Spanish slaves.

In a gruesome aftermath of the battle, the Spanish doctor used fat removed from the dead Indian's bodies to make medical unguents to treat the wounded soldiers. All of his bandages and unguents had been destroyed by the fire in the city. While the doctor attended to the wounded, soldiers butchered the dead horses and foraged in villages near to Mabila to gather enough food to sustain the army. On their searches for food, they found many Indian corpses some distance from Mabila.

De Soto made a fateful decision following the battle at Mabila. Indians told him, before the ambush, that ships awaited him at Ochuse (Pensacola, Florida). He received further confirmation of this from the Indians after the battle. He had planned to go to Ochuse, establish a settlement there, and coordinate with Cuba for the shipment of men and supplies. He would have returned to Cuba with the pearls, furs, and other valuable items he had gotten from the Indians. But after the battle he was empty-handed. He felt that if he returned with nothing to show for the nearly year and a half he had been away his enterprise would end in failure, investors would defect, and he feared the report his men would give (more than 100 had died). As a result he decided he could not take the army to Ochuse to meet Maldonado. He felt compelled to push on within the interior until he found valuable commodities he could take back to Cuba to solidify his claim on La Florida.

When he announced his plan to the army, he faced the possibility of revolt. They had followed him for roughly a 1,400-mile trek through what would be six southeastern states in the US only to arrive at a close brush with death and the loss of all their possessions except for the clothes on their backs, their armor, and their weapons. They knew that Ochuse was perhaps ten days march from Mabila. They were tired, many wounded, and winter would set in soon. They wanted to abandon La Florida and return to Cuba. From there, many had plans to start again in New Spain or Peru where they felt they would have better chances for becoming wealthy. How De Soto had kept them motivated this far must have included the lure of gold at each new Indian region and access to Indian slaves—particularly the several hundred Indian women taken along their route.

Garcilaso the Inca summed up the situation following the battle at Mabila when De Soto discovered talk of mutiny:

> *These things, considered by a man so zealous of his honor as was the governor, produced in him hasty and desperate resolutions…. Thus as rapidly as he could, without revealing anything of his anger, he gave orders that they would again go inland and withdraw from the coast, so as to deprive the ill-disposed of the occasion from disgracing themselves and stirring up all his men to rebellion.*

> *This was the first beginning and the chief cause of this gentlemen and all his army being lost. From that day, as a disillusioned man whose own people have betrayed his hopes and cut off the road to his ambition and destroyed the plan that he had made for settling and holding the land, he never again*

succeeded in doing anything profitable to him...actuated only by indifference, he went about thereafter wasting his time and his life without any gain, always traveling from one place to another without order or purpose, like a man tired of life and desirous of ending it, until he died as we shall see below.

Remarkably, De Soto's officers and the men of his army, now numbering perhaps 500, followed his order and marched or rode off northwest with him. They left Mabila on November 14, 1540, with only a few days' supply of food, facing unknown lands and weather growing cold and wet. They headed into the Moundville area and met hostility almost immediately.

1-Mabila
2-Apafalaya
3-Chicaza
4-Quizquiz
5-Pacaha
6-Caluza
7-Quiguate
8-Coligua
9-Quipana
10-Utiangüe
11-Ayays
12-Anilco
13-Guachoya

De Soto's Route

At a town on the Black Warrior River they found that the entire population had abandoned their community and had taken all their corn and other food across the river. The Indians on the other side of the river made it clear that they wanted the Spaniards to leave their land. De Soto and his army camped beside the river as some of the men built two boats to ferry the army across. During the night, Indians attacked the Spaniards at their camp. De Soto then had men dig foxholes on the shore from which soldiers attacked the next band of Indians that attempted to steal into the camp. This precaution kept the Indians at bay for the week it took to construct the boats.

Each boat held thirty soldiers and several horsemen with their mounts. Gonzalo Silvestre, Garcilaso the Inca's source of information on the De Soto expedition, was one of the three horsemen. As the first boat neared the shore, the Indians fired volley after volley of arrows at them, wounding three Spaniards. Once the boat touched the shore, Silvestre and the other two mounted horsemen leaped ashore and routed the Indians who ran into a canebrake where the horses could not pursue them. The soldiers came ashore and took up positions to defend their beachhead. The boats then began shuttling back and forth across the river bringing the rest of the army to the opposite shore of the Black Warrior. The full army had crossed the river by December 1.

De Soto moved his men to a town where he captured Chief Apafalaya who ruled that region. The town and other villages near it supplied food for the army. Apafalaya led the Spaniards toward the region of Chicaza bordering the Tombigbee River near Columbus, Mississippi. There on the high banks looking across the river they saw a familiar site: hostile warriors massed on the opposite shore warning them not to approach. When De Soto sent an Indian messenger across the river to treat for peace, the warriors executed the man in full sight of the Spaniards. The only course of action was to build another boat. De Soto also sent Gallegos across the river upstream of their position with a company of men to secure a landing spot; he and his men had to swim across the river—a considerable challenge considering the time of year and the temperature of the water. These men had only minimal clothing. Some had only a tunic of deerskin and no shoes, since they had lost everything else in the battle at

Mabila. When Gallegos and his men crossed the river, the Indians of Chicaza withdrew from the river bank, allowing a safe crossing for the main army by December 16th.

The army found the main town of Chicaza abandoned. De Soto decided that this would be there winter quarters. The town had only twenty houses and many of the men in the army slept outside in the snow until they could fell sufficient trees and build additional houses. Fortunately, this region produced much corn and soon the Spaniards had accumulated enough food to see them through the winter. Also, the army was lucky that the Chicaza people stayed away from the Spanish winter camp for some time, giving them the freedom to accumulate their store of food and build their houses.

Then the Indians began to attack the encampment at night in small numbers, harassing the Spaniards night after night. They kept this up for so long that the army became complacent, assuming each new attack was just another minor annoyance. In time, they would pay dearly for their complacence.

During the winter, soldiers captured a few Indians, and one of them was of some importance. De Soto sent this man to the paramount chief of Chicaza requesting that he come and make peace with the Spaniards. In due time the chief appeared with two lesser chiefs named Alibamo and Miculasa. The Gentleman from Elvas wrote:

> They presented the governor with one hundred and fifty rabbits and some clothing of their land, namely blankets and skins. The cacique of Chicaza came to visit him frequently and sometimes the governor ordered him summoned and sent him a horse to go and come.

During one of the chief's visits, he told De Soto that one of his subordinate chiefs refused to pay tribute and that he planned to wage war on that tribe. He asked De Soto to accompany him on the campaign. This was a ruse, according to our anonymous chronicler. He continued:

... for it was planned that while the governor went with him and the camp was divided into two parts, some would attack the governor and others those who remained in Chicaza. [The chief] went to the town where he lived and came with two hundred Indians with their bows and arrows. The governor took thirty horse and eighty foot and went to Saquechuma, as the province of the principal man was called, [the chief] told [De Soto] had rebelled against him.

They found an enclosed town which had been abandoned by the Indians, and those who were with the cacique set fire to the houses in order to conceal their treachery. But since the men taken by the governor were very watchful and prudent, as well as those who remained in Chicaza, on that occasion they did not dare attack us.

The governor invited the cacique and certain of the principal Indians to visit and gave them some pork to eat. And although they were not accustomed to it, they lusted after it so much that Indians would come nightly to certain houses a crossbow shot away from the camp where the hogs were sleeping and kill and carry off as many as they could. Three Indians were seized in the act, two of whom the governor ordered to be shot with arrows and the hands of the other cut off. In that condition he sent him to the cacique ....

The situation at Chicaza grew tense. Animosity between the Indians and the Spaniards grew when four Spaniards went into the Indian village nearest their quarters and stole some furs and skin blankets. That alone should indicate how desperate the conditions were in their winter camp. When De Soto heard what the four men had done, he sentenced them to death. His officers and priests were horrified by the sentence.

When a messenger from the chief arrived to make a complaint, Ortiz the translator, at the urging of Gallegos, mistranslated his words telling De Soto that the chief wanted clemency for the four Spaniards, rather than the punishment the chief demanded. Likewise, Ortiz told the Indian messenger that De Soto said he would punish the men as the chief requested. This diplomatic dishonesty on the part of Ortiz and Gallegos saved their comrades' lives and also mollified the Indian chief for a short while. But that peace would not last.

On March 8, De Soto went to the chief and demanded he provide 200 Indian porters as the army planned to leave Chicaza. De Soto sensed that the chief would not obey and saw the hostility smoldering in the Indian village. He returned to Chicaza and ordered Moscoso to put the army in readiness, anticipating an attack. But the soldiers failed to take the threat seriously and the camp remained unprepared for the attack that came that night.

The Indians of Chicaza attacked late at night in four well-formed battalions, approaching the Spaniards' winter camp from four separate directions. They set the houses alight while the Spaniards slept. The three mounted sentries, who should have sounded the alarm when the Indians approached, instead fled at the sight of them. The Indians had caught the Spaniards totally unprepared and in a state of panic. Many of their horses died in the conflagration. At first De Soto alone managed to mount his horse and engage the enemy. Many of the soldiers stumbled out of their burning quarters without their armor or weapons. De Soto's first lunge with his lance left him hanging upside down under his horse because his page, in haste, forgot to tighten the cinch. The soldiers who made it out of the burning houses ran into the nearby woods for shelter.

The night would have ended with the decimation of De Soto's army if the Indians had pressed their attack, but the smoke from the fires and the riderless horses charging about caused so much confusion they withdrew. During the fire, Francisca Hinestrosa, wife of one of the soldiers, burned to death. She had successfully escaped her burning house but went back inside to retrieve some pearls. She became trapped and died in the fire. The Gentleman from Elvas tells us that eleven Christians, fifty horses, and 400 hogs died (100 hogs survived).

In the fire, many of the Spaniards lost all of their clothing, saddles, and weapons. At dawn, the demoralized army occupied an abandoned Indian village where they went to work finding skins to cover their nakedness, building new saddles, and building a forge to re-temper the steel weapons that had been burned in the fire. The lance heads they recovered were attached to new hardwood shafts.

A week after the first attack, the Indians returned to finish the job. They came again at night in three waves from separate directions. This time the Spanish sentries sounded the alarm and the soldiers stood ready with their newly repaired weapons to repel the Indians. The Indians, seeing they had lost the element of surprise, withdrew, but not before the soldiers captured some of them. From those captured Indians, De Soto obtained information on the country that lay ahead. He planned to continue his march to the northwest, and on April 26, 1541, the army departed Chicaza.

De Soto sent several scouting parties forward to learn the lay of the land and discover sources of food—Indian villages. Juan de Añasco found a highly fortified city the Spanish recorded as Alibamo about four days from Chicaza. This city stood within a tall palisade penetrated by only three gates which were so low a horse could not pass under them. From the cover of woods at the edge of the plaza in front of Alibamo, Añasco saw on a parapet at the top of the palisade:

many armed men daubed over with red ochre and with their bodies, legs, and arms painted black, white, yellow, and red, in the manner of stripes which made them look as though they were in breeches and doublet. Some had feather plumes on their heads and others horns, with their faces black and the eyes ringed round in red in order to look more ferocious. As soon as they saw the Christians approach, with loud cries and beating two drums, they came out in great fury to meet them. It seemed best to Juan de Añasco and those with him to keep away from them and to inform the governor.... In sight of the Christians, they made a fire and seized an Indian—one by the feet and others by the head—and pretended they were going to throw him into the fire, first giving him many blows on the head, signifying that so they would do to the Christians.

Añasco was wise to retreat from Alibamo. The Indians at this city with the same name as a chief who the Spanish met at Chicaza clearly knew who the Spaniards were and had no fear of them. They may in fact have taken part in the successful raid on Chicaza that reduced the Spanish army to their pitiful condition. When Añasco reported to De Soto, the governor should have decided to bypass Alibamo. Instead, in characteristic De Soto prideful fashion, he attacked the city with the army deployed in three companies. The arrow fire from behind the palisade took a heavy toll on the Spaniards. The Indians knew where to aim: at exposed heads, necks and thighs. Wounds in those areas could be deadly. De Soto received a direct hit with an arrow on his helmet with such force that he saw stars. Garcilaso the Inca gave the following description of the fortification of Alibamo:

It was square, with four equal curtains made of embedded logs, the curtain of each wall being four hundred paces long. Inside the square were two other curtains of wood, which crossed the fort from one wall to the other. The front curtain had three small doors so low that a mounted man could not go through them. One door was in the middle of the curtain and the other two were at the sides near the corners. In line with these three doors were three others in each curtain, so that if the Spaniards should take the first ones, the Indians could defend themselves at those of the second curtain, and of the third and the fourth. The doors of the last curtain opened on a river that passed behind the fort.... This was the intention of the Indians, to make a fort in which they could be sure that the Castilians would not attack them with the horses by entering the doors or by crossing the river, but would fight on foot like themselves, for as we have said already on other occasions, they had no fear whatsoever of the infantry.

De Soto and his men fought all day on foot, as the clever Alibamo Indians had devised, and they eventually entered the city, fighting past each of the four concentric defenses. The Indians fell back and finally escaped across the river using bridges they had built. When De Soto searched the city he had captured at great cost, he found it utterly devoid of anything useful. The fortified city proved to be a clever strategy used by the Indians to eliminate the Spaniards.

It is a testament to the military prowess of the Spaniards that about 500 Spanish soldiers successfully routed several thousand Alibamo warriors. Garcilaso the Inca wrote that 2,000 Indian dead were found at the end of the battle for Alibamo. The Spaniards lost no one during the battle, but the Indian arrows injured thirty soldiers, of whom fifteen died. But the Spanish victory accomplished nothing. The soldiers had to scour the countryside to seize enough food to sustain them for only a few days.

On the last day of April, the army quit Alibamo and continued on their trek to the northwest. Eight days later they entered territory abutting the Chucagua (Mississippi) River. The Indians called this land Quizquiz. The town of Quizquiz (near Memphis, Tennessee) was undefended when the army arrived; their men were preparing the fields for planting. De Soto's men took the village easily, capturing many women and some old men and children. The chief's house, a fortified structure, stood atop a tall artificial mound so steep that the only way up was two stairways cut into the side of the slope.

Among the hostages seized at Quizquiz, the mother of the paramount chief had the most value to De Soto. He instructed a captured Indian from the city to inform the chief that if he would come in peace, he would release his mother and the other captives. In due course the messenger returned to tell De Soto that the chief agreed to peace but only if his mother and the rest of his people were released first. De Soto, surprisingly, complied. He had no real choice. His soldiers were nearly naked and starving.

After a day's wait, the paramount chief came with a large army of warriors, apparently intent on eradicating the Spanish pests. When he saw that De Soto's army stood ready to fight, the Indian chief withdrew. De Soto sent him a message demanding that he supply the Spaniards with canoes with which to cross the Mississippi. The paramount chief of Quizquiz withdrew from the area and the Spaniards never saw him again.

Romantic but highly inaccurate depiction of De Soto at the Mississippi

De Soto first saw the Mississippi River, called by the Spanish Río de Espiritu Santo (river of the Holy Spirit) on May 9, 1541. A year later it would be his final resting place. For the next couple of weeks, the Spanish army moved from village to village foraging for food. During that time they also began construction of four large boats with the capacity to carry about seventy soldiers. While the boat building continued, a fleet of 100 dugout canoes carrying 7,000 Indians painted with red ochre appeared on the opposite shore of the Mississippi and paddled across to the army's position on the eastern bank of the river. Their chief rode in one of the canoes, seated beneath a canopy. A row of archers stood in each boat. The Indians said they came in peace. Several canoes broke away from the rest and came close to shore with presents of baked loaves of fruit.

Refusing De Soto's invitation to come ashore, the chief signaled and the canoes began to paddle away from the shore. De Soto's soldiers began firing at the retreating Indians with their crossbows, injuring or killing several Indians. So much for diplomacy! Every one of the twenty-seven days it took to build the boats, the Indians came and taunted the Spaniards. On June 18th, under a sliver of moon, the boats crossed the Mississippi, meeting no resistance. On the western shore of the river, De Soto would send two separate scouting parties to look for gold or other wealth upriver and to the northwest. These expeditions learned about the Plains Indians and their cattle (bison), but accomplished little else.

De Soto led an expedition in September and October to examine the territory the Indians called Tula to the west in Arkansas. The Indians along the Mississippi told him that Tula was populous and wealthy. He headed west between the Boston Mountains to the north and the Ouachita Mountains to the south along the Arkansas River, traveling to the vicinity of Fort Smith, Arkansas. There he attacked the Tula, and in heavy hand-to-hand fighting, seven of his men were wounded. The Tula women fought alongside the men. In one skirmish, Francisco de Reynoso attempted to steal food from a Tula house. Four women there attacked him and would have killed him if other soldiers had not come to his aid. They found Reynoso on the ground, subdued by the four women, one of whom had him by the genitals. His screams had brought the soldiers to his aid. They killed all four Tula women.

This Spanish army fought their way into Tula and fought several battles there before the Tula finally provided them with gifts of bison skins. In Tula, De Soto learned that the country became more desolate and unpopulated toward the southwest, but that a rich and productive region, Utiangüe, lay to the southeast, situated on a large body of water.

It was time to select a winter camp where the army would have access to sufficient food and a safe haven. De Soto decided, sight unseen, that the army would camp at Utiangüe for the winter and then march to the sea, which he thought was only a few days south from that location. At the sea, he would have two bergantines built to be sent to Cuba and Mexico, while he would remain on the coast establishing a settlement. On November 2, De Soto and his army arrived at Utiangüe, a city not on the Gulf Coast but on the Arkansas River, not far from the modern city of Little Rock. One thing the Tula told him was true; the population of Utiangüe was very large, extending many miles along the lower Arkansas River and the western shore of the Mississippi.

De Soto's army occupied part of Utiangüe, erecting a defensive palisade to protect them through the winter. Enslaved Indians did the work of felling trees, skinning logs, digging holes, and building the palisade according to De Soto's specification. They completed the work in a few days. He and his men spent a bitter cold winter huddled within their fortified camp. They did not suffer from starvation because the Indians of the region provided ample food. During the winter, De Soto learned more about the conflicts between the various tribes west of the Mississippi. Unfortunately, Juan Ortiz, the indispensable interpreter, died that winter. After he lost Ortiz, De Soto depended on a young boy of Cofitachequi who had learned Spanish.

In late winter and early spring, the Spaniards ventured out into the countryside raiding villages for slaves, both men and women. The army now numbered about 400 men and had no more than forty horses. The rigorous march from Chicaza to the Mississippi, up the Mississippi, the trek into the territory of the Tula, and back to Utiangüe totaled nearly 900 miles. During that time, the bitter cold, battles with the Indians, and disease had taken their toll on men poorly clad, marching without shoes, and subsisting on a scant diet composed primarily of corn.

Departing Utiangüe on March 6, 1542, De Soto led his army for a push to the east to the town of Anilco, which, if his young Indian interpreter had understood properly, lay near the Mississippi. De Soto apparently planned to go down the Mississippi to the Gulf Coast where he would implement the plan he had devised mistakenly for Utiangüe. On the way to Anilco, they passed through other Indian villages including Ayays. They generally found the Indians of this region more cooperative and willing to provide food. Their route took them along the western shore of the Arkansas River; on March 28th near Bayou Meto, they crossed the river on rafts made from timbers taken from Indian houses. A day later the army arrived at Anilco.

An enemy of the Anilco, the chief of the Guachoya, sent a messenger saying that he wished to be friends with the Spaniards. Two days later, the chief arrived with gifts of woven cloaks and deerskins—much appreciated by the ill-clad Spaniards. De Soto decided to relocate to Guachoya, having learned that it lay along the Mississippi River.

He arrived at Guachoya on April 17th. The Indians of Guachoya had fled across the river, believing that the Spaniards had come to attack them. De Soto sent Juan de Añasco across the river with a small detachment to encourage the Guachoya to come back to their town. He needed them there to plant and harvest the corn that would sustain the Spaniards while they put his plan into effect. Añasco got sidetracked, filling his canoes with stolen Indian corn, but the same day, the chief of Guachoya sent a man to De Soto promising that he would return in a day.

True to his word, the chief returned with a flotilla of canoes and landed at Guachoya on the west side of the great river his people called Tamaliseu. With him he brought more presents of fish, woven capes, and skins. De Soto interviewed the chief to learn more about the region, particularly how far away the sea was. Lacking confidence in his Cofitachequi interpreter and perhaps doubting the veracity of the chief of Guachoya, he sent Añasco out again to scout down the river in search of the sea. Añasco traveled over land along the western shore of the river—an arduous way to travel. Why he and his men didn't go down river in Indian canoes is a mystery; it certainly would have been quicker and easier.

Perhaps they felt less vulnerable on land since both sides of the river held Indian tribes hostile to each other and potentially hostile to Añasco.

Añasco returned on April 25th to report that in the week he was gone, he never found an Indian trail nor did he get anywhere near the sea. He reckoned he had covered about fifteen leagues (about forty miles) in the time he had been gone. He and his men and horses barely had the strength to return to Guachoya. This news greatly troubled De Soto. But he had one more hope. The powerful chiefdom of Quigualtam lay across the river, according to what the chief of Guachoya told him. Perhaps Quigualtam would be his El Dorado.

De Soto sent a messenger to Quigualtam claiming to be the son of the Sun and demanding that the chief come to him, submit to his dominion, and bring him the most precious gift in his land—De Soto hoped that would be gold. By now it should be clear that De Soto was not rational. He had seen no gold in all of his travels on both sides of the Mississippi. In fact, the only gold he had seen was in Florida near Tampa Bay, and that probably came from Indian salvors who had found wrecked Spanish treasure ships. The reply from the chief of Quigualtam was that if De Soto expected him to bow down in obedience, first De Soto should dry the Mississippi—surely not an impossible task for the son of the Sun.

The terminal phase of the expedition began for De Soto at this point. After slogging thousands of miles across a great expanse of La Florida, he had found no sign of wealth to rival New Spain or Peru. Rage took hold of the conquistador and he railed against that arrogant Indian. He said he would personally cross the river and humble the chief of Quigualtam, but in fact he couldn't raise himself off of his bed. He had been ill for days. De Soto's spirit was beaten and he descended into depression. From his sickbed he sent some of his soldiers on a fruitless campaign of war as allies of the Guachoya against the people of Alnico where, with the backing of the Spanish soldiers, the warriors of Guachoya visited atrocities on the men, women, and children of Alnico. In desperation, De Soto even sent an armed contingent across the river to attack Quigualtam. That senseless attack only made the chief of Quigualtam stronger in his resolve to "kill all the Spaniards and hang their bodies from the trees."

On May 20, 1542, De Soto realized his time was up. He wrote his will and called his principal officers to his bedside. He told the men to elect a new governor, but Baltasar de Gallegos asked the Adelantado to appoint a new man to succeed him. De Soto then named Luis de Moscoso as the new governor. De Soto died the next day. Initially, the men buried his body in the city and then rode horses over the grave to obscure the location. They feared that when the Indians learned De Soto had died, they would become emboldened and attack the Spaniards. When they overheard Indians talking about De Soto dying, they denied it and said he had only gone on a visit to see his father, the sun, something he did periodically. The Indians weren't buying that. Finally, on a moonlit night, some of the soldiers took De Soto's body, wrapped in one of the fabric capes and weighted with sand, paddled out in a canoe to the middle of the Mississippi and consigned his body to the big muddy river where the Indians couldn't find it.

Adelantado Hernando de Soto's dream of a golden empire in La Florida came to the logical conclusion. A lesser man might have settled for building a permanent colony at Apalachee or Cofitachequi, but De Soto's dream of glory and wealth would not permit so plebian a conclusion. He pursued his dream until his health and spirit gave out after a grueling trek of thousands of miles among a people much different from the Indians of Central and South America—a people he never mastered.

Chapter 6
Back into the Southwest

L uis de Moscoso now had the dubious honor of leading the Spanish army in North America, a force of between 300 and 400 men supported by an enslaved Indian contingent of perhaps twice as many. The question of the day was what to do.

By this time, there was no hope of finding fame and fortune in North America; all they wanted to do was survive and make it to Cuba or Mexico. But which way to go? If Moscoso could have called in a helicopter, he would have had a 300 mile flight to the gulf coast, and the journey by water would be multiples of that distance due to the sinuous nature of the river. Of course, all Moscoso knew was that the sea was farther away than Añasco could travel in three or four days on horseback.

The Spaniards still had no idea how extensive the land of La Florida was. Some of them believed that Mexico could not be more than a few days' march to the west. After all, they had walked more than two thousand miles to reach the Mississippi. How much farther could Mexico be? In fact they had only walked about 600 miles west in a straight line from

Cofitachequi. If they set out from Guachoya walking in a relatively straight route to Tampico, the closest port of New Spain, they would have to walk nearly 1,000 miles.

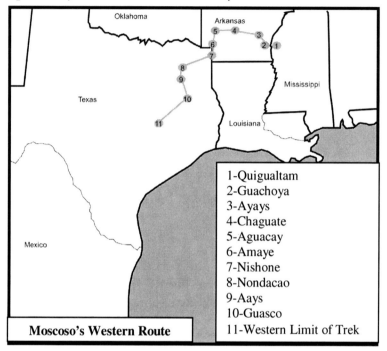

Moscoso's Western Route

1-Quigualtam
2-Guachoya
3-Ayays
4-Chaguate
5-Aguacay
6-Amaye
7-Nishone
8-Nondacao
9-Aays
10-Guasco
11-Western Limit of Trek

After some debate, the officers and Moscoso decided to walk to Mexico. They reached that decision for several reasons: they had no skill as sailors and weren't sure that they could even build seaworthy boats that could withstand the Caribbean waters; they didn't think it could be that far to go overland to Mexico; and they still hoped they might have the good fortune to find a land rich in gold or silver on their way. Although the route would have taken them through such land, the Indians would not have been experienced in exploiting precious metals.

Their course took them slightly north of west to nearly the western limit of Arkansas, passing through the Indian towns of Ayays, Chaguate, and ending at Aguacay. At Chaguate, Francisco de Guzmán deserted the army. He had lost a beautiful Indian woman gambling, and because he loved her, he ran off with her. Moscoso sent men back to Chaguate to retrieve Guzmán, but they couldn't find him. The chief protected him and "would entertain and honor him as a son-in-law who had restored a much-beloved daughter to him…." No manner of persuasion could convince Guzmán to leave his beloved Indian woman. He chose to remain among the Indians of Chaguate where, presumably, he and his new wife lived out their lives together.

At Aguacay they changed course and headed south to Amaye and Nisohone at the border with Texas where they headed southwest to the Indian towns of Nondacao and Aays. Then they headed down the Neches River to Guasco. At Guasco, two parties ventured out scouting the territory. One went a short distance southeast and returned to Guasco. The other party went southwest for a great distance, possibly reaching the Brazos River before they turned back. In all, the Moscoso land expedition traveled about 560 miles before returning along the same route back to the Mississippi River—they covered more than 1,100 miles between June 5th and early December, 1542.

At Guasco, before they agreed to return to the Mississippi, some of the men wanted to continue overland to Mexico. The believed they were in the land that Cabeza de Vaca had crossed, they saw evidence of turquoise and woven clothing used by the Indians and still held out hope that they could discover a golden land that Cabeza de Vaca had missed or had not disclosed in public. But those wanting to go back to the Mississippi won out and they returned the way they came, still driving their small herd of pigs along with them.

On their westbound trip they had abused the Indians and could expect a hostile reception on the way back to the Mississippi. But they persevered, and though suffering greatly, arrived back an Alnico in the midst of winter. The people of Alnico were also in desperate straits. The time of their attack by the Indians of Guachoya had prevented them from planting corn, so they were in no shape to take in several hundred Spaniards and at least an equal number of Indian slaves.

Moscoso moved the army to Aminoya, about sixty-miles upstream of Guachoya. The food supply at Aminoya sustained the army through the winter. As soon as the weather permitted, the army with their Indian slaves went to work cutting timber to build seven bergantines to take them down the Mississippi and across the sea to Mexico. They found every scrap of steel they had including crossbow bolt tips and hardware, saddle stirrups, and bits of armor to re-forge into saws, hammers, and nails to build the ships. The local Indians supplied woven capes which the Spaniards unwove to obtain cordage for caulking.

Fortunately they had a Portuguese man named Francisco who knew how to convert raw timber to lumber and could supervise the boat building, although he was not a shipbuilder. They found a local plant fiber that the Indians could twist into rope for the ships rigging. In order to obtain sufficient materials to complete the boats, Moscoso had to send men to neighboring villages to obtain sufficient capes and plant fibers.

The Indians of Quigualtam and those of Guachoya conspired to kill the Spaniards when they saw their work of boatbuilding. They most likely wanted to prevent them from escaping and returning with more of their kind. Moscoso added to this unrest by seizing all the Indian corn he could and stockpiling it for the planned trip down river.

By the first of July, 1543, Moscoso and his army were ready to depart. They had about 500 Indian slaves and they knew they didn't have room or sufficient drinking water in the seven bergantines to carry all of them plus themselves and their remaining horses. They felt it would be more humane to free their slaves where they were than to take them part way down the river and release them in unknown territory. Privately, Moscoso told some select men that they could take a few slaves with them. In fact, two Indian women taken from Coosa stayed with the Spaniards and sailed with them.

A Spanish woman named Ana Méndez, who had come as a servant to Don Carlos Enríquez also remained among the Spaniards at this time.

The day before their departure, they slaughtered the hogs and salted the meat for their use during the voyage, loaded the boats with all the corn they had, laid on all the fresh water they could carry, and prepared for sailing. They also butchered about thirty horses and added their meat to the ships stores. They departed Aminoya on July 2, 1543, with about 322 people and twenty horses. The horses rode in pairs of Indian log canoes lashed together and towed behind the bergantines.

They hadn't seen the last of the Indians of Quigualtam. On July 3rd, the bergantines had reached the channel and were making good progress down the flooded Mississippi, when they spotted Indians on the east side (Quigualtam side) of the river. Moscoso sent men ashore who captured an Indian woman and then raided her village, taking all the food they could find. Finally, they set fire to the village. This brought an understandable reaction. Quigualtam had been preparing for the departure of the Spaniards. He had an impressive armada of 100 canoes, each carrying seventy warriors. As described in the first chapter, Quigualtam knew how to deploy these boats in clever tactical maneuvers. When they came out to attack the Spaniards on July 4th, Moscoso sent some men back in a few canoes to paddle upstream and force the Indians to withdraw.

Juan de Guzman took twenty-five men in five canoes and they struck out toward the fleet of canoes from Quigualtam. As they neared the Indians, the wall of canoes parted and Guzman pressed on, thinking the Indians were backing away. Soon he found his five canoes surrounded as the massed Indian canoes closed off his escape. The outcome was predictable. Only four Spaniards managed to escape and swim back to the bergantines.

The Indians of Quigualtam followed the Spaniards down the river for two days, coming very close to disabling the seven boats, and causing additional casualties. In the end, the chief of Quigualtam called off his attack at noon on July 5th. As quickly as they had attacked, they withdrew. The voyage down the Mississippi from that point on proved uneventful until they were attacked by an unknown tribe with fifty canoes. These Indians actually boarded the rear-most boat and freed an Indian woman, injuring several Spaniards in the fight. That was the last battle on the Mississippi for Moscoso and his men.

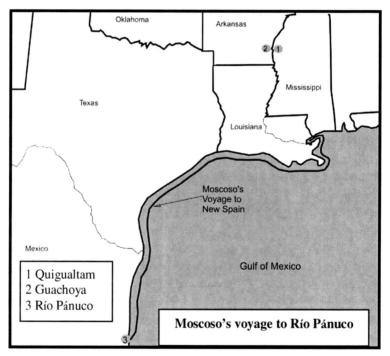

Moscoso's voyage to Río Pánuco

1 Quigualtam
2 Guachoya
3 Río Pánuco

They reached the mouth of the Mississippi on or about July 16th. There they went ashore to rest a while before putting out to sea. A local tribe of Indians assaulted them and one of the Spaniards was hit in the thigh by a fishing spear hurled with an atlatl or spear thrower. They had not seen this weapon used in North America in all their travels, although it was common in Mexico and Central America. The tip of the spear, made of deer antler, had two wide prongs that caused a great deal of damage. The injured man later died from the wound.

After a two day rest, Moscoso ordered the boats to head into the Gulf of Mexico. They had no maps, no compasses or other navigational instruments except an astrolabe that Juan de Añasco had carried all the way from Mabila for just such a purpose. He argued that they should sail directly across the gulf for Mexico. Other more timid souls felt they should hug the coast until they reached the Río Pánuco at Tampico.

Actually, the astrolabe would have been of little use—it would have given them their latitude if they knew how to use it, and would have told them whether they were being driven north or south of the latitude of the Pánuco, if in fact they even knew its latitude (Tampico is seven degrees of latitude below the mouth of the Mississippi River). In any case, given the construction of the bergantines, the remnants of De Soto's army probably took the best course. They decided to follow the coast where they could put ashore when needed to get drinking water and food.

None of the people on those seven boats had any idea how far away Mexico was. By the coast, it is just under 1,000 miles from the mouth of the Mississippi to the entrance to the Pánuco. At four knots of steady progress that distance would take them about ten or twelve days, assuming they rowed and sailed non-stop, around the clock. It took considerably longer than that. They sailed away from the Mississippi River on July 18th and arrived at the Río Panuco on September 10th. They had been at sea for fifty-three days—or to be more accurate, at sea or anchored on shore when the weather prevented their sailing.

The area at the mouth of the Pánuco was no metropolis. In fact, the men who went ashore and explored the area had to look hard to find anyone. They finally found an Indian who could speak some Spanish and confirmed their whereabouts. They sailed up the river to the town of Pánuco where the alcalde mayor, astounded that survivors of the De

Soto expedition had entered his hamlet, immediately sent word to Viceroy Antonio de Mendoza at Mexico City.

Soon after all the men from the seven boats made it to Pánuco, they began to fight, and not merely verbal exchanges—they tried to kill each other. They had begun to realize the value of what they had left behind. With them they had brought a few furs that the people of New Spain found very valuable. Then they thought of the fertile lands of Cofitachequi, Apalachee, and Chicaza. They realized the folly of having chased a dream of gold when what they had could have provided a golden opportunity to trade for furs, to raise cattle, and to operate lucrative trading ports in North America. They took out their frustration on each other. The tension became so bad that Viceroy Mendoza ordered that the surviving 311 people be conducted back to Mexico City in small groups of no more than twenty to keep the violence to a minimum. When the De Soto survivors reached Mexico City, they continued to squabble.

Luís de Moscoso remained in New Spain and settled in Xochimilco where he sired a son by his first cousin, Leanor de Alvarado. Accused of living illegally with her, he married Leanor. Moscoso worked for Viceroy Antonia de Mendoza and returned to Peru with Mendoza in 1550. He died there in 1551. Some other survivors of the De Soto expedition, such as Juan de Añasco, remained in the New World seeking riches. Others returned to Spain and spoke of La Florida in derogatory terms. Gonzalo Silvestre went to Peru as a soldier where he met Garcilaso the Inca and told him some of the stories about the De Soto expedition. Subsequently, Silvestre returned to Spain and continued his acquaintance with Garcilaso, who had also gone to Spain. Garcilaso eventually published his account of the De Soto expedition based on his dialogs with Silvestre.

Viceroy Mendoza listened to what the survivors could tell him about La Florida. He had harbored designs on that land since Cabeza de Vaca had appeared in New Spain.

De Soto's survivors had entered New Spain one year after Francisco Vázquez de Coronado limped back from the American Southwest, concluding Mendoza's second sponsored expedition into La Florida (Fray Marcos and Estevám had gone first at Mendoza's behest). Now we need to go back to 1538 and trace Coronado's expedition into North America.

The Seven Cities of Antillia

In the eighth century as the Moors invaded the Iberian Peninsula, the Bishop of Porto in Portugal along with six other bishops boarded boats and sailed off into the Atlantic seeking a land where they could live free from the Arabic forces. They took many people with them to an Island in the sea where they founded seven cities—the Seven Cities of Antillia. Antillia came from the combination of two Portuguese words meaning "the island out before."

The legend of Antillia became embellished over the years to where the mythical island had copious gold and magnificent palaces with the people living an idyllic existence in a utopia. The legend of the Seven Cities of Antillia became transmuted to Seven Cities of Gold. Spain and Portugal eventually both claimed credit for the founding of Antillia by bishops from their countries.

The legend of a wealthy island to the west led to the identification of the islands encircling the Caribbean Sea as the Antilles. As the Spanish became more familiar with those islands, they began to envision that North America could be the land of the Seven Cities of Gold. In the sixteenth century, Spanish explorers still thought of North America beyond the province of New Spain as an island. Coastal exploration would eventually make clear the extent of North America above the Rio Grande. But until that happened, conquistadors entering that northern territory still held hopes that the legendary Seven Cities of Gold would be located there.

As stated earlier, De Soto and Mendoza knew of each other's designs on the North American territory. Mendoza also had competition from Hernán Cortés who was backing voyages up the Pacific coast with an aim toward settlement there. It had been two years since Cabeza de Vaca and his three companions had come to New Spain. Mendoza was anxious to pursue his own dreams of finding and claiming the Seven Cities of Antillia or the Seven Cities of Gold as the Spanish also called them. Since the fabulous cities were west of the Azores and had not been found in Central or South America yet, many believed they lay in the land to the north, then designated as La Florida. Mendoza feared De Soto would get there first.

In 1538, Viceroy Mendoza appointed Francisco Vázquez de Coronado, who had accompanied him from Spain, to serve as governor of the region of New Galicia in the northwestern part of New Spain. Coronado, the son of Juan Vázquez de Coronado y Sosa de Ulloa and Isabel de Luján— a lady-in-waiting to Queen Isabel of Castile—came from Salamanca.

Mendoza ordered Coronado to support the mission of Fray Marcos and Estevan in their discovery of lands to the north. Marcos's mission was ostensibly to bring the Native Americans to Christianity through kindness and gentle persuasion, but certainly Mendoza hoped that their quest would shed light on the location of the Seven Cities of Gold. In evidence of that, Mendoza ordered Marcos to claim land in his name and in the name of Charles V, an order that Marcos duly carried out at his overlook near Cibola.

Coronado had seen Fray Marcos and Estevan safely on their way into the unknown land beyond New Galicia, and was as inflamed as Mendoza when Marcos returned to New Spain in the summer of 1539 with his vision of a city (one of seven) larger and grander than Mexico City, in the North American wilderness. Mendoza and Coronado immediately began to plan a full-scale expedition to conquer this shimmering land.

Cortés had heard rumors of Fray Marcos's report even before the printed copy reached Mendoza. In July, Cortés dispatched Francisco de Ulloa to sail north from Acapulco on a voyage of discovery of this fabled northern land. We will cover that in more detail later, but Mendoza had his spies just like Cortés, and Ulloa's voyage added impetus to the plans of Mendoza and Coronado, as did the attempts by Cortés to get a royal injunction to prevent Mendoza from proceeding with his plans. Pursuant to that, Cortés sailed to Spain to press his case; the pre-eminent conquistador failed and never returned to the New World.

In Mexico City, out of work soldiers heard about Fray Marcos and his discovery everywhere they went, particularly in church where the priests spoke proudly of their Franciscan comrade's accomplishments. Although his written report lacked hyperbole, apparently Fray Marcos spoke publicly in gleaming terms about the promise of the Seven Cities of Cibola. He may have never mentioned gold in connection with Cibola but soon everyone assumed that he had found the Seven Cities of Gold. Coronado had no trouble recruiting both soldiers and financial backers for the largest and best equipped expedition yet into North America.

Pedro de Castañeda de Náçera was an eager volunteer who remained throughout Coronado's adventure. Castañeda left a detailed journal of the expedition and his narrative plus dispatches and letters in the Spanish archives provide the historical record of Coronado's quest for the Seven Cities of Gold.

At least 300 Spaniards (including three women) volunteered for the expedition, many of them of noble birth or high social standing. More than 1,000 Indian "allies" were provided as well as black slaves to support the expedition. Small cannon, called culverins, together with a large stock of the more portable firearms and other weapons ensured that Coronado's army would be invincible, or so they thought. Herds of thousands of sheep and steers provided food on the hoof to accompany the army, with about 1,500 horses and pack animals to carry the Spaniards and their belongings. The total count of cattle at the beginning of the journey was not recorded, but half way through Coronado's campaign, they counted 500 steers and 5,000 sheep (some were born on the trek). The estimated cost of this expedition is staggering— 600,000 silver pesos (equivalent to about $40 million today). Mendoza invested 85,000 pesos and Coronado (with his wife's help) put up 71,000 pesos in a joint partnership. The rest of the funds came from many of the Spanish participants and other investors who remained in New Spain.

The various elements of the expedition came together at Compostela in New Galicia in January 1540. The next month, Mendoza reviewed the troops. Here is the scene described by George Parker Winship writing in 1896:

> It was a splendid array as it passed in review before Mendoza and the officials who helped and watched him govern New Spain, on this Sunday in February, 1540. The young cavaliers curbed the picked horses from the large stock farms of the viceroy, each resplendent in long blankets flowing to the ground. Each rider held his lance erect, while his sword and other weapons hung in their proper places at his side. Some were arrayed in coats of mail, polished to shine like that of their general [Coronado], whose gilded armor with its brilliant trappings was to bring him many hard blows a few months later. Others wore iron helmets or visored head-pieces of the tough bull hide for which the country has ever been famous. The footmen carried crossbows and harquebuses, while some of them were armed with sword and shield. Looking on at these white men with their weapons of European warfare was the crowd of native allies in their paint and holiday attire, armed with the club and the bow of an Indian warrior.

Coronado moved his army north from Compostela, with Fray Marcos as his guide, headed for Culiacán on the coast opposite Cabo San Lucas at the tip of Baja California. The journey soon turned arduous. They had too much baggage and the inexperienced men who didn't have servants or Indian porters began to discard their belongings along the trail.

The King of Spain had ordered that the natives should be treated with respect, and, in response, Viceroy Mendoza ordered Coronado to establish rules of conduct toward the Indians. Coronado announced at the time of his army's departure that, "no man-at-arms was to enter an Indian's house, or take anything, or burn a house without permission from his captain, under penalty of death." At a village called Chiametla (near modern Mazatlán), an Indian caught Lope de Samaniego, the camp-master, foraging in the village for food. The Indian shot and killed Samaniego with an arrow. In retaliation for the death of Samaniego, Coronado ordered the hanging of every Indian who belonged to the village. So much for setting a good example.

By Easter, March 28th, the army reached Culiacán, the northernmost Spanish settlement in New Spain. The local settlers had to find sufficient food to feed the huge army and their livestock. The food, of course, came from Indian villages in the area. Coronado had only recently married the beautiful Beatriz de Estrada, and one of the soldiers, named Trujillo, concocted a story about her which he told while at Culiacán. Castañeda retold this story:

> Trujillo pretended that he had seen a vision while he was bathing in the river, which seemed to be something extraordinary, so that he was brought before the general [Coronado], whom he gave to understand that the devil had told him that if he would kill the general, he could marry his wife, Doña Beatris, and would receive great wealth and other fine things. Friar Marcos of Nice preached several sermons on this, laying it all to the fact that the devil was jealous of the good which must result from this journey and so wished to break it up in this way.... The general ordered Trujillo to stay in that town and not to go on the expedition which was what [Trujillo] was after when he made up that falsehood...

After several weeks rest at Culiacán, Coronado, as De Soto had done, took an advance party of eighty mounted soldiers and most of the Indian allies forward to scout the terrain. The rest of the army would follow in two weeks and bivouac in the Sonora valley awaiting further orders. On May 26th, he had advanced north about 300 miles to Los

Corazones (the hearts); the travel was so arduous that some of the sheep wore down their hoofs and had to be abandoned, and some Indians and black slaves had died on the journey. Cabeza de Vaca had passed this way and had named Los Corazones in honor of the feast of deer hearts the local Indians had given him as a sign of respect. Coronado received no such respect when he passed through the Sonora valley.

California

Arizona

New Mexico

1-Compostela
2-Culiacán
3-Benson, AZ
4-Hawikuh
   (Cibola)
5-Alarcon Cross

Baja California

Mexico

Gulf of California

Coronado's Route to Cibola

Coronado's route took him to the San Pedro River valley where he had to turn east to skirt the Santa Catalina Mountains. His path took him to Chichilticale (Nahuatl for red house), named for a pueblo built of red adobe that Fray Marcos remembered seeing on his previous trip to Cibola. His detachment had crossed what is today the Mexican border very near Benson, Arizona. Coronado was now within about 250 miles of his goal, the first of the Seven

Cities of Cibola. Coronado stayed at Chichilticale for two days, letting the horses graze on what little grass they could find.

Traveling north along the San Pedro River valley they passed east of the Little Dragon Mountains and the Galiuro Mountains about sixty miles east of Phoenix, before following the Gila River along the western edge of the modern Apache reservation. Continuing north they crossed the Salt River and entered into an area they called "despoblado," meaning unpopulated or deserted. In this region they lost men and horses due to the difficult conditions and lack of food and water.

Near Young, Arizona, they ascended the Mogollon Rim. It had taken about two weeks to reach this point since leaving Chichilticale. Coronado and his men would not have made it if his horses hadn't found sufficient water and grazing along the creek beds and in the wooded hills.

The Spaniards crossed the Mogollon Rim east of Colcord Mountain and headed into an area of barren desert plain. They had a little over 100 miles to reach Cibola. Food and water would be a serious concern for men and horses as they crossed the desert. Traveling through undulating lands with juniper and piñon trees, drinking water for themselves and their mounts was foremost in their minds.

After about forty miles of desert they came upon the bed of the Zuni River that would lead them to Cibola. They were at the juncture of the Zuni with the Little Colorado River in an area of the country that even today is despoblado. Coronado named the Zuni River Río Verméjo (Red River) due to its iron-rich color. The date was July 7th, and they were only two days from the Cibola of which Fray Marcos had spoken so glowingly. Here they encountered local Indians who attacked an advance party of Spaniards. During the night, the Spaniards saw signal fires blinking in succession along the Zuni River, warning the Cibolans of the coming of the Spaniards.

**Coronado leading his detachment to Cibola
Fray Marcos holding up the skirt of his cassock**

The next night they camped within five or six miles of Cibola. The Cibolans kept up such a ruckus of whoops and shouts during the night that many of Coronado's soldiers were terrified—so terrified that they saddled their horses backward in the morning. With his army still in the Sonora valley of Mexico, Coronado mounted his horse and led his small contingent of Spaniards and large complement of Indian allies forward to the gates of the first golden city. We know today that the name of the city was Hawikuh; it is now a ruined pueblo on the Zuni Reservation of New Mexico.

At the time of Coronado's arrival, Hawikuh consisted of 200 multi-story houses "looking as if it had been all crumpled up together," according to Castañeda. It stood on a rocky ledge on the south side of the Zuni River. Old men, women, and children had left the pueblo, anticipating a great battle with the Spanish invaders. As Coronado rode toward the city, Indian warriors came out of the pueblo, blocking their way. Coronado sent two friars with a small mounted guard to speak with the Indians and to deliver the Requerimiento—the announcement required by the king to be read to all Indians of the New World before subjugating them. It gave them, theoretically, the opportunity to submit peacefully to the dominion of the King, the Pope, and to accept Christianity as their new religion. If they refused, then the conquistador could use whatever force was necessary to subdue them and bring them to the "true faith." The English translation of the Requerimiento runs nearly 1,000 words long. Aside from its length, the problem of communicating this document through a succession of Indian interpreters to the language of the subjects in question made it unlikely the Indians about to be attacked could understand what the Spaniards were saying. Trying to communicate it through sign language was even more hopeless. Nonetheless, Coronado's religious representatives presented the required statement. Here are some excerpts from the official document:

> On the part of the King ... we his servants notify and make known to you, as best we can, that the Lord our God, Living and Eternal, created the Heaven and the Earth, and one man and one woman, of whom you and we, all the men of the world at the time, were and are descendants, and all those who came after and before us....

> Of all these nations God our Lord gave charge to one man, called St. Peter, that he should be Lord and Superior of all the men in the world, that all should obey him, and that he should be the head of the whole human race, wherever men should live, and under whatever law, sect, or belief they should be; and he gave him the world for his kingdom and jurisdiction.

> The men who lived in that time obeyed that St. Peter, and took him for Lord, King, and Superior of the universe; so also they have regarded the others who after him have been elected to the pontificate, and so has it been continued even till now, and will continue till the end of the world.

> One of these Pontiffs, made donation of these isles and Tierra-firme to the aforesaid King ....

> So his Highnesses is king and lord of these islands and land of Tierra-firme by virtue of this donation: and some islands, and indeed almost all those to whom this has been notified, have received and served their Highnesses, as lords and kings, in the way that subjects ought to do, with good will,

without any resistance, immediately, without delay, when they were informed of the aforesaid facts....

Wherefore, as best we can, we ask and require you that you consider what we have said to you, and that you take the time that shall be necessary to understand and deliberate upon it, and that you acknowledge the Church as the Ruler and Superior of the whole world, and the high priest called Pope, and in his name the King...and that you consent and give place that these religious fathers should declare and preach to you the aforesaid.

If you do so, you will do well, and that which you are obliged to do to their Highnesses, and we in their name shall receive you in all love and charity, and shall leave you, your wives, and your children, and your lands, free without servitude, ...

But, if you do not do this, and maliciously make delay in it, I certify to you that, with the help of God, we shall powerfully enter into your country, and shall make war against you in all ways and manners that we can, and shall subject you to the yoke and obedience of the Church and of their Highnesses; we shall take you and your wives and your children, and shall make slaves of them, ...

Naturally, the warriors of Hawikuh had no idea what the Spanish clerics were telling them. They listened for perhaps a few of the opening sentences and then shot a volley of arrows at the advance men. Seeing that hoped for provocation, Coronado hollered "Santiago" and charged off into battle, the rest of the Spaniards and their allies hurrying to keep up. Coronado looked resplendent in his gold chased armor and made an inviting target for the warriors of Hawikuh. He was hit in the face and foot with arrows. The pueblo Indians also hurled stones and several struck Coronado hard, knocking him from his horse. Some of his men carried him back behind the Spanish lines where he would be safe. None of his wounds was life threatening.

In spite of the loss of a number of horses, defective crossbows, and ineffective harquebuses, Coronado's men and his Indian allies captured Hawikuh in about one hour of battle, the defenders having fled to the safety of a neighboring mesa stronghold, Dowa Yolanne, about twelve miles to the northeast. Presumably the Indian "allies" brought from New Spain were the most effective fighters in the battle of Hawikuh, since Coronado couldn't have had more than about seventy-five Spanish soldiers.

Once the dust cleared and Coronado examined this first of the Seven Cities of Gold, he discovered that there was no gold, no silver, no precious gems, and the two-hundred buildings of perhaps four stories did not rival Mexico City, and certainly did not rival the truly golden city of Tenochtitlan captured by Cortés that the Spanish then occupied. Coronado had seen even before he entered Hawikuh that Marcos had deceived him, but the prospect of starving to death in the desert made it inevitable that he would take the Indian town.

Fray Marcos had clearly misspoken; his reputation disintegrated, and Coronado told him to return to New Spain. Coronado and his men had begun to doubt Marcos long before they reached Hawikuh because the road to Cibola had been more arduous than Marcos had led them to believe. Now they knew he had greatly exaggerated the kingdom of Cibola. They couldn't even count on there being seven cities, but it would take a great deal more than this one disappointment to make Coronado abandon his dream of finding cities of gold in North America.

Coronado prepared a long letter to the Viceroy giving his progress. He wrote that, "He [Fray Marcos] has not told the truth in a single thing that he said, but everything is the opposite of what he related, except the name of the cities and the large stone houses." Actually, Marcos didn't get the name correct either; the natives called their land Shíwana (later called Zuni). Coronado had an Indian artist paint two cloths with pictures of the animals of the region. Those along with his letter and some colored crystals, he entrusted to Juan Gallegos to carry to Viceroy Mendoza. Gallegos would travel with Melchior Díaz as far as the Sonora valley where the rest of the army remained. Gallegos would continue from there to Mexico City and Díaz would bring the army to join Coronado. Fray Marcos was happy to leave in the company of Gallegos, since he feared for his life if he remained with the Spaniards at Hawikuh. Gallegos and Díaz reached the army in Sonora in late August or early September. Gallegos and Marcos were in Mexico City by the middle of September.

All the cities of Cibola or, as we now know it, Shíwana, were deserted. The Ashiwi people (their name for themselves) had relocated to the stronghold of Dowa Yolanne and would remain there as long as the Spaniards occupied their territory. However, a few men came to Hawikuh on occasion, and from them Coronado learned of two provinces that seemed worth visiting: Tusayán to the northwest and Tiguex to the east.

Pedro de Tovar went with a small force in search of Tusayán, described by the Ashiwi people as seven wealthy cities—the Ashiwi learned fast; if the Spaniards wanted seven cities, then that's what they would tell them they would find. Tovar left with twenty men-at-arms, a friar, and an unknown number of Indian allies. He found Tusayán in northeastern Arizona, a Hopi pueblo on Antelope Mesa. The Hopi saw the Spaniards coming and came out to meet them. They drew a line on the ground with sacred cornmeal, indicating that Tovar and his men should go no farther. After reading the Requerimiento, the Spaniards crossed the line. One of the Hopi punched a horse in the nose, gravely insulting the Spaniards. War would have erupted, but other Hopi men came from the pueblo bearing gifts and food. Tovar called his men back into order and accepted that the Hopi's gesture meant they wished peace with the Spanish.

Hopi Pueblo ca. 1906

The Hopi soon sized up the Spaniards. Questions about great cities, gold, and jewels led the Hopi to tell the Spaniards that, unfor-tunately, they had no such thing in their province, but farther to the west, the Spaniards would find a tribe of giants with all the wealth they could want. Those people lived on a great river. Would Tovar fall for this standard Native American ploy that so many of his country-men accepted?

Tovar had orders to return to Hawikuh within thirty days. He didn't have time to go any farther so he returned to Coronado and reported his findings. Coronado immediately dispatched García López de Cárdenas back to the Hopi people and beyond to find the giants of the big river. Cárdenas took twelve men and a contingent of Indian allies. At the Hopi pueblo he took guides who led him to the Colorado River. Castañeda wrote:

After they had gone twenty days' march they came to the banks of a river, which are so high that from the edge of one bank to the other appeared to be three or four leagues [about ten miles] in the air. The country was elevated and full of low twisted pines, very cold, and lying open toward the north, so that, this being the warm season, no one could live there on account of the cold.

147

They spent three days on this bank looking for a passage down to the river, which looked from above as if the water were six feet across, although the Indians said it was half a league wide. It was impossible to descend, for after these three days Captain Melgosa and one Juan Galeras and another companion, who were the three lightest and most agile men, made an attempt to go down at the least difficult place, and went down until those who were above were unable to keep sight of them. They returned about four o'clock in the afternoon, not having succeeded in reaching the bottom on account of the great difficulties which they found, because what seemed to be easy from above was not so, but instead very hard and difficult. They said they had been down about a third of the way and that the river seemed very large from the place which they reached, and from what they saw, they thought the Indians had given the width correctly.

Having found the Grand Canyon, but unable to reach potable water, and having found no giants or gold, Cárdenas led his disillusioned men back to Hawikuh. After Coronado heard this report, he set his sights on the land of Tiguex to the east. Remarkably, in addition to hearing about Tiguex from the Ashiwi people at Hawikuh soon after he took the city, Coronado found himself greeting a contingent of Indians from the Cicuyé (Pecos Pueblo) people of eastern New Mexico. Their chief spokesman, a man the Spaniards dubbed "Bigotes" because of his long mustache, told them about a large river to the east where many populous pueblos stood. He presented Coronado with gifts of bison robes, strong shields made of multiple layers of bison skin, and a helmet made of the same material. Bigotes showed Coronado a picture of a bison painted on the torso of one of the other Cicuyé Indians.

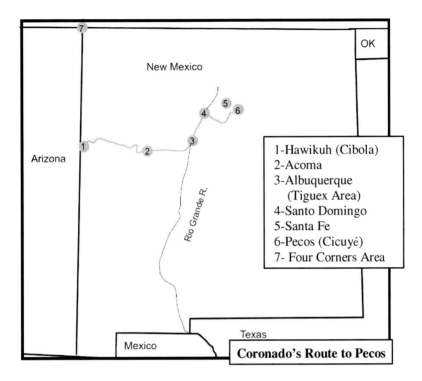

1-Hawikuh (Cibola)
2-Acoma
3-Albuquerque
   (Tiguex Area)
4-Santo Domingo
5-Santa Fe
6-Pecos (Cicuyé)
7- Four Corners Area

Coronado's Route to Pecos

Coronado ordered Pedro de Alvarado to accompany the Cicuyé along with a guard force of twenty soldiers and Fray Juan de Padilla. Alvarado and the others left Hawikuh at the end of August, and their course took them east over very difficult terrain about 100 miles to the high mesa village of Acoma. From there they continued another roughly sixty miles to the location of Tiguex, a complex of pueblos on both sides of the Rio Grande near Albuquerque. Alvarado sent word back by a messenger to Coronado advising him to bring the army to Tiguex for their winter quarters. Then Alvarado continued with Bigotes up the Rio Grande valley to a spot about twenty-five miles from Santa Fe where he turned east and arrived at Cicuyé, a journey of eighty miles from Tiguex. Cicuyé, strongly situated and defended by an encircling stone wall, was the largest city that the Spaniards would see in North America. Within, hundreds of four-story

149

houses, plazas, and courtyards provided lodging for thousands of people. This pueblo boasted 500 warriors and claimed never to have been captured or breached by invaders.

At Cicuyé, Alvarado met a man who would play a major role in the Coronado venture. This man was a slave of the Cicuyé people who came from a wealthy land to the east he called Harale. He offered to take Alvarado there. Alvarado called him El Turco (the Turk) because of his appearance. Alvarado and El Turco went east and south, possibly as far as west Texas before Alvarado decided to return to Tiguex to report to Coronado; he brought El Turco with him. By the beginning of winter, Coronado, Alvarado, and the army had set up winter quarters in Tiguex. El Turco had a willing listener when he finally met Coronado.

According to Castañeda, El Turco told Coronado:

In his country there was a river in the level country which was two leagues wide, in which there were fishes as big as horses, and large numbers of very big canoes with more than twenty rowers on a side, and that they carried sails; and that their lords sat on the poop under awnings, and on the prow they had a great golden eagle. He said also that the lord of that country took his afternoon nap under a great tree on which were hung a great number of little gold bells, which put him to sleep as they swung in the air. He said also that everyone had their ordinary dishes made of wrought plate, and the jugs, plates, and bowls were of gold.

When shown samples of gold, silver, and other metals, El Turco easily distinguished gold and silver, saying that the people of Quivira, his country, called gold "accochis." El Turco said that when the Cicuyé captured him they took away his golden bracelets. Coronado's lust for gold enflamed, he sent Alvarado to Cicuyé to retrieve El Turco's bracelets. When Alvarado asked about the bracelets there, Bigotes said El Turco was a liar, there were no gold bracelets. Alvarado put Bigotes in chains along with an elderly chief of Cicuyé and marched them back to Tiguex where they remained prisoners for six months. By this act, he turned the Cicuyé people against the Spaniards.

At Tiguex, Coronado demanded much of the people of the pueblos. His huge army consumed all of the Indians' stores of winter food. Then he demanded three hundred sets of cotton clothes for his men, and before the Indians could comply, he sent his men out to strip the Indians of the clothes they were wearing. In another incident, a Spanish officer asked an Indian to watch his horse. The Spaniard then entered the Indian's house and raped the man's wife. The husband complained to Coronado and identified the Spaniard by pointing out his horse. Coronado took no action against the rapist.

Finally, the Tiguex people had reached their limit and all the pueblos rose up in revolt. Coronado sent Cárdenas to talk with the Tiguex leaders at the pueblo of Arenal to end the uprising. He found the villages fortified and the people ready for war, so that is how he responded. With the assistance of the Indians from New Spain, he soon routed the people from the pueblo where the rape had occurred.

The Tiguex leaders from that pueblo approached two of Cárdenas's officers and indicated they wanted peace by crossing their arms. The two officers returned this sign for peaceful surrender. The Indians then put down their weapons and surrendered. The officers brought the Indians to Cárdenas's tent where he decided to make an example out of them. He ordered 200 stakes to be erected in the plaza where the Indians were to be burned to death.

The captured Indians, seeing the preparations, decided to die in combat rather than submit to that humiliation. They grabbed whatever they found at hand to use as weapons and attacked the Spaniards. But they were soon cut down by Spanish swords and lances. Only a few of the Indians escaped into the village and eluded capture when night fell.

Coronado took no action against Cárdenas for his treachery. However, Cárdenas stood trial later in Spain and was imprisoned for his mistreatment of the Tiguex prisoners.

Meanwhile, word of his violation of the peace spread throughout the pueblos. The Indians of the Southwest knew they could not trust the Spanish to keep their word. The Tiguex revolt continued at all twelve pueblos throughout the winter months.

The army laid siege to one of the pueblos with the most inhabitants. The Indians resisted all the Spaniards' efforts to scale the walls and take the city, with heavy losses on both sides. Finally, the lack of water within the pueblo brought victory to Coronado. First the Indians within asked the Spaniards to allow their women and children to leave unharmed. The Spaniards consented to that. The warriors in the pueblo resisted for two more weeks then, under cover of darkness, sneaked out of the pueblo. But the Spanish discovered them and attacked, killing many. The army captured the rest of the warriors and put them in chains.

While the winter revolt was raging, Coronado had taken the elderly Cicuyé chief back to his pueblo (Pecos) and promised to bring Bigotes back in the spring when he, Coronado, planned to set out for Quivira, the fabled city of gold that El Turco had told him about.

Eventually Coronado negotiated a troubled peace, or at least an end to open aggression, along the Rio Grande. Now the time had come to locate Quivira, but not all the Spaniards believed El Turco's story. Castañeda wrote:

A Spaniard named Cervantes, who had charge of [El Turco] during the siege, solemnly swore that he had seen the Turk talking with the devil in a pitcher of water, and also that while he had him under lock so that no one could speak to him, the Turk had asked him what Christians had been killed by the people at Tiguex. He told him "nobody," and then the Turk answered: "You lie; five Christians are dead including a captain." And as Cervantes knew that he told the truth, he confessed it so as to find out who had told him about it, and the Turk said he knew it all by himself, and that he did not need to have anyone tell him in order to know it. And it was on account of this that he watched him and saw him speaking to the devil in the pitcher.

So some of Coronado's men had misgivings about El Turco, but Coronado was beguiled. Some of his officers advised that he send a reconnaissance expedition forward rather than move the whole army. Coronado insisted on taking all of his forces with him to Quivira.

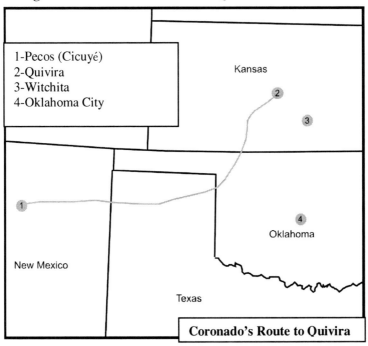

1-Pecos (Cicuyé)
2-Quivira
3-Witchita
4-Oklahoma City

Kansas

New Mexico

Oklahoma

Texas

Coronado's Route to Quivira

On April 23, 1541, the Spanish army, with all their livestock, marched away from the Tiguex pueblos and followed the Rio Grand north, then moved east to Cicuyé where Coronado released Bigotes. At Cicuyé, Coronado obtained two additional natives of Quivira named Xabe and Ysopete to assist as guides along with El Turco. Coronado obtained supplies of food at Cicuyé in spite of El Turco saying that loading the horses with packs of food was unnecessary and would limit the amount of gold they could return with. The people of Cicuyé gave the food willingly; undoubtedly glad to see the back of Coronado and his army.

In four days, Coronado's army crossed the Pecos River and proceeded on a northeasterly course taking them through west Texas, across Oklahoma and into Kansas. They had never experienced anything like the Great Plains. As far as they could see, a flat, featureless sea of grass extended to the horizon. Without a compass, men could get lost and never find their way back to camp. They burned fires all night as beacons so that lost men could find their way back. The grass was so dense according to Castañeda:

> ...that a thousand horses, and five hundred of our cows, and more than five thousand rams and ewes, and more than fifteen hundred friendly Indians and servants, in traveling over these plains, would leave no more trace where they had passed than if nothing had been there—nothing—so that it was necessary to make piles of bones and cow-dung now and then, so that the rear-guard could follow the army. The grass never failed to become erect after it had been trodden down, and, although it was short, it was as fresh and straight as before.

They encountered Apaches living in bison-skin teepees. The Apaches told the Spaniards that farther east they would find a great river that people inhabited for a length of at least eighty leagues (200 miles). The Mississippi River was about 500 miles to the east. The Apaches struck camp the next day, bundling their hide tents and poles together, and moved out with their dogs pulling travois with the Indians' bundled belongings strapped to them. The Spaniards also encountered another tribe of the plains, the Teyas or Texas, whose name would one day designate the largest of the lower forty-eight United States.

In thirty-seven days Coronado's army had covered about 600 miles since leaving Tiguex, an indication of the relatively undemanding country they had traversed. While in the plains, they met an old blind Indian who told them he had met four Spaniards years before when he traveled far to the south. The four had been headed to New Spain. These they took to be Cabeza de Vaca and his companions.

Apache Man ca. 1905

Ysopete had denied that gold existed in Quivira and contradicted much of what El Turco had told Coronado. Now the conquistador could see no evidence of a great city within sight on that sea of grass. The Spaniards were running out of food and water and would have to hunt bison and other game to supplement the food left from what the Cicuyé had provided. Coronado conferred with his officers and decided to send the main army back to Tiguex under Tristán de Luna y Arellano.

Coronado continued on his quest with thirty men on horse and six foot soldiers, El Turco—now in chains—and with Ysopete and some Texas Indians guiding him toward the north. They traveled for six weeks living off the land; after four weeks they had reached the Arkansas River near its southernmost extent in Kansas. Coronado named the river after Saints Peter and Paul. For the next three days they marched along the river's north bank which took them in a northeasterly direction to Lyons, Kansas, where a small village was identified as Quivira, consisting not of many-storied stone houses but of a small collection of wickiups. The people lived a nomadic existence, following the bison across the plains. Coronado found one Indian with a copper gorget and a few copper bells (possibly obtained in trade from Indians who had gotten them from De Soto's expedition). Coronado seized these items and sent them back to Viceroy Mendoza with a letter giving a report of his progress.

In spite of his profound disappointment at Quivira, Coronado erected a cross there and claimed the land for Spain. The only other satisfaction he got there was personally strangling to death El Turco, who had confessed, according to Castañeda, that the Cicuyé had asked him to "take [the Spaniards] to a place where we and our horses would starve to death."

Plains Indian wickiup dwelling ca. 1903

Although some historians designate Lyons, Kansas as the place closest to Coronado's farthest location, he reported that he had reached forty degrees north latitude. If his sighting of the noon sun was correct, then he had made it to the border between Kansas and Nebraska, about one and half degrees farther north than Lyons. Perhaps archaeologists will one day discover the inscribed cross he erected at Quivira.

The Spaniards remained at Quivira for nearly a month, talking to Indians and seeking a report on a land more profitable than the fertile and pleasant plain they were on. Finally Coronado, fearing that his small force could not survive the winter at Quivira, led his men back to Tiguex, leaving Ysopete and two soldiers at Quivira. They rejoined the army at Tiguex forty-days later at the end of September or early October. The army under Arellano had reached there in the middle of summer and found the Indians along the Rio Grande profoundly disappointed to see the Spaniards. Likewise at Cicuyé, the Spaniards found they were so unwelcome that the Indians of that great pueblo fired upon them. Undoubtedly they had hoped that El Turco would have left the vast army to die, lost in the plains.

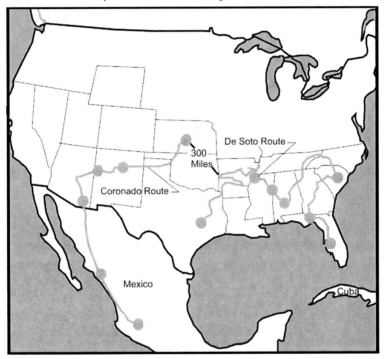

Coronado's and De Soto's men came within 300 miles of each other

Coronado and his army spent an unpleasant winter, foraging among the pueblos for food, meeting resistance at each site. They found many pueblos abandoned but containing stores of food. At one abandoned pueblo they found pottery that appeared to be decorated with silver. During this period they foraged as far north as Taos Pueblo.

Due to shortage of food and clothing, even after pillaging the pueblo stores of food and stripping the Indians naked, the soldiers began to grumble and talk of returning to New Spain. Coronado had other ideas—he planned to take the entire army back to Quivira and continue his explorations of that pleasant country. His plans would have to change.

At the end of winter as Coronado was preparing for his return to Quivira, the Spaniards held a fiesta. Coronado took part in the festivities by riding his horse in a competitive joust where the contestants galloped toward a suspended ring at the end of the course, the object being to spear the ring on the end of their lance. Coronado's saddle girth had not been tightened properly, or perhaps the girth broke. He tumbled off his mount and Rodrigo Maldonado's horse trampled him, severely wounding Coronado's head. He nearly died. Then came into play one of the quirks of that period: before Coronado left Spain, a man in Salamanca had cast his horoscope and predicted that he would conquer a great, distant country, only to die in a fall. Coronado couldn't get that prediction out of his battered head.

Coronado chose the officers he knew most favored abandoning his expedition and instructed them to convince the other officers and the soldiers to decide to return to New Spain. They certainly had little difficulty with that task. Castañeda wrote that Coronado pretended to be more ill than he really was. In any case, the army marched out of the Rio Grande country in early March, 1542. They left the pueblo Indians they had enslaved behind.

Coronado's route took him first to Hawikuh and then, after a rest, proceeded to Chichilticale where he met Juan Gallegos who was bringing reinforcements to Coronado. Gallegos and Coronado had cross words when Gallegos learned that Coronado had abandoned the expedition for no good reason—at least in Gallegos's opinion.

> ## First North American Martyr
> ## Fray Juan de Padilla
>
> Franciscan Fray Juan de Padilla insisted on staying with the pueblo Indians to minister to them and teach them about Christianity. Along with Fray Padilla, Fray Juan de la Cruz, Fray Luis de Ubeda (or Escalona), a Portuguese man named Andres da Campo, two black slaves named Lucas and Sebastián, a mestizo, and two Indians from New Spain remained with Padilla. Padilla, accompanied by Campo, Lucas, Sebastián, and the two Mexican Indians returned to Quivira. There Fray Padilla encountered a band of hostile Indians. Seeing they were intent on his murder, he calmly released his companions so they could make their escape, knelt in prayer, and died at the hands of the unknown Indians.
>
> Fray Juan de la Cruz and Fray Luis de Ubeda remained behind at Tiguex and suffered a similar martyrdom at their Rio Grande mission. Andres da Campo eventually turned up in Pánuco after a two year ordeal, supposedly carrying the bloody robes of Fray Juan de Padilla.

By the time Coronado's army reached Culiacán, they were in open revolt. By the time he reached Mexico City and Viceroy Mendoza, Coronado commanded at best 100 men. The Viceroy, realizing the depth of his financial loss as well as his personal disappointment, instituted an investigation into Coronado's handling of the whole enterprise. The commission report found Coronado not guilty of any crimes but said of him, "He is more fit to be governed... than to govern." The viceroy removed Coronado from the governorship of New Galicia. Coronado never recovered the huge financial loss of the 71,000 silver pesos he had invested in the expedition, and he continued in poor health until he died in Mexico City twelve years later.

Viceroy Antonio de Mendoza, who had lost 85,000 silver pesos on the failed Coronado expedition, had the means to recover from that staggering loss, and he continued to enjoy royal favor. Emperor Charles V appointed him Viceroy of Peru in 1549. Mendoza boarded a boat in Panama and sailed to Peru, taking office late in 1550. He died in Lima two years later at about fifty-five years old.

García López de Cárdenas was convicted of crimes against the Indians of the pueblos and confined to prison in Spain where he died.

While the main thrust of Viceroy Antonio de Mendoza's quest for the Seven Cities of Gold in North America was the land expedition led by Coronado, he also launched an expedition by sea. As early as 1533, Mendoza's rival, Cortés, had sent Fortún Jiménez north along the Pacific coast; Jiménez returned after finding Baja California, which he thought was an island.

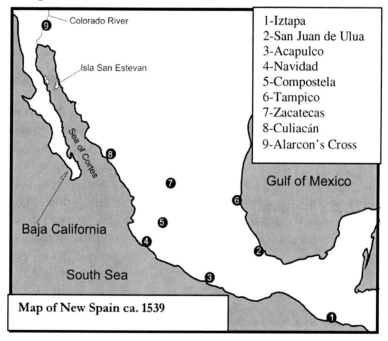

1-Iztapa
2-San Juan de Ulua
3-Acapulco
4-Navidad
5-Compostela
6-Tampico
7-Zacatecas
8-Culiacán
9-Alarcon's Cross

Map of New Spain ca. 1539

In 1539, Francisco de Ulloa, also sailing for Cortés, pushed up the coast from Acapulco and entered the Gulf of California. He was looking for the northern extent of the land. He found that Baja California was not an island but an 800-mile-long peninsula. He apparently went up to Isla San

Estevań where strong tidal flow may have blocked his progress, then sailed down the gulf, around the tip at Cabo San Lucas and up the western side of the peninsula about 600 miles, naming the land California.

Not to be outdone by Cortés, Mendoza sent Hernando de Alarcón up the west coast of Mexico to carry additional supplies for the land expedition of Coronado and also to search for the Seven Cities of Gold—the story of Fray Marcos made Mendoza think that Cibola might lie near the coast.

Naming of California

A popular tale in Spain in the sixteenth century, *Las Sergas de Esplandián,* told of an island called California to the east of the Indies that was populated by Amazons. The women warriors would allow men to come to their island once per year to procreate. The land, as in all fables, was rich in gold, gems, and pearls. Cortés hoped that the land that Jiménez had first glimpsed was that fabled land. Cortés's men did not find wealth or Amazons at Baja California, but the gulf bears his name today—the Sea of Cortés.

Alarcón sailed with two ships, *San Pedro* and *Santa Catalina,* on March 9, 1540, from Navidad bound for the port of Culiacán (Pabellones), where he learned that Coronado had already moved north from that city. The *San Gabriel* joined Alarcón's fleet at this point.

The three ships continued up the coast, entering the Gulf of California, and pushing past the restricted passage at Isla San Estéban, entered the head of the gulf. They sailed up to the mud flats at the mouth of the Colorado River where they anchored.

Alarcón took two of the ships' boats and on August 26, with twenty-two men and some small cannon, began his exploration of the Colorado River—the first documented instance by European visitors. About fifteen miles upstream, the Spaniards encountered their first Indians of the Colorado, the Cocopa. When Alarcón went ashore to speak with these people, an old man, perhaps the chief, came up to him and struck him in the chest. The Spaniard wisely got back into his boat and sailed up the middle of the river under a favorable breeze. The Cocopa wore little clothing: the men a loin cloth, the women a bunch of feathers covering their groin. They painted their bodies with charcoal and wore leather discs with feathers on their heads. Their weapons were wooden clubs and bows and arrows.

Farther up river, Alarcón found the Indians more approachable and learned some of their legends. Their stories, their healing practices, and social norms were similar to those observed by Cabeza de Vaca as he traveled along the coast of Texas. They built their houses of wood—communal huts of wattle and daub—near the mountains and planted their corn in the fertile, watered land along the river. From these Indians Alarcón heard tales of Cibola, said to be thirty days journey away. Proceeding up river he heard a story of the death of Estevan and his greyhound. Further up the river he heard from the Yuma or Mojave Indians that men like himself, Christians, had invaded Cibola—Coronado had beaten him to Cibola.

Alarcón tried to get one of his men to travel to Cibola to tell Coronado of his position on the Colorado River, but none of the men would dare to make the trip. He had by this time been gone two weeks from the fleet. With the aid of the river current, he made the return trip in two days and found the fleet in good condition.

Wanting to join with Coronado, Alarcón made a second trip up the Colorado, this time going an estimated eighty-five leagues perhaps to Fort Yuma, Arizona. There he set up a large cross and placed letters at the base of it.

His trip back down river was uneventful until an Indian woman jumped into the water and climbed into his boat. She huddled under a bench and wouldn't come out. She told the Spaniards that she had left her husband because he had taken another wife and she had given him children. She said she wouldn't live another minute with that man.

Rejoining the fleet, Alarcón sailed back to report to the viceroy. That ended his attempt to find Coronado by sailing up the Colorado River. Unaware that Alarcón had left the Gulf of California, Melchior Díaz, who had been left in charge of the army in the Sonora valley, decided he had had enough inaction. He set out with Indian guides to locate the Colorado River and join Alarcón. He reached the territory of the Yuma Indians several days' journey up river from Fort Yuma. The Indians told him that Alarcón could be found farther downstream. Díaz found the cross left by Alarcón and found the letters hidden there. From the letters he learned that Alarcón had departed for Mexico.

As Díaz and his men began to make their way back toward the Sonora valley, they had to cross the Colorado on rafts. While they were building the rafts, he uncovered an Indian plot to kill all the Spaniards while they were divided on the river rafts. Díaz secretly drowned the ringleader of the plot and the Spaniards made their escape.

Díaz never made it out of Arizona. One day riding along on his horse, he saw a dog attacking one of their sheep. Riding toward the scene at a gallop, he threw his lance to frighten the dog and save the sheep. The lance stuck in the ground, but the butt of the lance wounded Díaz in the thigh as he passed by it. The wound turned septic and within about twenty days, Díaz died. His men buried him somewhere in the Sonora desert.

In spite of the failures of the Coronado expedition, the Viceroy of New Spain would continue Spanish exploration of the coast to expand their knowledge of western North America.

Chapter 7
Coastal Exploration and Settlement

Juan Rodríguez Cabrillo, or João Rodrigues Cabrilho to give him his true name, sailed under orders from Viceroy Antonio de Mendoza to expand Spanish knowledge of the Pacific coast of California. Cabrillo's early life is vague; Spanish historian Antonio de Herrera y Tordesillas wrote that Cabrillo was Portuguese, while modern historian Harry Kelsey wrote that Cabrillo was born in Spain at Seville or Cuéllar. Sources agree that Cabrillo was born in 1499, and he first shows up in the annals of New Spain in 1519 as a captain of a company of crossbowmen under Cortés. After his part in the conquest of the Aztec Empire, Cabrillo continued as a soldier in Peru, San Salvador, and Guatemala.

Cabrillo received valuable land grants and encomiendas in Guatemala where he made a substantial fortune in gold mining. In 1532 he returned to Spain where he wed Beatriz Sanchez de Ortega. By the mid-1530s, Cabrillo and his wife were back in Guatemala living in Santiago.

Governor of Guatemala, Pedro de Alvarado and Viceroy of New Spain, Pedro de Mendoza entered into a partnership in 1540 to explore the Pacific coast with several goals in mind: to search for the Seven Cities of Cibola (the sea-based phase of Mendoza's dream); to locate the Strait of Anián that the Spanish believed connected the Pacific to the Atlantic; and to establish a trade route to the Spice Islands. The two men put up 90,000 silver pesos (about $6 million today) to

fund that venture; they were equal partners. Alvarado sailed from Guatemala to Navidad, Mexico, with a fleet of twelve ships, sixty horses, and at least 400 men. In Mexico, he agreed to put down an Indian revolt in New Galicia. During that engagement in July 1541, Alvarado died when a fellow-soldier's horse fell on him—an inglorious end for the man who had pole-vaulted with his lance across a canal at Tenochtitlan making his

Pedro de Alvarado

escape with Cortés as the infuriated Aztecs chased them. At the time of the conquest of the Aztec Empire, Alvarado was second-in-command to Cortés.

Alvarado had selected Cabrillo to build his ships, and Cabrillo was to sail in Alvarado's fleet to discover the coast of the Pacific above New Spain. Cabrillo had learned the ship-building trade, having served as an apprentice in that profession as a young boy. He had set up a shipyard at Iztapa, a port that lies on a bay behind sheltering barrier islands on the southern coast of Guatemala, about forty-five miles

JUAN RODRIGUEZ CABRILLO.

from Santiago. After Alvarado's death, his partner Mendoza placed his trust in Cabrillo to assume command of the Pacific coast portion of the venture.

The fleet would be divided between Cabrillo and Ruy Lopez de Villalobos, who would take the balance of the fleet across the Pacific to the Spice Islands.

Cabrillo had command of two ships: the flagship *San Salvador* and the *Victoria*. Villalobos sailed in November of 1542 from Navidad with six ships bound for the Philippines. He died in a Portuguese prison in the Moluccas two years later. Cabrillo sailed before Villalobos, departing Navidad on June 24 (or 27), 1542. His crew of unknown number included sailors, soldiers, a priest, some black and Indian slaves, livestock and other provisions meant to last for two years.

Pedro de Alvarado
Failed Marriage Broker

Among many stories about Governor Alvarado, one humorous one illustrates the primitive condition of Guatemala during his tenure and the condition of many of the men who had settled there after their service as soldiers.

By royal decree, men would have to forfeit their lucrative encomiendas if they were not married—this was to increase the population and to prevent marriage to the Indians.

Alvarado returned from Spain with twenty well-bred maidens, daughters of noblemen. To showcase these beauties, he held a party and invited all of the wealthy bachelors of Guatemala to attend.

The young women, hidden behind a screen, looked at the grizzled old conquistadors and said, "They say that these are to be our husbands. What! Marry those old fellows? Let those wed them who choose; I will not; the devil take them! One would think by the way they are cut up that they just escaped from the infernal regions; for some are lame, some with but one hand, others without ears, others with only one eye, others with half their face gone, and the best of them have one or two cuts across their forehead."

"We are not to marry them for their good looks but for the purpose of inheriting their Indians; for they are so old and worn out that they will soon die, and then we can choose in place of these old men young fellows to our tastes, in the same manner that an old broken kettle is exchanged for one that is new and sound."

One of the "old fellows" overheard the young women talking. He left and married the daughter of a cacique.

1-Iztapa
2-Acapulco
3-Navidad
4-Culiacán
5- San Pedro, Santa Monica, San Buenaventura
6-Santa Barbara
7-Monterrey Bay
8-Cape Mendocino
9-Rogue River

Exploration of the Pacific Coast

On September 28th, Cabrillo's ships entered San Diego Bay, anchoring at Ballast Point—a trip of nearly 1,400 miles. He described the bay as "a very good enclosed port." While there he heard from the local Ipai Indians that Spaniards were roaming the land to the east, killing many Indians. This had made the Ipai wary of Cabrillo and his men, and had caused them initially to show hostility. The comment about men to the east was, of course, a reference to Coronado's land expeditionary force, by then back in New Spain.

After six days, Cabrillo sailed out of the bay and, keeping to the coast, headed northwest charting the waters and coast as they progressed along California. His fleet observed San Pedro, Santa Monica, San Buenaventura, Santa Barbara, and reached Point Conception on October 17, where they had to turn back due to an unfavorable wind that took them back to San Miguel Island.

In early November, the wind turned and they struck out again from San Miguel Island to follow the coast farther northwest. They reached Monterey Bay by November 18th, and then turned back, arriving at San Miguel Island on November 23, 1542. They made that site their winter quarters. Ashore on the island, Cabrillo slipped on the rocks, shattering his lower leg while engaged in a fight with Indians there. Bone splinters caused the wound to become infected and gangrene set in. He died January 3, 1543 at San Miguel Island.

Bartolomé Ferrelo (aka Ferrer) assumed command of the fleet after Cabrillo's death. The ships sailed from San Miguel Island on February 18, 1543 and pushed northward to Cape Blanco or the Rogue River just across the line that separates the states of California and Oregon today. Their solar sighting on February 28th indicated they had reached forty-three degrees of latitude. Ferrelo reported that they turned back at this latitude for a variety of reasons including sickness, inadequate supplies, excessive cold, and unfavorable winds. The contemporary record (translated ca. 1886 by George Davidson) contains this description of the sailing conditions they endured:

> ...there came a very violent rain-storm from the north, which made them sail all that night and the following day until sunset to the south with the foresails furled; and because there was a high sea from the south it broke over them each time by the prow and passed over them as if over a rock, and the wind shifted to the north-west and the north-north-west with great fury, so that it made them run until Saturday, the 3rd of March, to this south-east and to the south-south-east with such a high sea that it made them cry out without reserve that if God and His Blessed Mother did not miraculously save them, they could not escape. Saturday at noon the wind moderated and remained at the north-west, for which they gave many thanks to

Our Lord. They suffered also in provisions, as they had only biscuit and that damaged.

They put ashore once more at San Miguel Island on March 5 and then departed for Navidad, where they arrived on April 14, 1543, having lost only Cabrillo and one sailor.

This would be the last Spanish voyage of discovery of the Pacific Coast until Sebastián Vizcaíno explored the Pacific Coast in 1602/3. But Cabrillo and Ferrelo added greatly to Spain's knowledge of the west coast. They established that if North America and Asia was one continent, the connection was much farther north than contemporary maps had indicated. They also found no Strait of Anián connecting the Atlantic and the Pacific. If such a channel existed, it also had to be farther north. Their logs and sightings enabled more accurate navigational maps for Spanish sailors to follow. They also had ruled out any of the seven golden cities of Cibola having a Pacific Coast location—Hollywood came much later in history.

Spanish exploration and settlement attempts west of the Mississippi would from this point until the end of the sixteenth century come over land rather than up the California coast.

In the 1540s and 1550s, Spain lost a number of ships along the Gulf Coast and the straits along Florida, prompting a renewed interest in establishing ports that would provide a haven for the treasure fleet in storms and a secure area for shipwreck survivors. Hundreds of Spaniards—men and women—lost along the Gulf Coast ended up as captives of various Indian tribes. Some shipwreck survivors died at the hands of the Indians, some lived in slavery, and some received benevolent care but were unable to rejoin their families in Spain. For example, in 1545 a Spanish shipwreck left 200 people ashore, and none survived.

In 1553, a fleet of treasure ships bound for Spain went aground with more than 1,000 soldiers, sailors, and other men, women, and children bound for Spain. The passengers included five Dominican clerics. Only 300 managed to struggle to the Gulf shore; only a few made it back to New Spain alive. One of the survivors, Fray Marcos de Meña, was riddled with Indian arrows. His companions buried him in the warm sand, leaving only his face exposed, since he had not quite expired. Much later, Fray Marcos awoke, much refreshed from his sleep in the sand. He pulled out the arrows and hailed a couple of Indians going by in a canoe. They proved friendly and carried the monk back to Tampico. In 1554, fifteen Spanish ships wrecked on the Atlantic coast; these events and others prompted action by Spanish authorities to secure the coasts.

Viceroy Luís de Velasco

Don Luís de Velasco assumed the position of Viceroy of New Spain in 1550 with a mandate from King Felipe to establish those strategic ports along the Gulf Coast and along the Atlantic to protect the restricted waters of the Bahama channel where ships could founder on the shoals and reefs, and where the fleet was more vulnerable to pirates. Both King Felipe and Viceroy Velasco shared the philosophy that a more benevolent and less militaristic approach to the settlement of La Florida would win the Native Americans over to Spanish rule and the Christian faith. Velasco's freeing of the Indian slaves in New Spain gives evidence that he genuinely subscribed to this philosophy.

Dominican clerics would accompany expeditions into La Florida to take charge of the religious instruction of the Indians and to ensure that they received humane treatment. On December 29, 1557, the king approved Velasco's plans for settlement of Santa Elena on the east coast (at Parris Island) and another settlement on the Gulf Coast. In an unusual turn from the past, King Felipe gave the Viceroy of New Spain the authority to select the new Adelantado or Governor of La Florida. Previously, that decision had been the king's.

Velasco sent Guido de Las Bazares in September, 1558, to explore the Gulf Coast for a suitable settlement location. Bazares departed San Juan de Ulúa (now part of Veracruz, Mexico) on September 3, 1558, with a bark and a small, shallow-draft sailboat for coastal exploration. His goal was to find a port that would be close to the Coosa region, as identified by the De Soto expedition, and also provide short overland access to Santa Elena. The Spanish knew that De Soto's trek took him relatively close to the Atlantic shore when he marched from Apalachee to Cofitachequi. They thought correctly that his path had taken him within forty leagues of Santa Elena.

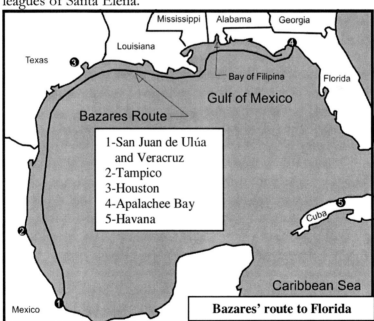

Bazares spent several months, making progress no farther than Apalachee Bay, although the viceroy expected him to sail around the Florida peninsula and up the Atlantic coast to

Santa Elena. He returned on December 14, 1558, reporting that he had found a suitable bay on the Florida coast and that the weather had prevented him from sailing farther than he had. Bazares recommended the Bay of Filipina (Mobile Bay today) as the location to establish the first settlement.

On October 30, 1558, after Bazares had departed on his exploratory voyage, Velasco appointed Tristán de Luna y Arellano as Governor of La Florida. Arellano's father was governor of Yucatán, and Arellano had served in New Spain for about thirty years; also he had accompanied Coronado on his quest for the Seven Cities of Gold and Quivira. Arellano seemed just the man to lead a major settlement effort into La Florida.

The viceroy's plan that he charged Arellano with was to erect three towns: one on the Gulf Coast east of the Río de Espíritu Santo (Mississippi River), one at Coosa (near present day Carters, Georgia), and one at Santa Elena. An overland trail from the port on the gulf to Coosa and then to Santa Elena would provide a route for supplies from New Spain to Santa Elena via the gulf port. Velasco expected that eventually a road would be established from the mining area of Zacatecas in northern Mexico to the gulf port, linking with the road to Santa Elena on the Atlantic. This way, silver could be shipped overland rather than through the riskier waters of the Florida and Bahama channels.

As governor of La Florida, Arellano would control all the land east of a meridian through the mouth of the Mississippi to the Atlantic coast and up to Newfoundland—about one-third of the North American Continent. His fleet of the settlers consisted of thirteen ships and smaller boats carrying 1,500 people including 500 soldiers and sailors, 1,000 colonists including women and children, black and Indian slaves (some who had been brought from La Florida). An Indian woman from Coosa traveled with the settlers—she had been brought to New Spain by Moscoso and the other survivors of the De Soto expedition. Arellano had 240 horses aboard. Six captains commanded the soldiers; several of the captains had been in La Florida previously, as had some of the soldiers. Six Dominican clerics led by Fray Pedro de Feria accompanied the fleet.

June 11, 1559, Arellano's fleet sailed out of Veracruz harbor bound not for the Bay of Filipina, as recommended by Bazares, but for the Bay of Ochuse (Pensacola Bay today), originally discovered by Captain Diego de Maldonado while sailing for De Soto. It isn't clear why Arellano disregarded Bazares' recommendation. They reached a position off the Mississippi River when unfavorable winds drove them back to the Yucatán. When a favorable breeze returned, they proceeded east about as far as Apalachee Bay before coasting west toward the Bay of Ochuse. This time they overshot it and ended up anchored at the Bay of Filipina (Mobile Bay). Arellano put the horses ashore there and sent them on a march overland to the Bay of Ochuse while he sent a ship east to locate their destination. Once the scouting party reported back, the fleet followed them to the Bay of Ochuse. They reached their destination on August 14, 1559.

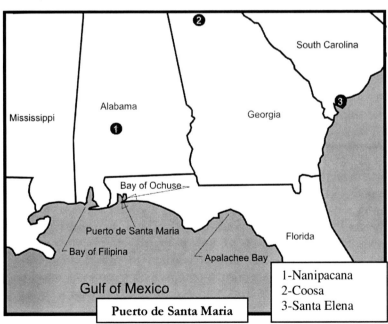

At the Bay of Ochuse, Arellano put his settlers to work building the first Spanish town in Florida. The town design had come from Viceroy Velasco. They named the town Puerto de Santa Maria; it was located where the Pensacola Naval Air Station stands today. Arellano's fleet sailed past Santa Rosa and Robertson Islands and into the west end of the bay. They staked out the town facing the inlet to the Gulf of Mexico.

While town building got underway, Arellano sent out two scouting parties into the interior to survey the land. Both parties were gone about two weeks and came back with disappointing news. They had found only a small Indian village and had nearly starved on their journey. With them they brought an Indian woman named Lacsoho to serve as an interpreter.

Little more than two weeks later a disaster of major proportions struck Puerto de Santa Maria. A fierce storm, most likely a hurricane, struck the fleet anchored in the bay, sending all but four ships to the bottom. One of the remaining ships ended up cast upon the land near the town. Because they had not yet built their storehouses in the town, Arellano had left most of the supplies, equipment, and provisions aboard the ships. Thus the storm of September 19th reduced his army and colonists to the point of starvation in an instant. Also, many lost their lives when the storm sank the ships.

Archaeologists Find Arellano's Fleet

At Emanuel Point in Pensacola Bay, Florida, in 1990, marine archaeologists found one of Arellano's ships wrecked during the hurricane of 1559. A quarter mile away, a second wrecked ship of the Arellano fleet was found in 2006. The archaeologists found intact ship's timbers, jars, rat and cockroach remains that were in the ship's hull when it sank in addition to ballast stones that marked the site. They also found Aztec pottery and obsidian blades belonging to Indians who accompanied Arellano's settlers from New Spain.

Arellano sent out several of his officers and 250 men traveling northwest in search of an Indian town that could provide sustenance to the colonists. They intersected the Alabama River and followed its course to Nanipacana. The town had a large quantity of corn and beans that the inhabitants had abandoned when they saw the Spaniards. Coaxed back to town by friendly overtures and gifts, the Indians said that their town had once been a large city but had been destroyed in the war with Spaniards who had come there years before—De Soto's expedition. Sixteen men went back to Puerto de Santa Maria to tell Arellano of the food supply at Nanipacana. By the time they reached the settlement, ships from New Spain had brought additional supplies to the starving colonists and soldiers on the coast. Arellano decided to remain at his new town for the winter.

During the winter, Arellano fell ill and was at times delirious with fever. In the late winter, the settlers had consumed all of their food and Arellano decided to relocate to Nanipacana 120 miles north of the Bay of Ochuse, taking approximately 1,000 people with him. He left a captain with fifty men and an unknown number of slaves at the new town to maintain possession of the port. Half of his settlers and soldiers traveled overland to Nanipacana and the rest went by boat following the coast west about forty-five miles to Mobile Bay and then up the Alabama River to the Indian village.

Arellano established his new encampment at Nanipacana and renamed the town Vera Cruz. Arriving as they did before the corn crops had been planted or had borne fruit, the food supply at Nanipacana soon ran out. By April, 1560, the Spaniards found themselves starving again, reduced to eating leaves and twigs gathered in the forest. Arellano sent out 200 soldiers and two friars under the command of several captains to search for the province of Coosa. They marched north following Indian trails for more than fifty days, starving as well and eating their leather boots, belts, and armor straps to stay alive.

At last, friendly Indians found the soldiers and conducted them to the main town of the Coosa, arriving there sometime before August 1st. The Coosa received the Spaniards with good will, feeding them, although not providing as much food as the starving men wanted. They sent a letter back to Arellano at Nanipacana urging him to relocate to Coosa, which they described as more favorable for settlement. Major Mateo del Sauz wrote to Arellano:

> I should consider it more fitting that you yourself should go [to the Coosa territory]. See to it that you are not deceived into being detained there, for at least if you do not find land suitable for settling, you comply with the duty of your position and close the mouths of base criticism. And now is the time, for now the dearth of food experienced hitherto will not have to be endured, the green corn and the beans being ready to gather.... I am fearful the people may rise against us when they harvest their crops; for now thinking we are only passing through, they give us burden bearers and all we ask for in order to get us out of the country.

During the summer, the paramount chief of the Coosa persuaded the Spaniards to join with him in making war on the neighboring Napochies. The day the Coosa and Spaniards left to wage war, the Indians conducted a ritual described by historian Woodbury Lowery as follows:

> The Coosa warriors assembled with bows as tall as themselves, strung with sinews which had been well cured and twisted, and carrying quivers of feathered arrows tipped with dart-shaped flints, which were poisoned, and in the use of which they were very skilful. A platform about eight feet high had been erected near [the Spanish] camp, which was not far removed from that of the natives. Suddenly there came running through both camps eight Indian chiefs, who seizing upon the cacique, lifted him upon their shoulders, and with great howlings and wild cries carried him to the steps of the platform, which he ascended and paced about with much gravity, while the braves grouped themselves below. He was then handed a fan of very beautiful feathers, with which he pointed three or four times

towards the province of the Napochies, with a motion like that observed by astrologers with the fore-staff. He was next handed some seeds, which he placed in his mouth, and again pointing with his fan in the direction of the enemy's country he ground the seeds between his teeth, and, scattering them as far as he could, cried out to his captains, who were watching him intently, "Friends, be comforted, for our journey will have prosperous outcome, and our enemies shall be conquered, and their forces crushed like these seeds which I have destroyed in my mouth.

Following the ceremony, the Coosa warriors and the Spanish soldiers accompanied by Fray Anunciacion began their march against the Napochies. At their enemy's principal town they found the inhabitants had fled into the woods. In the plaza they found stakes festooned with the scalps of Coosa warriors; those they took down and buried. Only an old infirm Napochie man remained there; they killed him. Then the Coosa began to destroy the food, but the Spaniards prevailed upon them to gather most of it to take back to Coosa. Leaving the town, they confronted the Napochies who surrendered and agreed to pay periodic tribute of chestnuts and fruit to the Coosa.

With peace concluded, the Spaniards and the Coosa returned to Coosa territory. Since Arellano and his large following of settlers and soldiers still had not arrived at Coosa, a captain and twelve soldiers rode back to Nanipacana to check on the welfare of the Spaniards there. As they neared the town they fired their harquebuses to announce their approach. They got no response. Entering Nanipacana, they found the town deserted with one Spaniard hanging from a tree. Their first thought was that the Indians had turned on the Spaniards and killed them all.

Finally, they found another tree with an inscription reading, "Dig here." Following that direction, they found an earthen pot with a letter inside. The letter told of sickness and starvation at Nanipacana and Arellano's ultimate decision to take the settlers and soldiers back to the Bay of Filipina where he hoped they would be re-supplied and could then travel to the Coosa.

Following Arellano to the Bay of Filipina, the thirteen soldiers from Coosa learned that Arellano and his people were back at the Bay of Ochuse. Arellano could not convince his settlers or soldiers to follow him back into the interior. They wanted to abandon the effort and return to New Spain.

At Puerto de Santa Maria on the Bay of Ochuse, Arellano had a near mutiny on his hands. He also had received written instructions from King Felipe that he expected Arellano to make settlement at Santa Elena his number one priority. He also received written instructions from Viceroy Velasco to establish the road from Coosa to Santa Elena. On August 10, 1560, Arellano sent three ships out to sail first to Havana and then to Santa Elena to begin the settlement there. Those ships got caught in a storm off Cuba and aborted the mission, one landing in Cuba, the other two sailing back to New Spain.

On August 26, 1560, Arellano met with the small party of soldiers from Coosa. They restored his confidence in the plan of relocating there as a staging point for going cross-country to Santa Elena. But many, perhaps most, of his settlers and soldiers were unwilling to go back into the interior. The next day, Jorge Ceron, camp master, wrote to Arellano a formal recommendation against going to Coosa. Over the next two days, the royal treasury official and all of the captains came out in opposition to Arellano's plan.

They gave the following reasons for not venturing into the interior: insufficient food to sustain them in the march; the horses and mules numbering about fifty were too weak; most of the soldiers were ill, naked, barefoot, and unequipped to make the journey; the people who had been to Coosa said the country was unfit to settle; and, even if the expedition Arellano proposed was necessary, they had lost all their arms and armor when they came down the turbulent rivers to the Bay of Filipina.

Arellano would not give up easily. He posted a muster list of 100 soldiers and fifty servants and insisted they be ready to depart for Coosa on Monday, September 2, 1560. Over the weekend, petitions circulated within Puerto de Santa Maria. Arellano was clearly a minority of one on this issue. He ordered the camp master to see to it that the soldiers and their servants had sufficient provisions for a march of fifty days. Some in the camp attempted to have Arellano declared unfit to command and have the camp master assume command, but the camp master refused to do so.

Finally, on Monday, Arellano, with the king's notary documenting his every move, ordered the provisions to be distributed to the men he had designated. None of the men appeared to receive the rations. Arellano then commanded that the mutinous soldiers be executed, but no one in Puerto de Santa Maria would carry out that order. Instead, the mutineers held council and decided to send a small detachment to Coosa to recall Major Sauz and all of his men to the Bay of Ochuse.

Sauz and his men abandoned Coosa and returned to Puerto Santa Maria by November, 1560. After a winter of discord and the silent treatment by Arellano, Fray Anunciacion said mass on Palm Sunday, (March 30, 1561) and forced a reconciliation between Arellano and the people of his settlement, but this came too late to save Arellano politically.

Prior to the mutiny, Fray Feria had sailed to New Spain to meet with Viceroy Velasco. Hearing the sorry state of affairs at Puerto de Santa Maria, Velasco gave orders that Angel de Villafañe would succeed Arellano as Governor of La Florida. Villafañe sailed from Veracruz and arrived at the Bay of Ochuse. He offered to take all there who desired to leave with him to Santa Elena. Everyone boarded Villafañe's ships except Arellano and a few servants. They boarded one of Arellano's vessels and sailed to Havana, then continued on to Spain where Arellano called for an official investigation to examine his governorship and restore his good reputation.

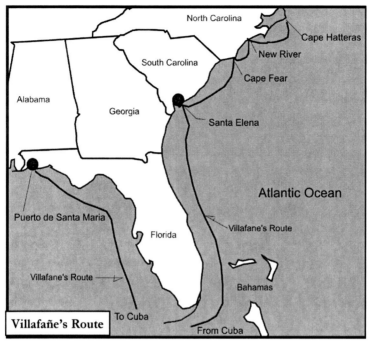

Villafañe sailed in his four ships with all but fifty soldiers he had left at Puerto de Santa Maria, bound first for Havana and then on to Santa Elena. At Havana, many took the opportunity to jump ship and even some of the officers refused to continue on the venture. Undaunted, Villafañe sailed to Santa Elena, reaching there on May 27, 1561. He proceeded upriver a small distance, claimed the territory for Spain, but decided that the land looked unsuitable for settlement. Back at sea, the ships sailed along the Atlantic coast to Cape Fear, which he called Cape Romano. He went a short distance up the river and claimed the land for Spain, but still found the area unsuitable due to a lack of harborage for ships.

Going farther up the coast, he reached the River de los Canoas (New River), and finding that also unsuitable for shipping, Villafañe sent one of his ships up to Cape Trafalgar (Cape Hatteras). That ship may also have taken aboard a young Indian the Spaniards called Paquinquineo. That young boy returns to our story in the next chapter.

On or about June 14th, a storm struck the little fleet off the treacherous outer banks of North Carolina sending twenty-six sailors to their deaths and separating the remaining ships. Villafañe abandoned his quest and arrived in Hispaniola on July 9, 1561.

Learning of Villafañe's return without settling at Santa Elena, Viceroy Velasco reported his failure to King Felipe. The king faced the situation that all expeditions into North America had failed to find any gold or silver other than what the Native Americans had salvaged from wrecked Spanish treasure ships. Furthermore, Spanish settlements had failed due to an inability to bring the Indians of most regions under Spanish rule and due to lack of sufficient food resources to accommodate a large influx of Spaniards. Minimal success in bringing the Indians to the Christian faith also added to the sense that La Florida was not fruitful ground for Spanish expansion.

On September 23, 1561 King Felipe announced that no further settlements would take place along the Gulf Coast or at Santa Elena; the one argument for continuing the efforts— defense against French settlement in La Florida—the king rejected as unfounded. His dismissal of the French would be short lived.

Villafañe sailed back to the Bay of Ochuse after about a month in Hispaniola and ordered Captain Biedma to abandon the settlement there. The small garrison at the Bay of Ochuse in Florida returned to New Spain abandoning Puerto de Santa Maria, Spain's only settlement in La Florida.

Tristán de Luna y Arellano found little sympathy with the king or council in Spain. He wrote to King Felipe:

> *I performed my duty well and obeyed the instructions which were given to me; but the maestro de campo, the other officers, and the soldiers conspired against me with the friars, not wishing to obey anything that I commanded, but on the other*

hand did just the contrary, attempting to give up the journey and prevent it from being carried forward. They even went as far as to make false reports and accounts which they sent to the Viceroy, so that he sent orders for me to give over my powers and papers to Angel de Villafañe, who proceeded with the expedition. Then, with your permission I came to make a report to Your Highness concerning everything. What I ask and supplicate is that, when you have seen and understood the aforesaid report, if I am found at fault in anything, I may be given the blame for it; but if I am not found to have been at fault, that it shall not be permitted that such a great injustice shall be committed as that done by the Viceroy in depriving me of the government of La Florida and authority of the expedition....

Arellano had depleted his personal fortune in the expedition to La Florida. He petitioned the crown for reimbursement for some of his expenses. The king's council replied, "There is no reason for making him the grant for which he asks." Case closed. Arellano returned to New Spain in 1567, but failed to find success there. Tristán de Luna y Arellano died at the home of his friend, Don Luís de Castilla, in Mexico City on September 16, 1573.

Chapter 8
Spain Settles the Atlantic Coast

Spanish ships had sailed up the Atlantic coast beginning with slave traders even before Ponce de León in 1513. We examined two voyages of discovery in the 1520s: Gomez sailing as far as Cape Cod in 1524, and Quexos reaching as far north as Delaware Bay in 1525. After Ayllón's landing at Winyah Bay in South Carolina and his failed settlement at Sapelo Sound in Georgia in 1526, the records show little Spanish interest in the Atlantic coast until 1559 and the failures by Arellano and Villafañe, which convinced Spain that the area was not worth the expense in men and other resources needed for its conquest.

Since Verrazano's voyage along the Atlantic coast in 1524 flying the French flag, Spain had been monitoring the French court to determine if France would follow that brief excursion with a settlement attempt. By the 1550s, Spain began again to look nervously at the Atlantic border of La Florida, concerned that they needed to protect it from incursions by France and also England. During most of the sixteenth century up to that point, Spain and France had been at war. At the Treaty of Cateau-Cambrésis in 1559, Spain reached a brief peace with France and England. The peace made Spain temporarily less nervous about the security of her Atlantic coast.

King Felipe's decision to abandon settlement attempts in La Florida proved premature. Ironically, Pedro Menéndez de Avilés, who would be one of the most important men in that cause, a man the king relied on to ensure safe passage of ships to and from the West Indies and who fought with distinction in the war with France, agreed with the decision to abandon La Florida. Neither the king nor Menéndez believed in 1561 that France would invade La Florida, held to be the exclusive domain of Spain based on a long history of Spanish explorers having annexed it for Spain, as well as the Papal donation of the land to Spain in the previous century.

Between 1559 and 1561, a Spanish ship sailed up the coast and made landfall at the Outer Banks of North Carolina. The Spanish took aboard a young Indian boy who had traveled there from his home in the north—about 100 miles to the north. We don't know whether the boy, dubbed Paquinquineo by the Spaniards, boarded the ship voluntarily or was kidnapped. We cannot be sure that he boarded one of the ships in Villafañe's fleet, but the timing seems correct and no other known fleet has been identified.

Paquinquineo was taken to New Spain and baptized with the name Don Luís in honor of the Viceroy, Don Luís de Velasco. The Indian boy's Dominican keepers began his education there. Later, in Spain, he came under the care of the Jesuits, who wrote that Don Luís was the son of a petty king in his homeland, a place he called Ajacán (or Axacán). They also described Don Luís as "a self-styled big chief and a big talker." While in Spain, Don Luís met King Felipe II and "received many favors from him."

He had sailed to Havana by 1566, and there he met Governor Garcia Osorio. Don Luís convinced Osorio to sponsor a mission to Ajacán. Don Luís would guide the ship to the Bahia de Santa Maria (Chesapeake Bay) and help establish a settlement there. He left Havana in the company of two friars and thirty soldiers. Somewhere along the Mid-

Atlantic coast the ship's master aborted the mission—Don Luís said he couldn't locate the entrance to the bay. Apparently, the ship sailed without an independent pilot. Some speculate that Don Luís decided he didn't want to bring thirty Spanish soldiers to his homeland.

Viceroy Luís de Velasco
The Emancipator

Paquiquino taking his name from the Viceroy of New Spain was most appropriate since Velasco had established himself as a protector of the Indians. He became the second Viceroy of New Spain on November 25, 1550, replacing Antonio de Mendoza. He remained viceroy until he died on July 31, 1564.

One of his early official acts was the freeing of 150,000 Indian slaves in New Spain. He also worked to reduce the abuses Indians faced in the gold mines, establishing hospitals for Indians and law enforcement for their protection.

When a flood devastated New Spain in 1558, Velasco worked tirelessly to aid the victims. When he died his estate was worthless; he had not enriched himself in the office of Viceroy as other Spanish officials in the West Indies had done. Instead he had used his own resources for the benefit of the poor and the Indians.

In 1570 a second attempt took place. This time, Don Luís sailed in August with eight Jesuits and a young novice named Alonso de Lara; there were no soldiers assigned to the mission this time. And Don Luís had no problem locating the entrance to the bay. The Spanish ship arrived on September 10, 1570, and sailed up the James River to College Creek. Don Luís led the nine Spaniards ashore and across the narrow peninsula area to his home west of Yorktown, Virginia. Their walk of seven miles should have taken them less than a day, passing through the site that would become Williamsburg 130 years later.

Don Luís helped the Jesuits establish their tiny mission on the shores of the York River. He certainly visited his relatives at their village nearby. At some point, Don Luís decided to leave the Jesuit mission and live at his village—a perfectly understandable desire for one who had been away from his people for ten years, having left as a child and now a grown man. He soon adopted the customs of a leading member of his tribe and took a wife, then another. This action brought him condemnation by the Jesuits. We can imagine how they railed against his "sinful bigamy," and his reversion to "savage" ways.

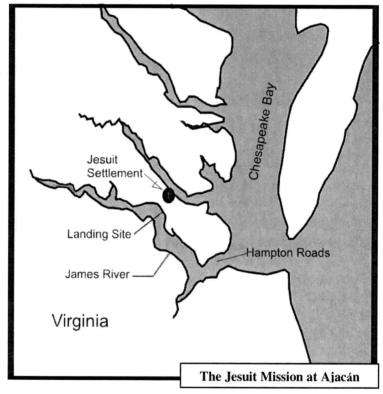

The Jesuit Mission at Ajacán

If the Jesuits thought they could cajole Don Luís back into the Catholic doctrine, they were gravely mistaken. Their constant demands for food also became tiresome for Don Luís and his people the Chiskiack, particularly since they had come to Ajacán at a time of famine due to a prolonged drought.

Abandoned by Don Luís, the Jesuits and young Alonso suffered through the winter, continually pleading with the Chiskiacks to feed them. The Indians provide food as long as the Jesuits had something to give in trade. In February, three Jesuits went to the Indian town to plead for help. They found Don Luís with his uncle and began to upbraid him for losing his faith and abandoning them. They went too far.

Don Luís and some of his people killed the three Jesuits in the woods before they could return to the mission. He intended to kill the others. On February 9, 1571, Don Luís and some Chiskiack warriors entered the clearing where the mission was. They told Father Juan Bautista Segura, the head of the mission, that they had come to help him by cutting firewood. Taking the axes offered for that purpose Don Luís and the other Indians killed the remaining five missionaries; they spared Alonso as ordered by tribal elders who overruled Don Luís' advice to kill the boy as well. Alonso lived to tell the story of the Jesuit mission of Ajacán, the only Spanish settlement in the Chesapeake Bay region.

Following the massacre, the Indians rifled through the priests' belongings. A legend developed around that event and was eventually written about by another Jesuit, Father Rogel. Here is his account written in 1610:

It happened that an Indian, coveting the spoils, went to a coffer in which there was a crucifix, and wishing to open it or break into it, in order to extract its contents, fell dead on the spot as he began to unlock it. Then another Indian possessed with the same covetousness, sought to follow the same intent, and likewise the same thing occurred. Then none dared further

approach the coffer, but they preserve it to this day with much
veneration and fear, without daring to approach it. And this
was told me by some old soldiers who came from Florida of
those who had been to Axacan, to whom it was told by the
Indians how the coffer was still in the country and no one dares
approach it, even now, after the lapse of forty years.

Later in 1571, a Spanish relief ship came to the river
looking for the Jesuits; when the men aboard ship saw
Indians dressed in the black robes of the Jesuits waving them
ashore, they became suspicious and stayed off shore. Indians
came out in a canoe but the Spaniards were ready for their
attack and they captured three of them. One of the men
confessed in Cuba that the Jesuits had been killed and
revealed that Alonso was still alive.

A year later, Pedro Menéndez de Avilés, Governor of
Cuba, personally led a punitive force to rescue Alonso and
punish the Indians responsible for killing the Jesuits.
Menéndez arrived at the mouth of the Powhatan River
(James River) in August of 1572, and a small boat separated
from his ship sailed up to College Creek, carrying the Indian
informant. They encountered Indians there and captured
several of them, one of whom wore a silver paten
(communion plate) obviously taken from the Jesuit's
belongings.

Taking the new captives out to the river, the officer in
charge ordered the Indians to bring Alonso to him. The
Indians agreed, but said he was two days journey away among
the Kecoughtan Indians. Their territory, ironically, was at the
mouth of the river very near where Menéndez' ship was
anchored. The boat crew waited at College Creek for Alonso
to arrive, but he never did. Their Indian captives, also
concerned that Alonso had not been brought to them,
attacked the men in the boat, but the Spanish crew subdued
them. They waited another day for Alonso and then fired
their guns at Indians standing on the shore, killing many.

After the massacre, the boat crew returned to the ship
where they found Alonso who had been delivered promptly

directly to the ship. With Alonso safe, Menéndez sent a raiding party up river with an Indian guide to bring Don Luís back to face Spanish justice. When the Spaniards returned without Don Luís, Menéndez examined the Indian captives with the assistance of Alonso. Some of the captives he found innocent of the murder of the Jesuits. They were released, but eight other captives implicated in the murder Menéndez hanged from the ships rigging.

The Martyrs of Ajacán

The leader of the Jesuit mission betrayed by Don Luís was Father Juan Bautista Segura, a native of Toledo, Spain, who entered the priesthood in 1566. In 1568, he became vice-provincial of La Florida. He ministered to the Indians of Apalachee Bay and elsewhere in Florida before conceiving of the mission to Ajacán after meeting Don Luís, the Indian of Ajacán, in Havana.

Segura selected another Jesuit priest, Father Luís de Quiros, and six Jesuit brothers: Brother Juan de la Carrera, Brother Gabriel de Solis, Brother Juan Baptista, Brother Cristobal Redondo, and two others. Alonso de Lara, a Spanish boy pledged as a novice accompanied the Jesuits on their mission to Ajacán.

The ship carrying Father Segura stopped at the new Spanish settlement at Santa Elena (Parris Island, South Carolina) where some of the clerics joined the mission and where Segura obtained some liturgical materials before continuing on to the Chesapeake Bay.

Father Segura and the seven other Jesuits died at the hands of Chiskiack Indians led by Don Luís, becoming the first Christian martyrs in the Chesapeake Bay region. In 2002, the Roman Catholic Diocese of Richmond began the process of canonization of the Spanish Jesuit martyrs of Virginia and designated St. Elizabeth Ann Seton Parish in New Kent County as the Shrine of the Jesuit Martyrs.

At the time that Don Luís was brought from his homeland to New Spain, France continued its ambitions for settlement in the New World. From 1555 to 1560, the French maintained control of a part of the Brazilian coast, securing their foothold in the New World at Fort Coligny on the Bay of Guanabara. French Huguenots initially planned to settle at that site in large numbers, but unrest in Brazil put an end to their plans. On March 16, 1560, the Portuguese governor of Brazil finally ejected the French from his territory with military force. This ended French Huguenots' plans for settlement in South America. They shifted their focus to La Florida, taking advantage of Spanish King Felipe's suspension of settlement attempts in that region.

Religious conflict raged in France pitting Catholics against Protestants (Huguenots) creating an impetus for the Huguenots to look for a safe haven in the Americas. They selected the Atlantic coast for their next expedition. In May of 1562, only eight months after King Felipe's announcement of the abandonment of Spanish settlement attempts in La Florida, Jean Ribault landed with 150 settlers near Jacksonville, Florida, took possession for the King of France and, on an island in the St. Johns River, erected a column with the coat of arms of the Queen of France.

First landing of the French in Florida

Ribault met with the local Timucuan Indians and exchanged trade goods for food. He then sailed up the coast to a spot near Parris Island, South Carolina and built a small log fortification he named Charlesfort, in honor of King Charles IX, leaving thirty soldiers to hold the fort until his return. To complicate matters, Roman Catholic Catherine de Medici, mother of French King Charles IX, had felt it her duty to warn Felipe II of Spain that French Huguenots were attempting to intrude on the Spanish lands claimed in America.

Angel de Villafañe had sailed along the South Carolina coast only the year before and had decided that Santa Elena was not suitable for settlement. Nonetheless, Spain considered that location within their sphere of control. Now the French had a fort there. Spain moved quickly to eradicate Ribault's settlement.

Timucuan Indian shows Laudonniere the column erected by Ribault

Spanish authorities considered the Huguenot Ribault a heretic. Worse still, the French settlement was in the perfect location for French corsairs to attack the annual treasure fleet as it sailed through the Bahama passage and up the coast before turning east to cross the Atlantic on their homeward voyage. French as well as English pirates plagued the Spanish treasure fleet and even sacked Spanish cities in the West Indies including Santiago, Havana, and Cartagena. One of the most daring French pirates, Jacques Le Clerc—complete with wooden leg— exemplified the numerous pirates sailing from Brittany and Normandy to prey on the Spanish vessels and ports.

Spain also saw through France's protest of innocence. Admiral of France Gaspard de Coligny repeatedly disavowed knowledge of the French pirates' operations while doing nothing to curtail them. He had set his sights on a French Huguenot settlement in the Americas and was directly involved in the attempts of Ribault and, later, René Laudonnière.

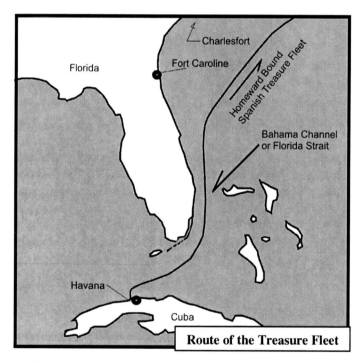

Ribault went to England to gain support for a second voyage to Charlesfort, but Queen Elizabeth had him arrested to prevent further French ventures. By this time she had Englishmen with designs on building an English outpost in North America. She didn't want Frenchmen as well as Spaniards in the way.

Meanwhile, the thirty men left at Charlesfort had argued among themselves and then sailed away in a longboat, abandoning the first French settlement in North America. King Felipe complained to the French about their incursion into La Florida and, getting no satisfaction, ordered the Governor of Cuba to destroy the French fort and the markers Ribault had left as evidence of French annexation of the land.

Hernando de Manrique de Rojas led the expedition from Havana aboard *La Concepción* to Charlesfort where he captured the only Frenchman left behind, who was living with the Indians; Manrique de Rojas burned the fort and returned with his prisoner to Cuba.

René Laudonnière, who had been Ribault's deputy on the first voyage, took up the challenge of maintaining a French presence in Florida with funding provided by Admiral Coligny. He led 300 men with three ships back to Florida in June 1564. The French ships landed on the St. Johns River and erected a small fort, called Fort Caroline in honor of the king (whose Latin name was Carolus). The colony consisted of a mix of soldiers and various artisans. But trouble soon erupted, and Laudonnière proved unable to govern the settlers, some of whom set out in boats to try their hand at pirating Spanish gold in the West Indies.

English privateer John Hawkins, returning from trading slaves in the West Indies, stopped at Fort Caroline mid-July 1565 and found the Frenchmen in poor condition. In addition to food, Hawkins gave them the friendly advice that the Spanish were aware of their colony and were bent on ejecting them. He generously left them with a ship to take them back to France if they decided to evacuate the colony.

Jean Ribault, recently released from prison in England, sailed in June 1565 on a relief mission with 600 French settlers and soldiers. This mission included women and children as well as men. In August, Ribault found the Fort Caroline colony in disarray, dispirited and ready to return home. They had made enemies of the Timucuan Indians and had failed to work together under Laudonnière's leadership. He set to work immediately, but the Spanish were sailing his way, led by one of the most accomplished admirals in service to Spain, Pedro Menéndez de Avilés.

Fort Caroline

In 1554, Menéndez had commanded Prince Felipe's (later King Felipe II) galleon on his voyage to England to marry Queen Mary. Seven years later, Menéndez successfully shepherded the treasure fleet from New Spain to Spain. On that voyage only one ship was lost, wrecked near Bermuda, but his son and other relatives had sailed on that ship. He petitioned King Felipe to allow him to return to America to search for survivors. The king agreed, but imposed the condition that Menéndez agree to colonize La Florida. This "honor" carried a huge financial burden since King Felipe would not provide financing for those ventures, yet would insist on a sizeable share in any profits to be had.

PEDRO MENENDEZ DE AVILES.

The King designated Menéndez Adelantado of La Florida. Before Menéndez sailed, King Felipe secretly gave him the additional order to "hang and burn the Luteranos" in Florida—Luteranos was the Spanish name for Protestants, in this case the French Huguenots. Once news had reached the king of the French settlement at Fort Caroline, Felipe augmented Menéndez' fleet with 300 soldiers paid by the royal treasury. Menéndez sailed with more than 1,500 men bound directly for the French Settlement rather than Santa Elena, his originally planned destination. Menéndez was forty-six years old with about thirty years of seafaring and combat experience, most in conflict with the French whom he hated. The French in La Florida didn't stand a chance.

After Menéndez had sailed from Cadiz and was well on his way to La Florida, King Felipe wrote to his ambassador in the French court:

> It is now my wish that you speak to the Queen Mother and say to her, that having understood that some of her subjects had gone to Florida to usurp that province, which we had discovered and possessed for so many years, I have given orders to send and chastise them as thieving pirates and perturbers of the public peace. And having made this provision I had thought to have done with it, but that the brotherly relations which I have had with the Most Christian King, the frankness and sincerity that should be observed with him and with her in all matters, have induced me not to conceal this from them.

195

King Felipe knew full well that Jean Ribault and Laudonnière had sailed on an officially sanctioned colonization scheme for the French king, but he maintained the fiction that the French colonists were pirates so that he could eradicate them without the action appearing an attack on France. He was giving back to the French king the same double-dealing diplomacy that he received from France. The pawns in this game of international power, as always, were the loyal subjects—in this case the French men and women in Florida where Menéndez was sailing with all due haste.

At Fort Caroline, the relief at Jean Ribault's arrival with reinforcements was short lived. On September 4th, Menéndez sailed into the mouth of the St. Johns River bent on executing every Protestant Frenchman he could find. In a nighttime confrontation with four French ships that blocked his entrance to the river, Menéndez sailed his 900-ton flagship, *San Pelayo*, until it was bow to bow with the much smaller French ship, *Trinity*, and hailed the French crew. "Gentlemen, from where does this fleet come?" The French answered, "From France." "What are you doing here?" Menéndez asked. "Bringing infantry, artillery, and supplies for a fort which the King of France has in this country, and for others which he is going to make." "Are you Catholics or Lutherans?" asked Menéndez. "Lutherans, and our General is Jean Ribault."

The French crew asked Menéndez who he was. He replied, "I am the General; my name is Pedro Menéndez de Avilés. This is the armada of the King of Spain, who has sent me to this coast and country to burn and hang the Lutheran French who should be found there, and in the morning I will board your ships; and if I find any Catholics they will be well treated."

Shots rang out, but before a real naval battle could develop, the French ships slipped away in the dark under pursuit by the Spanish ships. As the opposing fleets tried to outmaneuver each other, a storm struck the area, driving them south along the coast. Menéndez ordered his ships to gather at a site about thirty miles to the south that they had entered a week earlier. There he established an outpost that eventually grew into St. Augustine, Florida. This settlement, with so inauspicious a start, became the oldest continuously occupied European settlement in the United States. Menéndez expected the French to attack him there at his hastily erected fort.

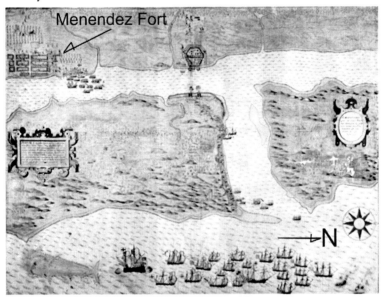

Saint Augustine with fortifications

Ribault decided the only way to survive the expected Spanish aggression was to make a pre-emptive strike. Unfortunately, his ships ran into a fierce storm that swept them southward, well past St. Augustine, and most were driven ashore where they were wrecked. Menéndez, who decided not to wait for the French to take the initiative, launched an overland attack on Fort Caroline with 500 soldiers. They took three days to slog through the swamps following Indian guides, but arrived at Fort Caroline eager for a fight. They attacked the nearly defenseless settlement early in the morning and killed 142 settlers. Laudonnière escaped with about fifty survivors and made it to the coast. On the shore, Laudonnière and the other survivors found Jacques Ribault, son of Jean, who took them aboard his ship; they returned to France. The Spanish changed the name of the fort from Fort Caroline to Fort San Mateo.

Menéndez then proceeded back to St. Augustine and found Jean Ribault and his men trapped on the seashore south of Matanzas Inlet (fourteen miles south of St. Augustine). Ribault had no recourse but to surrender. After Menéndez accepted his surrender, he had Ribault and all of the Protestants among his troop (about 130) murdered. Ten French Catholics and six cabin boys were spared. This marked the end of France's attempts to settle near Spanish territory on the Atlantic coast of North America.

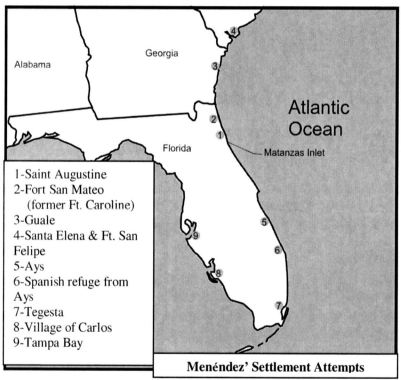

1-Saint Augustine
2-Fort San Mateo
(former Ft. Caroline)
3-Guale
4-Santa Elena & Ft. San Felipe
5-Ays
6-Spanish refuge from Ays
7-Tegesta
8-Village of Carlos
9-Tampa Bay

Menéndez' Settlement Attempts

Some questioned whether Menéndez should have spared the French prisoners. The chronicles offer two excuses for the murder of the Frenchmen: he had insufficient supplies to keep his own force and the additional men alive; the other excuse is best read as originally written by sixteenth-century Spanish historian Bartolomé Barrientos:

> He [Menéndez] acted as an excellent inquisitor; for when asked if they were Catholics or Lutherans, they dared to proclaim themselves publicly as Lutherans, without fear of God or shame before men; and thus he gave them that death which their insolence deserved. And even in that he was very merciful in granting them a noble and honorable death, but cutting off their heads, when he could legally have burnt them alive.

King Felipe approved of the action Menéndez had taken against the French. He wrote to him:

> And as for the judgment you have executed upon the Lutheran corsairs, who have sought to occupy and fortify that country, to sow in it their evil sect, and to continue from there the robberies and injuries which they have committed and are still committing, wholly contrary to the service of God and of me, we believe that you have acted with entire justification and prudence, and we hold that we have been well served.

Not all of the Frenchmen were killed or escaped to France. Menéndez wrote to the king the following summary of what had or would happen to those at large in Florida:

> The other people with Ribault, some seventy or eighty in all, took to the forest, refusing to surrender unless I grant them their lives. These and twenty others who escaped from the fort, and fifty who were captured by the Indians, from the ships which were wrecked, in all one hundred and fifty persons, rather less than more, are the French alive today in Florida, dispersed and flying through the forest, and captive with the Indians. And since they are Lutherans and in order that so evil a sect shall not remain alive in these parts, I will conduct myself in such wise, and will so incite my friends, the Indians, on their part, that in five or six weeks very few if any will remain alive. And of a thousand French with an armada of twelve sail who had landed when I reached these provinces, only two vessels have

*escaped, and with those very miserable ones, with some forty or
fifty persons in them.*

Having disposed of the French intruders, Menéndez was now
free to carry out his primary mission of settling La Florida.
King Felipe had given specific orders regarding colonization
of Florida. The king directed Menéndez to transport 500
colonists made up of 100 soldiers, 100 sailors, and 300
artisans, farmers, and laborers with the skills to support a
colony. The artisans included stone-cutters, carpenters,
blacksmiths, and barbers. The king's order required that 200
of the colonists would be married.

He had to erect two towns with at least 100 inhabitants
each, and each town would have a fort for protection. Four
Jesuit priests and a dozen monks were required to see to the
religious welfare of the colonists and to convert the Indians.
The king's order permitted the taking of 500 black slaves
from Spain, Portugal, the Cape Verde Islands, or Guinea,
with one-third of the slaves being women. Menéndez had to
ensure that none of his colonists were heretics, Jews, Moors,
or Marranos (secret Jews). His orders included the taking of
at least 100 horses, 200 sheep, 400 pigs, 400 lambs, and any
other livestock he thought he would need.

His first task after eradicating the French heretics was to
explore and chart the coast of La Florida from the gulf side,
around the peninsula, and up the Atlantic Coast to
Newfoundland. He was to provide a full report of all the
ports, bays, rivers, sea currents, shoals, and other hazards
along the coast.

In reward for these services, the king advanced Menéndez
15,000 ducats ($1.5 million today), which he would have to
repay eventually from profits in La Florida. He was
authorized a salary of 2,000 ducats ($200,000 today) from
rents and products of the land such as sugar cane or tobacco
production. The king granted Menéndez an estate of twenty-
five leagues square (about sixty-five miles square) and the title
of Marquess. He could also select two fisheries for his own

benefit: one of pearls and the other of fish. He received a license to trade with certain islands in the West Indies, and had, for a limited time period, duty free import and export rights. Further, he could keep all that he captured from pirates plying the waters around La Florida for a period of five years. His heirs or successors would keep the title Adelantado of La Florida in perpetuity.

Menéndez had the opportunity to become a very wealthy man if he could make a success of his ventures in La Florida. He spent all he had and all he could raise from other willing investors to acquire the ships, the supplies, the equipment, and material needed to support the colonies adequately. A contemporary account puts the total investment at one million ducats ($100 million today) spent during a fourteen month period.

The fleet and the personnel assembled by Menéndez exceeded what the king had ordered. He had a fleet of ten vessels ranging from sixty tons to more than 900 tons. The personnel numbered 1,500, including 820 soldiers, many of whom did double duty since they were also artisans. Twenty of them were tailors, fifteen were carpenters; there were also brewers, masons, millers, shoemakers, weavers, and silver-smiths—virtually every profession one would need at that time. One hundred and thirty-seven sailors manned the ships. The religious staff included seven priests.

The Adelantado planned to settle La Florida in this fashion: first, he would find a suitable port on the gulf side of the peninsula and establish a garrison there; then he would reinforce St. Augustine to provide a port to secure the safe passage of the treasure fleet through the Bahama channel; finally, he would establish a garrison at a suitable location at the Bahia de Santa Maria (Chesapeake Bay). The latter location he thought would provide access from the Atlantic to a vast inland sea—the Strait of Anián—that he believed lay just to the west of the mountains located about eighty leagues west or north of the bay. He thought that one of the rivers flowing into the bay, probably the Potomac, would provide access to that inland sea.

His plan would thus secure safer passage for the annual shipment of gold and silver to Spain and provide the path west, originally proposed by Columbus, for Spanish ships sailing across the Atlantic and through the Chesapeake Bay, up a river, and into the South Sea, where they would continue on to the orient. Menéndez dreamed of great wealth to come from wine, sugar plantations, cattle herds, pitch and tar for shipbuilding, salt, wheat, rice, pearls, and silk that he envisioned being produced in La Florida. He told the king that the wealth of La Florida would exceed that provided from New Spain and Peru.

In August, conditions at St. Augustine and Fort San Mateo (the former French Fort Caroline on the St. Johns River) had begun to deteriorate due to the scarcity of food. To make matters worse, Menéndez received word from the Indians that seventy Frenchmen, survivors of Ribault's fleet, had come together near Cape Canaveral and were building a fort there, using armament salvaged from one of the wrecked ships. Menéndez assembled a small fleet of boats with 100 soldiers aboard and ordered them south to attack the French. He marched to the same destination at the head of a company of about 150 soldiers. When they closed on the French fort, the occupants ran into the forest.

Some surrendered to Menéndez and he treated them kindly—why he didn't kill them is unknown. From Cape Canaveral, Menéndez and his men marched south to the Ays Indian village on the Indian River. After making friends with the Ays chief, he left his men about eight miles away from the Ays village on a lagoon abundant with fish so that his men could survive without placing demands on the Indians. He then traveled to Havana to arrange for new supplies for San Mateo, Saint Augustine, and his new encampment on the Indian River. He sailed with fifty of his men and twenty of the French prisoners in two open boats. It was late November, 1565.

Menéndez arrived in Havana after some delay caused by a storm, but encountered a storm of a different kind. Governor Osorio made it difficult for the Adelantado to recruit the necessary men and obtain supplies for his settlements in Florida. Menéndez also fell ill and remained unable to leave his bed for about two weeks. Finally, he dispatched a ship to New Spain to obtain chickens, corn, and other foodstuffs for the relief of his people at San Mateo, Saint Augustine and on the Indian River with the Ays.

Early in 1566, the men sent to bring supplies to the Florida settlers returned to Cuba and briefed Menéndez on what they had found. The Spaniards left near the Ays had faced starvation and had split up into smaller groups to spread out over the country in their frantic search for food. The Ays had become hostile toward them and the Spaniards had to relocate about fifty miles farther down the peninsula near the mouth of the Saint Lucie River.

At Saint Augustine and Fort San Mateo, the men of the relief ship found that about 100 colonists had died due to lack of food and clothing during the winter. After Menéndez received this bad news he heard worse news. A rumor reached him that the French had placed a garrison at Santa Elena—their old Charlesfort—and Menéndez concluded that the French there were Jacques Ribault and the people he rescued from the St. Johns River battle. However, this rumor later proved to be false; Jacques Ribault had sailed from the St. Johns River to France.

Another rumor that came to Menéndez proved true: he heard that at a village somewhere on the west coast of the Florida peninsula a chief named Carlos held a large number of Spanish men and women, victims of shipwrecks along that coast, and every year Carlos sacrificed some of them to his idols. Menéndez made it a priority to sail there as soon as he could to rescue those people and then to establish another Spanish outpost and garrison along Florida's west coast.

Menéndez sailed on February 10, 1566 bound for Florida with seven vessels and 500 men. When the fleet neared the southern tip of Florida, Menéndez separated from the ships taking two smaller shallow-draft vessels and 30 men in search of the captive Christians. On February 18th, a canoe approached one of the two boats and a man looking and dressed like an Indian hailed them. According to Barrientos, he said, "Welcome, Spaniards and Christian brothers. God and St. Mary have told us that you were coming. And the Christian men and women who are still alive here have directed me to wait for you here with this canoe, to give you a letter, which I have." The articulate Spaniard was naked except for a deerskin loincloth, tanned from the sun, and painted like the Indians. The marooned man produced a crucifix and said, "…the captive Christians … beseech you, by the death suffered by Our Lord for our salvation, not to pass by but to enter the harbor and rescue us from the cacique, and carry us to a Christian land."

The Adelantado learned that twelve men and women remained alive from an initial number of 200 who had wrecked on those shores twenty years before. The others had died in Indian sacrifices performed by Carlos and his father. The Caloosa Indians controlled this part of Florida from Cape Sable to the southern shore of Tampa Bay, using modern place names. The principal village of Carlos probably sat alongside Charlotte Harbor, perhaps near Cape Coral and the mouth of the Caloosahatchee River. That river provided a link between the Gulf Coast and the Atlantic via Lake Okeechobee. Communication between the Ays of the Indian River on the east coast and the Caloosa on the west coast via that waterway link probably led to the information concerning the captive Spaniards that came to Menéndez.

Menéndez sent the captive Spaniard who had greeted him back to Carlos to announce that he had arrived and wished to talk with the cacique. Soon, Carlos arrived with great pomp followed by 300 naked bowmen. Menéndez, uncertain of Carlos's intentions, had his two boats back away from the shore. Then some his men spread a carpet on the sand, and Menéndez and Carlos sat on it facing each other. Some of

Carlos's principal men joined him on the carpet and some of the Spanish harquebusiers stood behind the Adelantado.

Carlos and Menéndez pressed the palms of their hands together in a gesture of peace and Menéndez distributed gifts including a hat, shirt, and breeches for Carlos, and bread and honey for the chief's wives. Carlos presented Menéndez a bar of silver and some golden objects and jewels. The Caloosa had undoubtedly recovered these precious items from wrecked Spanish treasure ships—perhaps the very ones carrying their marooned captives.

Menéndez lured Carlos and twenty of his men aboard one of his boats and then sailed far offshore. He told Carlos through his interpreter, the captive Christian, that the King of Spain wanted to live in peace with the Caloosa but that a condition of the peace must be the release of the Christian captives. The Adelantado made it clear that failure to comply would result in the death of Carlos and his men. Carlos made the obvious choice under the circumstances and ordered the Spanish captives freed. Five Spanish men and three Spanish women were released, and Carlos promised the return of the remaining three who were at a distant village.

Now a series of maneuvers took place where Carlos attempted to lure Menéndez and some of his men to his village where he planned to slaughter them, and Menéndez, realizing what Carlos had planned, tried to play along to keep the chief under control and friendly without putting himself or his men in a dangerous situation. Much posturing took place on both sides. Finally, Carlos offered his sister in marriage to the Adelantado (who had a wife in Spain). Carlos asked Menéndez to take her to a Christian land where she would learn about their religion and then could return to the Caloosa and instruct them in the Christian ways. Menéndez apparently changed the subject without giving an answer to the marriage proposal.

While Carlos and Menéndez sparred in this way, other men of the fleet had found 2,000 ducats worth of gold in a nearby village. They reported to the Adelantado that Carlos had 100,000 ducats of gold hidden somewhere; they advised he hold Carlos hostage until he surrendered the gold that would have a value of $10 million today. Menéndez refused, insisting that he wanted to attain peace and trust with Carlos and would not be caught in a lie.

After repeated invitations, the Adelantado finally traveled to Carlos's village. He arrived with a large retinue in full regalia. He was accompanied by a dwarf, who was an excellent dancer, twenty gentlemen in their finery, and 200 harquebusiers. All the men wore armor and carried swords, pikes, banners, and marched into the village with pipers, drummers, trumpeters, a harpist, and a violinist. The Adelantado certainly knew how to travel in style.

Carlos spared no opportunity for display either. He sat on a raised throne in his house, with his rather plain, thirty-five-year-old sister at his side, with 100 of his men kneeling below him and several hundred Indian youths outside the house singing to accompany Indian dancers.

Once the Indian presentation ended, Menéndez gave a speech in the Caloosa language that he had jotted down on a piece of paper with the help of the Christian captive translator. After the speech, Carlos had his wife brought in, an attractive young woman of about twenty. Menéndez, still speaking the Caloosa language, complimented her on her beauty. At that, Carlos became concerned that the Adelantado intended to take his wife instead of his sister. He ordered that his wife leave, but Menéndez requested that she stay, and so she did.

The Indians served a feast of fish and oysters, and the Spaniards contributed bread, honey, sugar, and wine to the menu. After the meal, Carlos renewed the marriage proposal in a way that indicated he expected an immediate answer. Menéndez said that as a Christian he could not marry the chief's sister since she was not a Christian. Carlos suggested he rectify that by making her a Christian. The Adelantado's men advised that he do what was necessary to placate the

Caloosa so that the whole region could be brought into the Christian fold.

Menéndez reluctantly agreed and had Carlos's sister baptized on the spot, naming her Doña Antonia. She and the Adelantado exchanged marriage vows that night in a tent erected by the Spaniards. The chronicles give no details on the honeymoon. The next morning, Menéndez placed Doña Antonia and her seven Indian handmaidens in the care of one of his captains to take them to Havana along with most of his ships. Before leaving Carlos's village, the Spaniards erected a large cross in the plaza.

Meanwhile, at the small outpost near Saint Lucia, the Ays had killed fifteen of the Spaniards, and when another relief ship reached them, found that the garrison had fled to the safety of a small fort they had built, and were starving within because about 1,000 Ays warriors kept them under siege. The desperate soldiers seized the relief ship and set sail for Cuba, but ran into the Adelantado who was then exploring the Bahama channel on his way to San Mateo. Menéndez took control of the ship the deserters were in and, certainly against their will, forced them to join with his two ships on the course to the other Florida settlements.

During the winter, similar distress had struck Saint Augustine and Fort San Mateo. At Saint Augustine, mutineers had confined the camp master, spiked the cannons, and captured the relief ship that called there. They nearly made their escape but the camp master gained his freedom and brought the mutineers into custody; he burned the only boat at their disposal so that no one else could escape to the relief ship. However, about 130 mutineers had already reached the relief ship and they sailed away. The commander of the fort executed the leaders of the mutiny, but much damage had been done.

San Mateo erupted in similar violence with 120 mutineers escaping to one of the abandoned French ships, intending to leave behind twenty-five loyal men at the fort. Before leaving, the mutineers had alienated the Indians who then began to harass the small Spanish garrison. Menéndez arrived just in time to block the mutineers at San Mateo from leaving. He offered them all pardons if they would rejoin the garrison there. Thirty-five accepted the pardon and returned to their posts. The rest made their escape and sailed to Santo Domingo, Hispaniola, where they found the mutineers from Saint Augustine. These men began to spread the word about the appalling living conditions in the garrisons of Florida.

Menéndez left 150 fresh men from his force at Saint Augustine and San Mateo to reinforce those garrisons and set sail for Santa Elena on April 1, 1566. He had two shallow-draft boats and a ship in his fleet with a total of 150 men. Along with his men, he had the Frenchman that Manrique de Rojas had rescued at Charlesfort. This man named Rufin would serve as his interpreter with the Indians of Guale.

When Menéndez arrived at Guale, near St. Catherine's Island, Georgia, he found that the Guale Indians were at war with the Indians of Orista that bordered Santa Elena to the north. A group of forty Guale met him when he came ashore and, from their midst, a Frenchman who spoke Spanish, told

Menéndez that he had been part of a scouting party sent out by Jean Ribault. Some of those scouts had relocated to Santa Elena where they were living with the Orista. The Guale and the Orista were at war and two of the Orista warriors were captives among the Guale, who intended to sacrifice them to end a drought.

Menéndez spent a few days with the Guale, erecting a cross in their village and instructing them in the Catholic faith through the interpretation of a very nervous Huguenot. The Adelantado insisted that the Guale and Orista make peace and he took the two captive Orista warriors into his custody, replacing them with young Spanish boys as hostages. He warned the Guale chief that if any evil befell the boys, he would personally return and cut off his head.

The Adelantado then sailed about sixty miles north to Santa Elena and found the Orista a few miles up the Beaufort River. The Orista were rebuilding the village that the Guale warriors had burned in their most recent attack. Menéndez returned the two Orista warriors and urged the chief to make peace with the Guale. Rufin, it turned out, was married to one of the chief's daughters. Through Rufin, Menéndez had the Orista chief instructed in the faith, and the chief consented to baptism.

Having brokered a peace between the neighboring tribes and seeing the seeds of Christianity planted among them, the Adelantado set to work directing the building of a new fort at Parris Island at the mouth of the river. The Spaniards, probably with Indian help, completed the fort in fifteen days, armed it with six cannon, and manned it with 106 soldiers under Captain Las Alas; Menéndez named it Fort San Felipe, after the saint and his sovereign.

Menéndez left Santa Elena and his new fort and returned to the Guale. The drought had continued and the chief feared the corn would not grow. He pleaded with the Adelantado to pray to the Christian god for rain, but Menéndez refused, telling the chief that the rain had not fallen because of his bad behavior. The chief then talked to the two Spanish boys and convinced them to pray for rain. When Menéndez learned that the boys had done so, he threatened to strip them and whip them, but the chief pleaded for leniency. Finally, in desperation, the chief went into the plaza and prostrated himself at the cross, embracing it and pledging his acceptance of the Christian faith. You can surely anticipate the outcome as written in the Spanish archives—a thunderstorm erupted within a half hour and the rains lasted for twenty-four hours. Menéndez left a few Spaniards among the Guale to continue their religious instruction until proper priests could be brought to their domain.

Before leaving Guale, Menéndez learned that the Huguenot who had remained there had been spitting on the cross and telling the Indians that the Spaniards were not followers of the true religion. Learning this, the Adelantado convinced the unsuspecting Frenchman to travel to Santa Elena with some Guale Indians. He sent a letter to Las Alas ordering him to execute the heretic but to do so secretly. Las Alas in due course garroted the hapless Huguenot.

Menéndez left Guale and sailed down the coast to San Mateo, arriving on May 15, 1566. The fort was sound but still at war with the Indians. Similarly, Saint Augustine was in a state of war with the Indians and had suffered some significant damage. There the Indians had attacked at night with a favorable wind and had sent burning arrows into the roofs, destroying buildings and setting the powder magazine alight; the explosion caused extensive damage and casualties. To keep the Timucuans at bay, the Spaniards had begun burning their villages and fields, destroying their canoes, and pulling up their fish weirs. This, of course, fanned the flames of discord between the two cultures.

The Adelantado returned to Havana, arriving by the middle of June. He found his Caloosa bride depressed; all but two of her companions had died, no doubt from foreign diseases, and she missed her new husband. Menéndez, fearful of the consequences if Doña Antonia should die as well, returned her quickly to Carlos and came back to Havana with several more Christians that the Caloosa had held, plus Carlos's cousin and heir. The young Indian was baptized and named Don Pedro.

Almost immediately, Menéndez sailed again for San Mateo, arriving there July 8th, where a relief ship from Spain had just brought 250 men to strengthen the garrison. In a separate fleet of three vessels, Captain Juan Pardo was headed to Santa Elena to strengthen Fort San Felipe with 300 men. Menéndez had at his command a fleet of seventeen ships and 1,500 men, 500 sailors, and plenty of supplies recently shipped from Spain. He assigned an additional 250 men to each of his three forts on the east coast of La Florida and dispatched most of the remainder of the men in a fleet of eight ships to cruise the West Indies in search of pirates.

Menéndez planned to explore the St. Johns River and then sail to Santa Elena and check on the progress of Juan Pardo. The Adelantado found the terrain, the climate, and the Indians more favorable at Santa Elena and decided to make that locale his capital of La Florida. During his St. Johns River exploration he learned of a vast lake the Indians called Maymi, now called Lake Okeechobee, which could provide access to the land of Carlos.

When Pardo arrived at Fort San Felipe he found the garrison divided, with twenty soldiers having deserted, leaving only twenty-five at the fort. Menéndez joined Pardo at Santa Elena on August 20th. Menéndez realized that the Indians of Orista couldn't provide sufficient food for a large contingent of Spaniards at Santa Elena, so he ordered Juan Pardo to deploy 150 of his men into the interior to alleviate the food problem. The Adelantado had a plan to explore the interior and develop a road from Santa Elena across country to New Spain, a distance of which he still had no concept. His idea was for Pardo to build small forts along the route, stationing garrisons at each one—the other reason for Pardo deploying his men into the interior.

After giving Pardo his orders and making a call at Guale where he learned that the Indians were embracing

Christianity, Menéndez sailed to San Mateo. As usual, mutiny had erupted there again and the ringleaders had been hanged. Menéndez felt compelled to check on the progress of the fleet charged with hunting down pirates in the West Indies, but he also wanted to advance his conquest of La Florida. While at San Mateo he selected Francisco de Reynoso to lead thirty soldiers to the land of Carlos and to build a fort there. Once the fort was built, Reynoso was to search for a waterway leading to Lake Okeechobee. Menéndez planned to ring the coast of La Florida with forts manned with garrisons sufficient to keep his territory secure.

Menéndez had a sincere wish to convert the Indians to Christianity and realized that relying on soldiers to perform that task was foolish. King Felipe also shared this goal and, anticipating the Adelantado's need, dispatched in May, 1566, a contingent of Jesuit priests and monks under Father Juan Rogel and Father Pedro Martinez to establish ministries in La Florida.

They arrived off the Florida coast in September, but had difficulty locating Saint Augustine. In desperation, Father Martinez rowed ashore with a few others to ask the Indians for directions to the settlement. They traveled along the coast for many days from village to village, becoming more dejected. Finally, near Saint Augustine, they saw some Indians who gestured to them to come ashore.

When Father Martinez walked through the surf to the shore, the Indians seized him; he fought for a moment, then knelt down in the sand and bowed his head in prayer as an Indian struck him a death blow with his club. Father Rogel and the rest of the clerics abandoned the search for Saint Augustine and sailed to Havana, where the Adelantado found them in December.

In the southwest of Florida, Reynoso arrived on his mission from San Mateo to a chilly reception from Carlos. Don Pedro, Carlos's heir, had come with him. To compound Reynoso's problem, Doña Antonia decided to return to Havana on the ship that had brought Reynoso to the Coosa.

She apparently preferred life in Havana to life in Coosa, or perhaps she hoped to reunite with her husband, the already happily married Adelantado.

Several times Carlos set a trap to kill Reynoso, but each time friendly Indian women warned Reynoso. Carlos still had control over hundreds of Spanish captives throughout his realm, all shipwreck victims. He wanted to kill them in sacrifice as he had done before, but he dared not do that until his sister returned again from Havana for fear the Spaniards would take vengeance on Doña Antonia.

Menéndez heard of the difficulties among the Caloosa and, in January, 1567, he sailed for Florida with seven ships, 150 soldiers, Doña Antonia, Father Rogel, and Brother Francisco. Soon after they arrived at Carlos's village, they built a chapel and dwelling for the priest. The Adelantado wanted to locate the waterway that would establish a link with San Mateo. Carlos told him that he would find a river from Tampa Bay that would take him in that direction. Ironically, the river flowing to Carlos's village would have served his purpose better.

The Adelantado took a small force of Spaniards along with Carlos, whom he didn't trust to leave behind, and traveled to Tampa Bay. There he met with the Indians who still remembered the rough treatment by De Soto and Narváez. Eventually, Menéndez was able to sit down with them and discuss his wish to establish a river route to San Mateo, but he eventually abandoned the idea when he saw how precarious his position was. He left Captain Martinez de Coz with thirty soldiers at Tampa Bay to secure the area and provide religious instruction to the Indians.

Back at Carlos's village, the Spaniards strengthened the blockhouse they had built, and the Adelantado left fifty additional soldiers there to discourage Carlos from murdering any Spanish. Father Rogel remained there to study the Indian language and minister to the Indians and to the Spaniards when Menéndez left.

After a quick trip to Havana to restore order between the Governor of Cuba and a mutinous captain, the Adelantado took Brother Francisco and a small detachment of men to Tegesta (Miami) to establish an outpost there and to teach the Indians about Christianity. While there, he supervised the building of a blockhouse and the erection of a cross. Three days later, Menéndez reached San Mateo where he found the Indians and the Spaniards still fighting. He made an honest attempt to settle the dispute, but failed to instill any trust in the chief, Saturiba. In disgust, he sailed down to Saint Augustine and found the Spaniards fighting among themselves.

By May, 1567, he had restored some semblance of order there and departed for Fort San Felipe at Santa Elena. No one could fault Menéndez for his tireless efforts in attempting to maintain order among his widely dispersed garrisons.

During the previous year, Juan Pardo had carried out the Adelantado's order, trekking into the interior, establishing forts at intervals along the way. Pardo had traveled inland nearly 300 miles. Some of his men had gone even farther, reaching the Alabama River valley and retracing part of De Soto's route.

When Menéndez heard the progress report from Pardo he must have felt quite proud of his accomplishments. He had ringed much of La Florida with his three forts and four other garrisons; he had thus added a measure of protection for the treasure fleet against piracy and also provided some protection for survivors of shipwrecks that occurred with some frequency on those coasts. He had established his capital at Santa Elena, and had penetrated inland more than 300 miles from there. He had ejected the French from La Florida and had begun the conversion of the Indians to Christianity, albeit mostly with instruction by soldiers rather than clerics. He had accomplished all of this in spite of roadblocks erected by Governor Osorio in Cuba.

Unfortunately, his forces were deployed along about 800 miles of coastline, with only minimal military capability at each fort or garrison, and only sporadic supply deliveries to sustain the people at each of the seven locations. In several key locations, notably San Mateo, Saint Augustine, Charlotte Harbor, and Tampa Bay, the Indians clearly wanted to dispose of the Spanish intruders. Indian relations were slightly better, but tenuous, at the other locations. Recognizing this weakness, Menéndez ordered the building of additional blockhouses at San Mateo and Saint Augustine to strengthen their defenses.

With those final precautions, the Adelantado set sail for Spain in a tiny twenty-ton vessel on May 18, 1567. A month later he reached the Azores and, eluding English and French pirate attacks, arrived in his home town of Avilés in early July. After a couple of weeks renewing his acquaintance with his wife (the original, not the Indian), he traveled to Madrid to meet with the king. He had six Indians from La Florida with him. On their way to see the king, they passed through a village where a survivor of the De Soto expedition was living—perhaps Gonzalo Silvestre. Garcilaso the Inca wrote

215

of the event that as the Indians passed through the village, the old soldier came out and asked them if they were from Apalachee, Mabila, or Chicaza. The Indians replied, "Do you want to have news of those provinces which you left in such a bad condition?" Then they said they would prefer to shoot him with a volley of arrows, but settled for merely firing a volley high into the air.

During his appearance at the king's court, Menéndez was made the new Governor of Cuba and received the honor of a new title: Captain General of the West. That position carried with it a stipend of 200,000 ducats ($20 million today) and a fleet of twelve galleons, carrying 2,000 soldiers to secure the safety of the West Indies seas. In January of 1568, the king admitted Menéndez to the highly prestigious Order of Santiago.

Menendez had little opportunity to return to La Florida after this, since much of his time he spent on ensuring safe passage of the annual Flota carrying men and supplies to the West Indies and the return of gold and silver to Spain. He kept the garrisons and forts manned and supplied to the best of his ability, but relations with the Indians and international events worked against him.

France learned about the massacre of their settlers at Fort Caroline in 1566. The queen berated the Spanish ambassador to the French court, saying, "Neither Turks nor Moors would have been guilty of so great a cruelty as the Spaniards have practiced on the subjects of my son [the king]." She maintained a fantasy that Ribault and Laudonnière had settled in Nova Scotia, a land she called the "Isles of the Bretons" and not in Florida. Eventually she admitted that the settlers had located in Spanish territory, but blamed the expedition on Admiral Coligny, as if she had not played a role in it. Coligny became the scapegoat in the international tug of war. Nationalistic pride grew in France and religious differences were put aside as Catholics and Protestants bemoaned the Spanish treatment of French subjects in Florida.

French spies reported to the queen in 1567 that Menéndez' settlements were in a seriously weakened condition due to revolt, scarcity of supplies, and problems with the Indians—an accurate assessment. The time seemed right for a counter stroke against them by France, but no official expedition would take place. Instead, an impassioned Catholic mariner named Dominique de Gourges would lead a punitive raid on the Florida settlements. His mission was not sanctioned officially, but he probably had some encouragement by court officials.

De Gourges set sail from Bordeaux in a 250-ton ship with a 120-ton vessel and a fifty-ton vessel accompanying him. He had 100 harquebusiers and eighty armed sailors aboard. Ostensibly they were sailing on a slaving expedition, but De Gourges intended to restore French honor in the West Indies as well. He kept those intentions secret, not even telling his crew until they reached the Caribbean.

His ships sailed in August of 1567 and, after a call at Cape Blanco in Africa where they fought the natives to capture slaves, they sailed to the Caribbean. During the winter he coursed through the West Indies looking for prizes and trading with the natives. Early in 1568 De Gourges finally revealed his real mission: an attack on the Spanish fort of San Mateo—formerly French Fort Caroline.

Through a combination of luck and an alliance with the Indian enemies of the Spanish, De Gourges' small army took the blockhouses guarding the entrance to the St. Johns River and successfully attacked and destroyed Fort San Mateo. The surviving Spaniards he captured at the fort he dealt with the same way that the rumors said Menéndez had dealt with the French a few years before. De Gourges took the men to the spot where the Adelantado was supposed to have hanged the French survivors after having said that he was hanging Lutheran pirates not Frenchmen. De Gourges left the Spaniards hanging from trees with a pine plaque inscribed as follows. "I do this not as to Spaniards, nor as to Marranos, but as to traitors, robbers, and murderers."

Having restored France's honor, or so he thought, De Gourges sailed away from Florida on May 3, 1568, and headed for home, capturing several Spanish prizes along the way. Continuing the tradition he had started in Florida, De Gourges threw the Spanish crewmen overboard each time he captured one of their ships.

Of all the forts and garrisons established by Menéndez, only Saint Augustine and San Felipe remained as viable settlements by his last visit to La Florida in 1572. The settlement among the Caloosa, where Father Rogel had attempted to instill the Christian religion, came under increasing pressure from the Indians. Rogel had accomplished little other than to incur the wrath of the shamans. One day they decided to carry their idols into his chapel. Rogel saw them coming and called for Reynoso who ran at them with his lance, wounding one of them. The Spaniards had to take cover in their blockhouse to avoid disaster.

Finally, the Spaniards assassinated Carlos, and his friendlier heir became chief. Then the new chief announced that, in conformance with their custom, he planned to marry his sister. The horrified priest railed against that union and the chief became a foe of the Spanish. Soon he had plotted to kill the Spanish. Reynoso, having discovered the plan, rounded up the chief and fourteen of his principal men and executed them. The Indians revolted, burned the village and fled into the forest, leaving the Spaniards without a source of food or labor. That led the Spaniards to abandon the settlement on Florida's west coast.

Eventually, all the outlying garrisons were evacuated, and the Spanish concentrated on holding onto Santa Elena, with a renewed emphasis on Fort San Felipe, and continued to reinforce Saint Augustine, where discord repeatedly threatened its survival. Conditions there were so bad that when supply ships called at Saint Augustine, they anchored well offshore to prevent possible mutineers from commandeering the ships and abandoning the settlement.

Pedro Menéndez de Avilés visited Saint Augustine, his truly lasting accomplishment in La Florida, for the last time late in the fall of 1572. He sailed from there for Havana on December 20th with Father Rogel in a fleet of three small boats. A storm struck the Florida coast and the three were separated. The largest weathered the storm and sailed on to Havana. A second boat was cast ashore in Ays where the Indians killed the Spaniards and burned their boat. Menéndez and Rogel went ashore near Cape Canaveral where, with thirty men in their company, they fought their way back through hostile Indian country to Saint Augustine, arriving just in time to assist in repelling an attack on the settlement by English corsairs. In April, 1573, a boat arrived from Havana and carried the Adelantado back to Cuba. He returned to Spain with the treasure fleet that fall.

In 1574, Menéndez led a Spanish armada publicly proclaimed as on a mission to clear the European waters of pirates, but believed, at least in England, to be intended to invade England. On September 8, 1574, Menéndez wrote to his nephew:

> Expressing to His Majesty my discontent at finding myself separated from Florida, he has graciously told me that as often as it is possible to allow me to return he will gladly do so. And I hope to God he will do so in the spring, for I do not doubt that the affair of Flanders will be arranged this winter. And with that I shall be free to go at once to Florida, not to leave it for the rest of my life; for that is the sum of my longings and happiness. May our Lord permit it, if possible and if He sees fit.

Pedro Menéndez de Avilés never led the great armada of King Felipe. On September 17, 1574, he died at Santander, reportedly of indigestion. He was buried there and later reburied at his parish church in Avilés.

Chapter 9
Juan Pardo and the Melungeons

We touched briefly on Juan Pardo's exploration of the North American interior from the Spanish settlement at Santa Elena. His two excursions into what would become the southern United States deserve more attention because of the number of men and women who were left behind in the interior when Spain abandoned Santa Elena. Their fate added an interesting element to the subsequent history of British colonization of North America.

Captain Juan Pardo had arrived at Santa Elena in July, 1566, with 300 men to provide relief to the garrison at Fort San Felipe. The men in his company had come from Northern Portugal as well as the neighboring Spanish provinces of Galicia and Asturias. Juan Pardo may have been Portuguese—he signed his name João in the Portuguese fashion. That fact and the inclusion of some Portuguese men in Pardo's company will become important later in this story.

When Pardo and his men arrived, Captain Las Alas was in command at the fort. Las Alas refused to relinquish or share command with Pardo, so Pardo located his men outside the fort and began constructing the town of Santa Elena (later Beaufort, South Carolina).

In August Pedro Menéndez de Avilés arrived and explained his plan to continue the idea, first put forward by Viceroy Velasco of New Spain, to build a road from the Bay of Ochuse (Pensacola) to Santa Elena as part of a longer route connecting the silver mines of Zacatecas in New Spain to the port of Santa Elena. Arellano had failed in his settlement attempt at the Bay of Ochuse and in the interior in Coosa territory, but he had established the route from the Gulf Coast deep into the interior. Pardo's task was to complete the "road" as they called it from Santa Elena to Coosa territory. They did not mean road in the modern sense; they meant establish and perhaps mark the route through the forest as well as secure the route with a series of forts along its length.

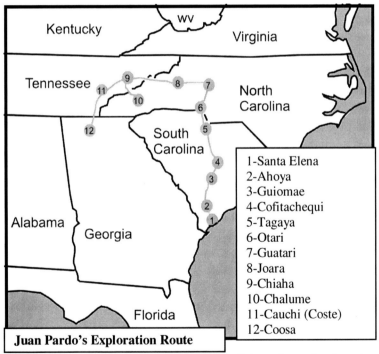

Juan Pardo's Exploration Route

1-Santa Elena
2-Ahoya
3-Guiomae
4-Cofitachequi
5-Tagaya
6-Otari
7-Guatari
8-Joara
9-Chiaha
10-Chalume
11-Cauchi (Coste)
12-Coosa

Pardo began his first of two expeditions into the interior on November 1, 1566, taking 150 men. At Guiomae, about eighty miles from Santa Elena, he built the first log outpost along his "road" to Coosa. The next village of note he recorded was Cofitachequi, a city we know well from the De Soto expedition twenty-five years before.

Leaving Cofitachequi, Pardo and his men passed through Otari and several other villages before arriving at Joara. During this phase of his journey, Pardo was among the Catawban-speaking tribes of North Carolina. The paramount chief of the region was a woman, with the title "Mico," who lived at Guatari on the Yadkin River. Joara (about eight miles northwest of Morgantown, North Carolina) lay at the crossroads of two Indian trade routes: one running north-south and the other east-west. Joara traded in salt and copper, and both Catawban and Cherokee people passed through this bilingual city. De Soto had found the people of Joara hospitable and the area pleasant, as did Pardo, who remained there for fifteen days. He erected a fort there naming it San Juan de Joara and later Cuenca.

Pardo left Sergeant Boyano in charge of the fort with thirty soldiers, and he moved on, initially attempting to follow the Catawba River north but then traveling along the river east to the Yadkin River and Guatari where he again rested for fifteen days. The Spanish wrote that they met thirty chiefs there, giving evidence of the power of the female Mico of Guatari. Pardo erected a fort at Guatari, Fort Santiago, and assigned a priest and four soldiers to remain there. While there, Pardo received a letter from Las Alas warning of a French attack, and he hurried back to Santa Elena with the rest of his men to help defend Fort San Felipe.

The French attack, of course, never came. At Santa Elena, Pardo received a letter from Sergeant Boyano saying that he had marched on and had defeated the Chiscas, an Indian group in the northeast portion of Tennessee. Boyano claimed he had killed more than 1,000 Indians there. When a messenger came saying the cacique of the Chiscas was coming to "eat" Boyano, he decided that he would take the offensive and carry the fight to the cacique. With twenty of his men he marched four days into the mountains to the fortified town of the Chiscas. He found that the town's weak point was its single entrance. Using their shields as protection from the arrows raining down from the wall, Pardo led his twenty men into the town and engaged the warriors. Soon the Indians withdrew into their houses, which Pardo's men put to the torch, burning to death, he said, 1,500 Indians. Boyano wrote that he had been wounded in the mouth and the Indians had wounded nine of his soldiers.

Boyano had written to Santa Elena asking if he should press on in the quest to reach Coosa. Receiving orders to do so, he left the fort at Joara in the hands of ten men. He headed west traveling four days before he came to Chiaha, a fortified town with twin towers located on an Island in the French Broad River. Boyano said that there were 3,000 Indian men in the city—no women or children—when he arrived. That must have seemed an ominous sign, but the people of Chiaha greeted him and his men warmly and fed the Spaniards well.

Leaving Chiaha, Boyano led his men down the French Broad River valley keeping the Great Smoky Mountains to his left, passing through Cauchi (De Soto's Coste). Following the Tennessee River and then the Coosawattee River, Boyano and his men reached Coosa (about sixty miles north of Atlanta). The Muskogean chief of Coosa offered food and other forms of hospitality to Boyano and his men; he also offered the help of men to build a fort for Boyano. Boyano decided not to build a fort at Coosa and, instead, returned to Chiaha, apparently satisfied with having reached Coosa without incident.

At Chiaha, the Spaniards awaited the return of Juan Pardo and planted wheat and barley there. This is an unusual occasion of the Spaniards engaging in agriculture anywhere in North America up to that time.

Pardo left Santa Elena in late August or early September, 1567, with 120 soldiers including harquebusiers and crossbowmen, and one Frenchman, Guillaume Rufin, to serve as his interpreter with the Indians. Rufin was the same

Frenchman who had been found at Charlesfort by Manrique de Rojas in 1564. Rufin had returned to Santa Elena with Las Alas.

Pardo followed the previously established route to Cofitachequi, Joara, and on to Chiaha. There he rested his men for a while and then set out in a southwesterly direction heading, he said, "in the direction of Zacatecas and the Mines of San Martin." Clearly that cannot be taken literally since even though Pardo probably didn't know how vast the continent was to the southwest, he certainly knew from the experience of De Soto and Arellano that heading southwest would take him near to Pensacola Bay and Mobile Bay, or in his terms the Bay of Ochuse and the Bay of Filipina, a distance of nearly 500 miles.

Pardo didn't get far. He marched several days to Chalahume (near Waynesville, Tennessee) and then to Satapo (in Swain County, Tennessee) where he learned that a confederation of several tribes with warriors numbering in the thousands had assembled to block his path. After conferring with his officers, Pardo decided that it would be foolhardy to proceed in the direction of Coosa. He and his men returned to Chiaha where he built a fort he named Fort San Pedro. Then he went west a few-days' journey into the mountains and built Fort San Pablo at Cauchi (now Bussell Island, Tennessee).

At each of the forts Pardo had constructed he left garrisons of men to maintain the forts for an indefinite period. He had the men take an oath that they would serve their king at the fort until they were relieved by fresh soldiers or given orders from the governor to leave. Not only men occupied these forts; there were some women along as well. In one account from a record dated 1584, an Indian uprising killed all the people at one fort except a piper, his wife, and daughter. It is possible that the wife was an Indian woman whom the piper had married. More than likely there were many marriages between these men isolated in the interior of La Florida and Indian women.

Pardo was back at Santa Elena on March 2, 1568. He would never see his men again. Sergeant Boyano had returned to Santa Elena with Pardo. Another figure from earlier in this tale, Alonso de Lara, who had narrowly escaped death with the Jesuits in Ajacán, came to Santa Elena in 1572. He decided he wanted no part of the religious life and became a soldier. Several years later under the command of then Lieutenant Boyano, Alonso and the lieutenant died in a skirmish with the Orista Indians.

One hundred and twelve men and some women remained at the forts distributed along the trail from Fort San Felipe (rebuilt and renamed Fort San Marcos in 1578) on the Atlantic coast to Fort San Pablo in the Cumberland Mountain Range of Tennessee. What became of them?

A cryptic account indicates Pardo's men and their wives may all have been killed except the piper with his wife and daughter mentioned earlier. But that seems unlikely given later reports of sightings of men of European origin living in the hills and valleys of the interior. Pardo's men came from Portugal, and the two neighboring Spanish provinces of Galicia, and Asturias. The men were never recalled from their posts at the forts.

Pardo left Marcos Jiménez in command at Chiaha with about forty-eight men, eighty-five pounds of lead, match cord and gunpowder. He distributed new sandals to the men. At Cauchi (Coste) he left twelve men and a "catechist" under the command of Pedro Flores, along with thirty-six pounds of lead, twenty-two pounds of gunpowder, and other arms and tools. At Joara, Pardo left Alberto Excudero de Villamar in command of thirty soldiers with 100 pounds of lead, eighty-five pounds of powder, and numerous tools for working wood and farming. At Guatari, he left Father Sebastián Montero and sixteen soldiers under the command of Lucas de Cañizares. The fort was an earthen structure topped with a palisade wall of logs and elevated towers at the four corners.

Pardo left fifty-one pounds of lead and thirty-four pounds of gunpowder for the men's use.

These men were seasoned soldiers, well-equipped to survive in the presence of the Indians. Also, Pardo had located the forts within the territories of Indians who had not shown hostility toward the Spaniards, perhaps because they had not been misused by Pardo and his men. De Soto had passed through the same region a generation before and, in spite of his demands for women and porters, had generally fared well among those tribes. Consequently, there seems no reason to think that all of Pardo's men would have died at the hands of the Indians.

More likely, these men remained loyal to their posts for many years. During that period, they took Indian wives and raised families, while waiting loyally for orders to return home. Some may have waited the rest of their lives. The soldiers would have maintained communications among all the forts to ensure that they didn't miss important messages and that they weren't caught by surprise. At some point the men of the first generation, or perhaps their children, would have decided that their mission no longer bound them and they would have moved with their Indian wives to band together with the others of Spanish-Indian or Portuguese-Indian heritage.

From this isolation among the Indians of North Carolina and Tennessee, a hybrid culture developed. They took up farming using a blend of Indian and Iberian practices adapted to the special environment of the mountain valleys of the Appalachian Mountains. As the soldiers had immunity to the diseases that attacked the Indians with such ferocity, these people of mixed ancestry likely would have prospered, while the Indians they came in contact with would have declined due to the infectious European pathogens. As the culture expanded, it spread along the fertile valleys and rivers, eventually reaching into the colony of Virginia by the seventeenth century.

In 1598, a Spanish expedition reached Stone Mountain, Georgia, and learned from a cacique that four days' travel north they would find men like them (the Spanish) who lived in houses built from trees felled with steel axes. They described the men as wearing their hair short and having beards.

In 1608, Captain John Smith reported hearing from the Indians in tidewater Virginia of men who lived in houses like the English built, men whom the Indians considered non-Indian, living in the interior of the Carolinas. Smith took this report to mean that survivors of the Lost Colony of Roanoke Island had penetrated into that area. They could equally have been survivors or descendents of the Pardo expedition.

A certain amount of leakage occurred from each of the Spanish expeditions; men deserted De Soto as he trekked across the southern region of La Florida. Similarly, some colonists fled from the Ayllón settlement to live with the Indians when those who remained on the coast were starving. In the west, survivors of the Narváez expedition became slaves of the Indians—some perhaps gaining their freedom in time as Cabeza de Vaca did. So, the Pardo soldiers left behind would not have been the only isolated Spaniards or Portuguese living among the Indians by the middle of the sixteenth century.

In 1654, unaccounted-for Iberians apparently operated a mine in the southern Allegheny Mountains. In April, 1673, Major General Abraham Wood sent James Needham, Gabriel Arthur, and eight Indians to explore the Tennessee River valley. Wood reported in a letter to a Mr. Richards in London:

> *Eight days' journey down this river [Tennessee River] lives a white people who have long beards and whiskers and wear clothing, and on some of the other rivers live a hairy people. Not many years since the Tomahittans sent twenty men laden with beaver to the white people. They killed ten of them and put the other ten in irons, two of which ten escaped and one of them*

came with one of my men to my plantation as you will understand.

After a small time of rest one of my men returns with his horse, the Appomatock Indian and 12 Tomahittans, eight men and four women. One of those eight is he which hath been a prisoner with the white people. My other man remains with them until the next return to learn the language. The 10th of September my man with his horse and the twelve Indians arrived at my house, praise be to God. The Tomahittans have about sixty guns. Not such locks as ours be, the steels are long and channeled where the flints strike. The prisoner relates that the white people have a bell which is six foot over which they ring morning and evening, and at that time a great number of people congregate together and talk he knows not what. They have many blacks among them, oysters and many other shellfish, many swine, and cattle. Their building is brick.

In 1714, French traders reported seeing "dark-skinned reddish-brown complexioned people who were neither Indian nor Negro, but had fine European features." Also in the early 1700s, an exploration party sent by the Governor of Virginia into the mountains found a family of non-Indians living and farming the land near Wise, Virginia. The family had not recently moved there. They had a well-built house and fields indicating they had been there a long time.

At a time just before the American Revolution, John Sevier, an Englishman born in New Market, Virginia, explored and settled in the Tennessee territory of Virginia. Sevier descended from the Spanish Xavier family of Navarre. He could well have been writing about his distant relatives when he reported finding in the 1770s people who were neither black nor Indian occupying the fertile valleys of present day Hancock and Rhea counties. Sevier described the European features of these people who claimed to be of Portuguese origin.

Note that a line from Rhea County in the southwest to Hancock County in the northeast of Tennessee passes near the fort at Cauchi (Coste), and the distance between the two counties is only a little over 100 miles, a journey that could easily be made in a week on foot. Probably by 1770, the descendants of the Pardo expedition had spread much farther than that 100-plus-mile swath of Tennessee.

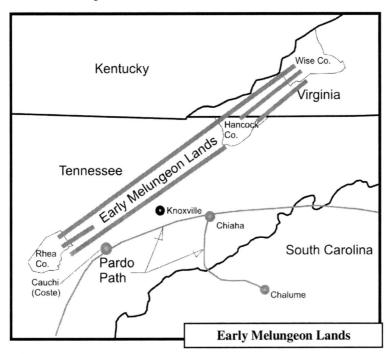

Early Melungeon Lands

In time this peculiar hybrid culture came to call themselves Melungeons. The origin of that name is highly debatable, as is the origin of the Melungeons themselves. The most common theory of the word asserts that it is a derivation of the French word mélange, meaning a mixture. That certainly makes sense, but the Portuguese-Indians descended from the Pardo soldiers would not have chosen a French word to describe themselves. The French traders who met them might have done so, but the people in question would not have adopted that name.

Another theory argues that Melungeon comes from a disparaging Spanish term meaning poor or lower-class person. A related theory links the name to Arabic melun jinn, meaning cursed soul. An Arabic origin makes more sense since the Portuguese and Spanish men who came with the conquistadors often had Moorish lineage. At the time of the Menéndez recruitment, people of Moorish blood were being persecuted and would have taken the opportunity to get out of Spain and Portugal. Finally, another theory ties the Melungeon name to the African Mbundu word malungu meaning "fellow countryman."

The Portuguese, who pioneered the Angolan slave trade, changed malungu to malungo meaning "shipmate." Thus the Melungeons were shipmates—certainly true. The proponent of this word derivation goes on to argue that the Melungeons were descendents of free blacks and Indians, the free blacks coming to Virginia in the 1620s and fleeing to the mountains of Virginia where they intermarried with Indians. Thus he argues, the Melungeons began in Virginia and spread to other areas from there beginning in the second quarter of the seventeenth century. That rather late origin doesn't explain the earlier evidence of Melungeons in Tennessee and the Carolinas, nor does it explain the European features that characterized the Melungeons throughout their history.

One more possible origin of the name is the old English word malengin meaning deceit or ill-intent. This theory holds that English settlers used that pejorative term to refer to the people they found in the fertile Cumberland Plateau already farming the land when they arrived as "pioneers." That certainly makes some sense. The first written record of the use of the word occurred in the minutes of a Baptist Church meeting in Stony Creek, Virginia, in 1813:

> *Then came forward Sister Kitchen and complained to the church against Susanna Stallard for saying she harbored them Melungins. Sister Sook said she was hurt with her for believing her child and not believing her, and she won't talk to her to get satisfaction, and both is 'pigedish', one against the other. Sister Sook lays it down and the church forgives her.*

This usage squares with the idea that the term Melungeon, at least in 1813 Virginia, was widely understood and had negative connotations. Like everything else about the Melungeons, it is not that simple. Researchers point out that there were Melungeons who were members of that church, and they argue the reference is to the obsolete English meaning of "deceitful people," rather than the original inhabitants of the Stony Creek area who were a people of uncertain origin and who at that time in Virginia were not called Melungeon.

Unfortunately, even DNA testing has not proved or disproved the link between the Melungeons and Pardo's soldiers. Some tests indicate a mixed ancestry of Mediterranean and American Indian ancestry; some include Arabic or Turkish heritage, and some include central-African ancestry. Part of the problem is that at this remote period more than 400 years after the Pardo expedition, it is difficult to find anyone whose ancestry has not included infusions of other cultures beyond that of the earliest Melungeons.

More important is what happened to the Melungeons when the later colonists invaded their territory. Soon their farms in the fertile lowlands were taken from them and they fled to the higher elevations where farming was more of a challenge. And later still, they became disenfranchised, being categorized as free people of color, mulattos, and other categories that denied their civil rights.

As is often the case with marginalized populations, people of Melungeon heritage attempted, often successfully, to hide their ancestry and "pass" as white in order to avoid discrimination and isolation. Now there seems to be a resurgence of people recognizing and celebrating their Melungeon heritage through genealogical research.

Perhaps advances in DNA will one day determine who the Melungeons were in the seventeenth and early eighteenth centuries. Similarly, some day scientific advances will make clearer the ancestry of the various Native American cultures that occupied North America when the Spanish conquistadors first arrived. By now it is apparent that many Native Americans may have a trace of Spanish or Portuguese genetic material due to the interactions between the Spanish explorers and the native people with whom they had contact. Some, indeed, had life-long contact with American Indian women.

Archaeological work began at a location in North Carolina called the Berry Site after the owners of the farm there. The farm has an Indian mound and in 1986 European pottery shards began to turn up in the excavated soil. Further investigation in 1994 established that sixteenth-century Spanish artifacts were mixed in the soil. The Berry site has been under annual excavation since 2001 and archaeologists connected with the project have established that the site contains the remains of the Fort San Juan de Joara of Juan Pardo. They have found traces of the post-in-ground houses Pardo's men constructed as well as ceramic jar fragments, weighing scales, and links from a chain mail vest.

Hopefully, one or more of the other forts constructed by Pardo and his men will be found some day. These finds clearly establish that North Carolina, which boasts the first English settlement site in what became the United States, can claim a history thirty years older than the "Lost Colony" of Roanoke Island; and that earlier history is Spanish—not English.

By the 1560s, in spite of Pedro Menéndez de Avilés' heightened patrols of the West Indies, English and French corsairs preyed on Spanish ports and ships. In 1567 and 1568, English privateer John Hawkins (or English pirate, from the Spanish perspective) sailed the Caribbean bringing slaves from Guinea for sale in the islands and looking for plunder. Sailing with him was young Francis Drake.

When Hawkins sailed boldly into San Juan de Ulúa in Mexico, he received a hot reception. He lost his most valuable ship there and barely escaped with his life. Farther up the coast, Hawkins put 114 men ashore because he knew they would starve at sea. Most of those Englishmen never made it home, dying at the hands of Indians, drowning, or being captured by the Spanish and subjected to the Inquisition before being burned to death. Two of Hawkins' men made it back home after sixteen years and told incredible stories of servitude, escape, recapture, and finally their successful escapes to England.

Sir Francis Drake

Francis Drake harbored a strong hostility to Spain after his brush with death at San Juan de Ulúa. Two years later he began a series of forays into the Caribbean to attack Spanish shipping and eventually Spanish ports. In July of 1572 Drake sailed boldly into Nombre de Dios with seventy-three men in two small ships of seventy tons and twenty tons. He captured that Spanish town in their Tierra Firme (Isthmus of Panama) and the considerable treasure held there.

The next year, Drake, teamed with French buccaneer Guillaume le Testu, stole twenty tons of gold and silver from the Spanish overland mule train that transported goods across the isthmus to the waiting treasure fleet. In 1577 with a royal commission, Drake led a fleet of five ships and 164 men on a mission to harass the Spanish off the Pacific Coast and to look for the Strait of Anián.

To do this, of course, Drake had to follow the route around South America pioneered by Magellan more than fifty years before. Drake was at sea for three years, during which he greatly troubled the Spanish. In one naval engagement off Peru he captured a Spanish ship and gained 37,000 ducats of gold (worth $3.7 million today).

Later, he gave chase to *Nuestra Señora de la Concepción*, which was bound for Manila in violation of the treaty between Spain and Portugal. The treasure Drake captured in this ship far exceeded that of the gold he captured off Peru. News of his capture of the *Nuestra Señora de la Concepción* led to the takeover of the throne of Portugal by Felipe II.

Sir Francis Drake's landing in New Albion (Pacific Coast)

Drake's exploits also included landing on the California coast and annexing that land for England, naming it "New Albion." Drake's raids and landing with impunity in territory claimed by Spain caused a renewed emphasis on securing the Pacific coast under Spanish control.

In 1576, Martin Frobisher made his first of several voyages to North America sponsored by Queen Elizabeth. The English queen and her court began to see opportunities to expand into the New World. She granted her first charter for colonization in North America to Sir Humphrey Gilbert in 1578. Spain certainly resented this move by the "heretic" queen. King Felipe could see clearly that, in addition to worries about French incursions, he would have to take steps to prevent English annexation of his territory in North

America. Although Gilbert failed miserably in Newfoundland, dying in the attempt, his half-brother Walter Ralegh moved quickly to plant English settlers in the mid-Atlantic region on land that Spain had strong interest in and a long history of attempted settlement.

In 1584, Ralegh, whom the Spanish detested almost as much as Sir Francis Drake, sent his first expedition to the Outer Banks of North America. He followed that quickly with a full-blown settlement attempt in 1585. Before the Spanish could hunt down and eradicate those English interlopers, Sir Francis Drake whisked them back to England. Spain needn't have worried about Ralegh's first colony; it was on the verge of collapse due to failure to deal effectively with the Indians and, as happened so many times to Spanish settlement attempts, a devastating hurricane.

In 1586, Drake had added an additional insult prior to rescuing Ralegh's colonists. Before coming to Roanoke Island, Drake had sacked Santo Domingo, Hispaniola, and Cartagena, Colombia, and then burned Spain's one successful North American outpost, Saint Augustine. In 1587, Drake and Ralegh participated in an English raid on Cadiz, the principal Spanish home port, severely damaging the armada that Felipe had assembled there in preparation for an all-out invasion of England.

That same year, Spain decided to abandon Santa Elena. Before leaving, the Spaniards destroyed Fort San Marcos and the town, burning the structures to prevent the English from occupying them. The next year Spain launched its attack on the English homeland and Drake and Ralegh played crucial roles in the English defeat of Felipe's Armada and invasion force. Near the end of the sixteenth century in North America, Saint Augustine—rebuilt after Drake's raid— remained the only Spanish colony still occupied in La Florida.

In the midst of the growing threat to Spain's monopoly in the New World, unauthorized incursions by Spaniards in the American Southwest and in South America caused King

Felipe to take steps to regain full control. He issued the Comprehensive Orders for New Discoveries in 1573, making it a capital offense punishable by death to enter into new American lands without a royal license. Felipe mandated that the word conquest be discarded in favor of pacification, and he gave the leading role to religious missionaries to stress the shift to a more benevolent approach to Spain's taking of lands from the Native Americans. As we will see, a royal proclamation in Spain more than 5,000 miles away would have little impact on the way the king's licensed agents treated the original occupants of North America.

Chapter 10
A Search for Silver in the Southwest

With growing threats to Spanish control in the Caribbean and in North America, new attempts to settle north of Mexico began in the last quarter of the sixteenth century.

In 1531, the coastal city of San Miguel de Culiacán was the northernmost settlement in New Spain. Fray Marcos's expedition in search of the Seven Cities of Cíbola had left from Culiacán in 1539. In 1546, the Spanish discovered silver ore in Zacatecas 360 miles north of Mexico City. This strike of silver shifted interest from exploration of the Pacific coast to the central highlands of Mexico.

Following Coronado's unsuccessful expedition to Cíbola and Quivira, Spanish slave traders and ranchers pushed north into the modern state of Chihuahua, Mexico, following the river valleys through the mountains toward the Sonora River and the Rio Grande. They may also have gone farther into the territory explored by Coronado.

Progress was slow in this vast area occupied by relatively poor Indian tribes with little wealth to attract the Spaniards. However those same Indians proved attractive to men looking to exploit them in the mines of Zacatecas. King

Felipe matched his order to treat the Indians more benevolently with a shift in leadership to Viceroy Velasco, who shared the king's approach to the Indians, and subsequent viceroys. But a secession movement in the 1560s and 1570s involving heirs of Cortés brought about a harsher government. Viceroy Martín Enríquez de Almanza arrived in 1568 to strengthen royal control of New Spain and the lands to the north.

In 1574, Almanza installed the Inquisition in New Spain and it set to work rooting out Luteranos—nearly 200 were burned at the stake that year in New Spain. However, Almanza carried on Velasco's policies of protecting the Indians. He instituted measures to ensure they had medical care and received salaries for the work they performed as peasants.

Lorenzo Suárez de Mendoza, second cousin of the first Viceroy of New Spain, Antonio de Mendoza, succeeded Almanza. During his three-year administration, the first sanctioned Spanish incursion across the Rio Grande took place.

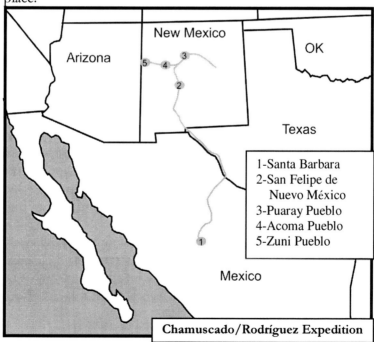

1-Santa Barbara
2-San Felipe de
   Nuevo México
3-Puaray Pueblo
4-Acoma Pueblo
5-Zuni Pueblo

Chamuscado/Rodríguez Expedition

On June 1, 1581, Franciscans Fray Agustín Rodríguez, Fray Juan de Santa Maria, and Fray Francisco López, protected by seven soldiers under the command of Captain Francisco Sánchez Chamuscado, followed the Río Conchos northeast to the Río Grande, a distance of about 260 miles from Santa Bárbara in Chihuahua. There is reason to believe that Chamuscado used the religious angle to cover his real interest—to look for mining opportunities in New Mexico.

The expedition crossed the river near the modern-day border town of Manuel Ojinaga, having trekked through a broad desert and entered into the west Texas desert with nineteen Indians, ninety horses, and 600 head of cattle.

Fray Rodríguez and Captain Chamuscado were on a quest to find—some say rediscover—the Pueblo civilization of New Mexico first encountered by Cabeza de Vaca and later Coronado. These new explorers had read the accounts of their predecessors and Fray Rodríguez wanted to minister to those people who lived in multistory stone houses and wore clothing made of cotton that they produced.

New Mexico

The land Fray Rodríguez and Captain Chamuscado were headed to was called Nuevo México by Coronado and had appeared as such in print at least by 1561 when Alonso de Zorita and Fray Jacinto de San Francisco requested permission from the Spanish king to undertake an expedition there. The king did not give them permission and Zorita contented himself with writing about the Indians and the period of Spanish conquest.

The Rodríguez/Chamuscado expedition followed the Rio Grande into New Mexico, and arriving at an abandoned pueblo, Chamuscado claimed the land for Spain, naming the pueblo San Felipe on August 21, 1581. Soon thereafter, they reached the Pueblos that Coronado and his men had lived among in the early 1540s. Continuing along the Rio Grande they turned east toward Coronado's Cicuyé Pueblo and followed the Pecos River into the plains, where they hunted bison with the Plains Indians.

By this time, provisions became an issue and the expedition retraced their steps to a Pueblo they called Piedrahita—possibly San Cristóbal Pueblo—where they wanted food. When the Indians didn't provide it, Chamuscado had warning shots fired over their heads. This caused the reluctant Indians to give the Spaniards cornmeal. However, word spread along the Rio Grande that the Spaniards had become hostile like those who had preceded them forty years before.

Wanting to see the Pueblos to the west, Rodríguez and Chamuscado led their band down the river and then across the desert to Acoma and Zuni Pueblos. By the onset of winter, the expedition had returned to the Pueblos of the Rio Grande valley, settling somewhere near Albuquerque.

Fray Juan de Santa Maria decided for some reason to return to New Spain. Against the better judgment of Chamuscado, Fray Juan and two Indian servants left the winter camp; he was killed by Indians two or three days later. Then, Pueblo Indians killed some of the Spaniards' horses. Chamuscado and his soldiers attacked one of the pueblos and captured two Indians, whom they sentenced to death to set an example and prevent further Indian attacks. Realizing their delicate situation—so few Spaniards among so many Indians—Chamuscado orchestrated a little morality play where he would start to execute the prisoners and then the two clerics would enter the scene and plead for mercy. He thought this would win over the Indians. It didn't work; the Pueblo Indians had grown tired of the demands of the Spaniards.

Captain Chamuscado decided they had worn out their welcome in the Province of San Felipe, as he had taken to calling the territory, and decided to return to Santa Bárbara to report their progress and assemble a larger expedition. The two friars wanted to stay in New Mexico among the Pueblo Indians whom they saw as fertile ground for their missionary efforts. They insisted on remaining at a pueblo they called Puaray (slightly north of Albuquerque). Soon after Chamuscado and his men departed, Fray Agustín Rodríguez and Fray Francisco López died at the hands of the Indians of Puaray.

En route to New Spain, Chamuscado became ill and died near Julimes, Chihuahua, Mexico. His seven soldiers and an unknown number of their Indian servants made it back to Santa Bárbara unscathed by mid-April, 1582. They had completed a round trip of at least 2,000 miles. One of the soldiers, Hernán Gallegos, requested that Viceroy Mendoza grant him a license to return to New Mexico with a new expedition. Mendoza turned down the request, placing his trust instead in Antonio de Espejo.

Antonio de Espejo sold his expedition to the viceroy as a mission to rescue the two Franciscans. Espejo was a relatively recent arrival in New Spain, having come with the first head of the Inquisition, Pedro Moya de Contreras. Espejo's real reason for the expedition was to search for gold or silver mining opportunities in New Mexico.

Espejo, as a tribunal official with the Inquisition, had apprehended and jailed one of the men that John Hawkins had put ashore after the battle at San Juan de Ulúa. Along with his brother, Pedro, Antonio de Espejo ran several cattle ranches and eventually became embroiled in a legal problem. His brother had killed one of the vaqueros who worked on their ranch. Pedro was found guilty of murder and Antonio guilty of being an accessory to murder. The brothers fled to Santa Bárbara in Chihuahua to avoid punishment. There they became interested in the silver mining business, and met the men who returned from the Rodríguez/Chamuscado expedition, who reported they had seen evidence of five promising mine sites.

Fray Bernardino Beltrán, a Franciscan stationed at Durango wanted to go to the aid of his Franciscan brothers left in New Mexico, not knowing they were dead. Antonio de

Espejo had heard reports that the two Franciscans had died but he kept that information to himself. Espejo put up his own funds to cover the costs of an expedition to take Fray Bernardino on his journey of mercy. By casting this as a religious mission, Espejo avoided a lengthy approval process that King Felipe's Comprehensive Orders for new Discoveries required. Instead of seeking approval from the viceroy, Fray Bernardino got permission from the Lieutenant Governor of New Galicia for the expedition.

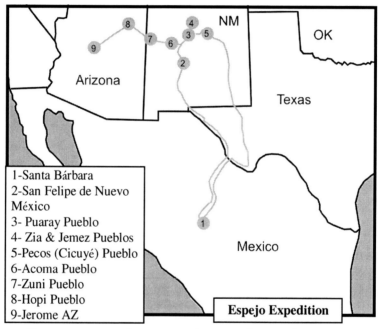

1-Santa Bárbara
2-San Felipe de Nuevo México
3- Puaray Pueblo
4- Zia & Jemez Pueblos
5-Pecos (Cicuyé) Pueblo
6-Acoma Pueblo
7-Zuni Pueblo
8-Hopi Pueblo
9-Jerome AZ

Espejo Expedition

Fourteen armed men and Fray Bernardino followed Antonio de Espejo out of Santa Bárbara in November, 1582, taking the same route along the Río Florida and the Río Conchos to the Rio Grande and the Pueblos of New Mexico. Some women and children as well as Indian servants swelled the size of the party to about fifty people. In February, 1583, when they entered the Rio Grande Valley, the Indians told them that the two missionaries were still alive. As they got closer to Albuquerque they learned that the Tewa Indians of the upper Rio Grande had killed the Franciscans. They also learned that the people of those more northern pueblos had united to fight the Spaniards if they insisted on proceeding north.

Espejo pushed on up the Rio Grande toward Puaray, which they found deserted by the inhabitants but the larders full of food. The Spaniards helped themselves to the food and continued north. As they entered the area of the Keres people (perhaps at Santo Domingo Pueblo), they confirmed that the Tewa people had killed the two missionaries. Coronado had mistreated the Tewa when he was among them, demanding food, fighting with them, and burning one of their cities.

Some among the expedition argued that they should return to New Spain since they had confirmed the death of the two Franciscans, but Espejo insisted on continuing their explorations. He led the expedition west to Zia and Jemez and then to Acoma and Zuni.

At the Zuni pueblos, Espejo met several Aztec Indians who had come there with Coronado. The Zuni Indians told of a lake to the west and nearby veins of metallic ore. Fray Bernardino had had enough. He insisted the time had long since come to return to New Spain since their mission to rescue the missionaries had ended. He argued that Coronado had found no trace of precious metals and Espejo would likewise fail in his quest. Finally, the two men agreed that Espejo would go west to the Hopi pueblos and then return to the Zuni to begin the retreat to New Spain.

Espejo and ten of his men with some Zuni guides, some of his servants, and eighty Zuni warriors marched to the Hopi about ninety miles to the northwest. The Hopi confirmed the story of mineral deposits to the southwest. Espejo sent five of his men back to Zuni and he traveled six days with the balance of his force to examine the ore (somewhere near Jerome, Arizona). The record doesn't offer a conclusive report of whether or not the ore was valuable.

Espejo returned to Zuni hoping to buy himself more time, but Fray Bernardino would not relent. He was leaving for New Spain with or without Espejo; he left Espejo behind at Zuni. Fray Bernardino returned to his monastery in Durango with no apparent incidents, following the route back via Acoma, the Rio Grande, and the rivers in Mexico.

Antonia de Espejo left Zuni with his men, servants, and other Indians. On his way to the Rio Grande, he had a hostile interaction with the people of Acoma, and also some Querechos, before arriving at Puaray, where he encountered more hostility, but no warfare. He continued on to Cicuyé, reaching that pueblo in July, 1583. Another surviving Mexican Indian from the Coronado expedition met Espejo at the pueblo.

Continuing on to the Pecos River, Espejo and his party followed the river back to New Spain. They arrived at Santa Bárbara on September 10, 1583, having covered as much or more ground than the Rodríguez/Chamuscado expedition.

Antonio de Espejo set sail for Spain intending to request royal permission to mount an expedition to New Mexico. He died at a stopover at Havana. Surprisingly, King Felipe was encouraged by the reports from these two expeditions into New Mexico; he sent instructions to the Viceroy of New Spain to select a suitable leader to undertake another settlement attempt. Almost fifteen years would elapse before that royal directive took effect.

Meanwhile, some were unwilling to wait for a license to explore and settle New Mexico. We don't know how many unauthorized excursions Spaniards made into New Mexico, but the record shows what at least two accomplished and what the consequences were.

In 1590 a Portuguese man, Gaspar Castaño de Sosa, had been considered and then rejected as a candidate to lead a sanctioned expedition into New Mexico. Castaño made no secret of his expedition; he even sent word to the viceroy that he intended to expand into New Mexico. He and Luís de

Carvajal had a license to settle the territory of Nuevo León in New Spain—a newly settled (1583) territory in northeast Mexico. Their interest, as in most of the northern expansion within New Spain, had been minerals, particularly silver. Since the discoveries in Zacatecas, speculators followed the mountains northward through the central portion of Mexico looking to make more silver strikes. Carvajal and Castaño had some initial success in Nuevo León, but there was insufficient ore to sustain their operation.

Luís de Carvajal

Carvajal was a Spanish adventurer who first came to New Spain in 1567 and served as alcalde of Tampico. In 1568, Carvajal apprehended seventy-seven of the men John Hawkins had put ashore after the battle at San Juan de Ulúa. This accomplishment put him in a good light with the viceroy, who commissioned Carvajal to undertake several assignments, including punishing the Indians in coastal Texas for the massacre of several hundred Spanish shipwreck survivors near Padre Island.

Carvajal fell afoul of the authorities when he engaged in Indian slave trading. He returned to Spain and, in 1579 petitioned the king for a charter to settle a new territory northwest of Tampico to be called Nuevo León. He received his charter and sailed with 100 families—mostly relatives of him or his wife. Along with those colonists, he brought 100 soldiers and sixty married laborers. They arrived in New Spain in 1580 and began the establishment of Nuevo León.

Initially successful, Carvajal, supposedly a converso (i.e. a converted Jew) was arrested by the inquisition along with a number of his family members including his niece, Isabel. Under torture, Isabel confessed that they were practicing Jews (Marranos). In all, 120 of Carvajal's associates (including Isabel and eight others of his immediate family) were condemned to death by the Inquisition and burned at the stake on December 8, 1596, in Mexico City. Carvajal was convicted of heresy and sentenced to banishment for six years, but he died in prison.

When the Inquisition took Carvajal, the governor of Nuevo León, into custody as a crypto-Jew, Castaño decided to act on his own. Castaño left Almadén in Nuevo León in July of 1590 with about 170 colonists, including women and children, hauling all of their possessions in ten two-wheeled carts, driving livestock in a northwesterly direction toward the Pecos River. Castaño had no trouble attracting colonists interested in the potential for more rich silver strikes in the new territory to the north. He had dropped some silver into ore brought back from New Mexico to insure that it "proved" valuable. Word of the rich ore sample did the trick. By late in December the colonists reached the Gallinas River (at Gallinas, New Mexico). As the mountains closed in on the river valley, progress with the carts would be difficult. Castaño sent forward a scouting party to determine their course.

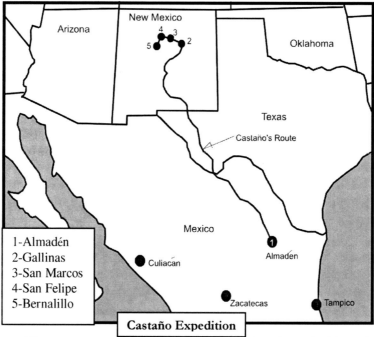

1-Almadén
2-Gallinas
3-San Marcos
4-San Felipe
5-Bernalillo

Castaño Expedition

The scouts reached Pecos Pueblo (Cicuyé) and although they initially received a friendly welcome, hostility soon erupted. The warriors of Pecos wounded several of the scouts and seized their arms and equipment. The scouts reported back to Castaño who set out with forty men to Pecos. When Castaño reached Pecos, he attempted to use trade goods to pacify the Indians, but his overtures didn't gain him entrance. Finally, he and his men stormed into the pueblo and the Indians abandoned their city.

Castaño replenished his food supplies from Pecos and then traveled west to the Rio Grande. The first pueblo he reached on that river was Tesuque; the people there appeared friendly at first. He erected a cross in the plaza and took formal possession of the city for Spain and himself. He continued this process along the river at each pueblo he found.

At the end of January, 1591, Castaño began the movement of the colonists along the Pecos and through the mountains to the Rio Grande. This arduous trek through heavy snows took them over a month. They followed the Rio Grande down to the vicinity of Bernalillo, all the while looking for evidence of silver or gold ore. Their prospecting turned up no trace of those minerals in all of their searches from San Marcos Pueblo down to San Felipe. While exploring along the river, Castaño named it the Rio Grande— the first instance of this designation. That naming of the river was his only lasting accomplishment on this expedition.

Near Bernalillo, an armed party of twenty Spaniards led by Juan Morlete arrested Castaño for his illegal incursion into New Mexico. Morlete assumed command of the would-be colonists and marched them down the Rio Grande to the Conchos River and back to New Spain.

Morlete took Castaño to Mexico City where he had to face Viceroy Luís de Velasco II. He was handed over for trial on charges of violating the king's Comprehensive Order by "marching into New Mexico with a company of soldiers recruited on his own authority, without an order or permit to do so." Two years after leaving New Mexico under arrest, Castaño was sentenced to six years' banishment to the

Philippines; he died aboard a ship bound for the Moluccas when the Chinese galley slaves revolted and took over the ship.

The next documented illegal entrada into New Mexico started out legally as a mission to punish unruly Indians near Santa Bárbara in Chihuahua. Governor Diego Fernández de Velasco ordered Captain Francisco Leyva de Bonilla (another Portuguese soldier) to lead the punitive expedition to Chihuahua. Captain Bonilla had other ideas that he discussed with his willing men. He recruited an unknown number of Spaniards and Indians and went in search of gold and silver in New Mexico. His route took him from Culiacán to Santa Bárbara and north along the Conchos River and then the Rio Grande. They entered New Mexico in 1593.

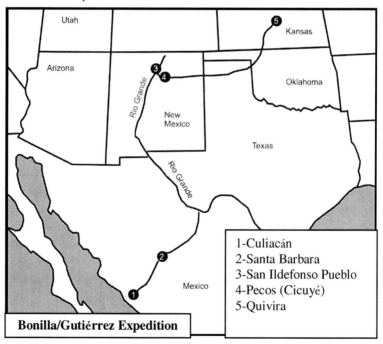

1-Culiacán
2-Santa Barbara
3-San Ildefonso Pueblo
4-Pecos (Cicuyé)
5-Quivira

Bonilla/Gutiérrez Expedition

Antonio Gutiérrez de Humaña accompanied the expedition and shared the leadership with Captain Bonilla. The now illegal band spent about a year on the Rio Grande with their headquarters at San Ildefonso Pueblo, searching the surrounding hills and mountains for signs of silver or gold. They apparently had no difficulties moving among the Pueblo Indians, perhaps because of a large number of Indians traveling with them.

Eventually, having found nothing of interest along the Rio Grande, they became enthused by stories they heard among the Pueblos concerning a fabulous land called Quivira somewhere to the east. This, of course, is the same ruse the people of Cicuyé (Pecos) used on Coronado to get rid of the Spaniards. It worked again. Captain Bonilla and Gutiérrez led their expedition to Pecos and then followed the river through the Glorieta Pass and to the plains beyond. On the plains they met the Querecho (Apache) Indians and hunted bison with them.

The expedition continued northeast across the plains and eventually reached Quivira. There, as had happened with Coronado, they realized that they had been duped—there was no great wealth, certainly no gold and silver to be had at Quivira. In a rapidly deteriorating state of frustration, they pushed on for a few more days until an act of violence ended the trek.

Gutiérrez and Captain Bonilla had become hostile toward each other. The two men retired to their respective tents on the plains and refused to talk. Finally, Bonilla entered Gutiérrez' tent, responding to his summons. As the captain approached Gutiérrez, the man stood up and stabbed a knife into Bonilla's body twice. Captain Bonilla bled to death in that tent somewhere near Quivira in Kansas.

The Indians from New Spain who had followed the Spaniards on this illegal expedition abandoned Gutiérrez at this point. One of the Indians, Jusepe, a servant of Gutiérrez, ended up back at the pueblos after spending a year among the Apache. He settled at the Pecos Pueblo, where he was living when he heard about a new Spanish expedition in the area. Jusepe told the story of Captain Bonilla's illegal entry to members of the final, legal entrada, the expedition of Juan de

Oñate. The fate of Gutiérrez became known later when Spaniards revisited Quivira. The Indians of the plains killed Gutiérrez and his followers sometime after his murder of Captain Bonilla.

Juan de Oñate Salazar emerged from the viceroy's twelve-year-long vetting process as the winner in the contest of who would lead a royally sanctioned expedition to settle New Mexico. In September of 1595, Viceroy Luís de Velasco II and Oñate signed the agreement designating Oñate as Captain General of Spanish forces and Governor of New Mexico.

Juan de Oñate was the first of the Spanish conquistadors born in New Spain; he was of Basque ancestry. His father, Cristóbal de Oñate, had come to New Spain where he settled in Zacatecas and made a fortune in the silver mines there. His mother came from a highly placed family whose ancestors had distinguished themselves in the expulsion of the Moors. Her name was Catalina Salazar y de la Cadena.

Juan de Oñate

The conqueror of New Mexico had earned his stripes fighting Indians on the fringes of New Spain in the 1570s and 1580s as the mining operators pushed northward. Oñate married well; his wife, Isabel de Tolosa Cortés de Moctezuma, was the granddaughter of Hernán Cortés and great-granddaughter of the Aztec emperor. Juan settled down to operate the silver mines he owned in Zacatecas while his application to lead the New Mexico expedition languished in the Spanish bureaucracy.

Following the agreement placing him in charge of the expedition to New Mexico, Oñate began recruiting his forces.

He selected two brothers, Juan de Zaldivar and Vicente de Zaldivar, to accompany him on his quest. He would rely heavily on both of them. The Zaldivar brothers were his nephews and were nephews of Captain Juan de Zaldivar who had accompanied Coronado into Arizona and New Mexico more than fifty years before.

With help from the Zaldivars and his own efforts, Oñate soon had 500 colonists ready to depart for New Mexico, but the bureaucrats had another hurdle for the conquistador. New Spain had a new viceroy, Gaspar de Zúñiga Acevedo y Fonseca, and he put all major initiatives on hold. He demanded changes in the contract Oñate had signed with the previous viceroy. This delayed the expedition until the spring of 1596. As Oñate began the movement of his colonists, supplies, and equipment to Santa Bárbara for their departure, word arrived that the king had suspended the authorization for the expedition.

Oñate was a wealthy man by this time, having inherited his father's interests in the silver mines and controlling his wife's inheritance as well, but he couldn't sustain the loss of the 500,000 pesos (about $10 million today) he said he had invested in the expedition. As in nearly all Spanish expeditions authorized by the King of Spain, the royal treasury contributed nothing—all the financial risk impinged on the conquistadors and other private investors. Oñate stood to gain the title of Adelantado for himself and his heirs, an annual salary, encomiendas, an estate of land thirty leagues (about 75 miles square), and silver and gold mines exempt from royal taxation. He learned that the reason for the suspension was that critics in Spain had questioned his ability to lead the expedition.

By 1597, the members of the expedition had assembled at Santa Bárbara and were anxious to depart, but it would take another year before Oñate secured final approval from the king to begin the trek to New Mexico. On January 26, 1598 Oñate led ten Franciscans, his colonists, and soldiers out of Santa Bárbara with their possessions, equipment, and supplies carried in a train eighty-wagons long stretching back miles as they headed up the Conchos River valley. About 400 men (130 of whom brought their wives and children) rode or marched along the route. Drovers moved 7,000 head of cattle including horses, steers, sheep, goats, and oxen. These colonists planned to stay and they brought with them the seeds and farming tools they would need to grow their own crops and fodder for their cattle.

Oñate did not follow the route of Espejo and others all the way up the Conchos to the Rio Grande. Instead, with an advance party he veered north across the desert of Chihuahua and reached the Rio Grande, following the river about twenty miles upstream to El Paso, which he named long before a city sprang up there.

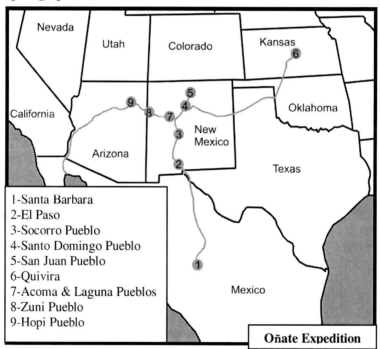

1-Santa Barbara
2-El Paso
3-Socorro Pueblo
4-Santo Domingo Pueblo
5-San Juan Pueblo
6-Quivira
7-Acoma & Laguna Pueblos
8-Zuni Pueblo
9-Hopi Pueblo

Oñate Expedition

On April 30, 1598, Juan de Oñate annexed the American Southwest into the Viceroyalty of New Spain, with these words recorded by his majesty's notary:

*...[Oñate took] possession of the land on the third day of
the Ascension of the Lord ... with the help of Juan Pérez de
Donís, his majesty's notary and secretary of the expedition and
jurisdiction of the said kingdoms and provinces, in the name of
the Most Christian king our lord, Felipe, second of this name,
and of his successors (may they be many and very happy), and
for the royal crown of Castile and the monarchs who have ruled
over it for and on behalf of that kingdom and my said province,
....*

Oñate's statement of formal possession was preceded by
a long religious speech referring to the Trinity, all the beasts
of the world and the heavens including cherubs, and St.
Francis—in total about 360 words. Then he justified his
authority by reciting all of the acts by the king and viceroys
granting him his position as Captain General, Governor, and
Adelantado. After the taking possession part quoted above,
Oñate rambled on for about 900 words giving the authority
of the Pope back through the pontiffs to the beginning with
St. Peter, justifying the Papal Donation of the lands to Spain.
Then he offered the following scope of his possession:

*I take and seize tenancy and possession, real and actual,
civil and natural, one, two, three times, one, two, and three
times, one, two, and three times, and all the times that by right
I can and should, at this said Río del Norte [Rio Grande],
without excepting anything and without limitations, including
the mountains, rivers, valleys, meadows, pastures, and waters.
In his name I also take possession of all the other lands,
pueblos, cities, towns, castles, fortified and unfortified houses
which are now established in the kingdoms and provinces of
New Mexico, those neighboring and adjacent thereto, and those
which may be established in the future, together with their
mountains, rivers, fisheries, waters, pastures, valleys, meadows,
springs, and ores of gold, silver, copper, mercury, tin, iron,
precious stones, salt, alum, and all the lodes of whatever sort,
quality, or condition they may be, together with the native
Indians in each and every one of the provinces, with civil and
criminal jurisdiction, power of life and death, over high and low,*

from the leaves of the trees in the forests to the stones and sands of the river, and from the stones and sands of the river to the leaves in the forests.

Then the Adelantado nailed a cross to a convenient tree, knelt down and pronounced these words required by law:

Cross, Holy Cross that thou art, divine gate of heaven, altar of the only and essential sacrifice of the body and blood of the son of God, way of the saints and the attainment of His glory, open the door of heaven to these heathens, establish the church and altars where the body and blood of the son of God may be offered, open to us the way to security and peace for their preservation and ours, and give to our king, and to me in his royal name, peaceful possession of these kingdoms and provinces for His blessed glory, Amen.

In this twenty-first century one can hardly conceive of the degree of hubris expressed in this formal possession of the land of the American southwest, nor conceive of the magnitude of the ego possessed by Juan de Oñate evident in the roughly 2,600 words he spoke to the vacant desert along the Rio Grande on that last day in April, 1598. He would repeat a version of this highly refined legal text at every pueblo he visited, following which he would demand the citizens of the pueblo to submit to an "Act of Obedience and Vassalage," signifying their acceptance of his jurisdiction over them. By this time in history, some of those Pueblo Indians may have understood enough Spanish to know what Oñate intended; however, they clearly had no choice but to submit or die resisting the Spaniards. As we will see, some chose death.

In the long, formal speech of possession delivered on the Rio Grande, Oñate enumerated seven reasons—justifications, really—for his possession of New Mexico.

- The death of the Franciscan missionaries: Fray Juan de Santa Maria, Fray Francisco López, Fray Agustín Rodríguez, whom he designated as the "first discoverers" of New Mexico

- "… punishment and correction of sins against nature and humanity among these bestial natives …."
- "Baptism and salvation of so many children among these heathens …."
- Civilize and improve the lot of the Indians, and "increase their trade and mechanical arts …."
- Clothe the naked
- Introduce new crops and livestock
- Govern the Indians "in peace and justice …" and provide security against their enemies.

The rest of the expedition followed Oñate's path across the desert—a journey of about 350 miles. They suffered greatly from lack of food, water, and the glaring sun during the day and bitter cold at night. By the time they reached the Rio Grande, many settlers wanted to go home but Oñate refused to let anyone leave the expedition.

Slightly north of Los Cruces, New Mexico, Oñate and the Zaldivar brothers separated from the rest of the expedition with about sixty men and moved quickly up the Rio Grande. Oñate had two purposes for moving in advance of his large expedition: he wanted to visit each of the pueblos and hopefully establish friendly relations with them; and he wanted to prospect for silver and gold.

At Socorro Pueblo, the Indians were cautiously open, willingly exchanging gifts with the conquistador. The small band of Spaniards advanced up the river to the Keresan Pueblo named San Felipe by Castaño seven years earlier and proceeded north exchanging gifts and pledging peace with each Indian community they encountered. Original records from the Oñate expedition identify nearly 200 pueblos (forty-two of them unnamed) that he or his men visited during their travels in the American southwest.

In July, Oñate had reached Santo Domingo Pueblo about 330 miles north of his initial stop on the Rio Grande and, as at the preceding pueblos, administered an Act of Obedience and Vassalage to the Indians there as well as representatives from other "provinces." Continuing north along the river, he reached San Juan Bautista Pueblo (Khe-Wa Pueblo) and summoned leaders from the Puaray, Keres, Zia, Tewa, Pecos, Picurís, and Taos along the upper Rio Grande, its tributaries, and the Pecos River.

Young Tewa Woman ca. 1906

These pueblos represented the remaining Indian cultures of the Rio Grande valley that Oñate had yet to "pacify." On September 9, 1598, He met with the Indian representatives he had summoned and held a formal ceremony of their submission. Notice that the Indians were the ones supposedly submitting, but the architect of the ceremony was Oñate, following a well-established protocol created by Spanish clerics and bureaucrats. The Indian representatives listened to the Adelantado's speech translated by interpreters of unknown fluency in the Indian dialects and then were required to:

> ... *rise, as a sign that they rendered obedience and vassalage to God and the king, for they had been seated up to this time, and approach the father commissary [Fray Alonso Martínez] and himself [Oñate], fall on their knees, and kiss their hands. The Indian captains of these kingdoms rose and knelt before the governor and the father commissary and kissed their hands as a sign of obedience and vassalage, as they had been instructed.*

Having taken the Indian representatives as submitting to Spanish rule, Fray Alonso Martínez assigned each of the other clerics to minister to a specific pueblo or group of pueblos. Oñate told the Indian leaders to kiss the hand of the Franciscan assigned to them and take him into their protection.

The notary recorded the conclusion of this ceremony in the following gilded prose that couldn't possibly have represented what the Indians really felt:

> *And when the padres had been pointed out to them, the Indians rose with demonstrations of joy and went to their priest and kissed his habit and embraced him, and some of the Indians told their priest that he must baptize their children.*

The rest of the expedition caught up to Oñate and his advance party at San Juan Pueblo late in August, a week or two before the last ceremony of submission recorded above. About the time of the ceremony, Jusepe Gutiérrez arrived at San Juan Pueblo, having heard at Pecos that Spaniards were back in the territory. Jusepe, former servant of Antonio Gutiérrez de Humaña, told Oñate about his experience with Bonilla and Gutiérrez on the expedition to Quivira. Jusepe's story satisfied one of Oñate's responsibilities: to determine what had become of Bonilla and Gutiérrez and bring them to justice if possible.

Vicente de Zaldivar and a detachment of sixty men went with Jusepe as their guide to Pecos and then into the plains of Texas to explore that region and presumably to learn of Gutiérrez' fate. They spent two months living among the Indians of the Great Plains, hunting bison, making jerky, and studying the habits of the Apache hunters. Their attempt at capturing a live bison to take back to San Juan Pueblo proved to be beyond their capability.

About the end of November, Vicente de Zaldivar and his men returned to the Rio Grande, having received an order to do so from the Adelantado. Oñate had decided during his inspections of the Rio Grande pueblos to strike out to the west in order to locate a path to the South Sea (Pacific Ocean). One of his goals was to establish a link between New Mexico and the Pacific Coast.

The Adelantado had sent orders to Vicente to assume command of the expedition at San Juan Pueblo, while Vicente's brother, Juan, with reinforcements, was to join Oñate on his journey into the west. Juan de Zaldivar selected thirty soldiers and left San Juan Pueblo to catch up to the Adelantado.

Oñate's route took him to Laguna and Acoma pueblos, a journey of about fifty miles south and then west from Albuquerque. He had supposedly already pacified Acoma in October and apparently passed through their territory with no trouble, making his way with thirty men another eighty miles to the Zuni Pueblos across the desolate and rugged country west of Acoma.

Acoma had seen Spaniards before. Coronado's men had been there in 1540. They were greatly impressed with the strength of the city's defenses. Pedro de Castaneda, one of Coronado's men who left a written record described Acoma:

> The village was very strong because it was up on a rock out of reach, having steep sides in every direction, and so high that it was a very good musket that could throw a ball as high... There was a broad stairway for about 200 steps, then a stretch of about 100 narrower steps, and at the top they had to go up about three times as high as a man by means of holes in the rock....
>
> There was a wall of large and small stones at the top, which they could roll down without showing themselves, so that no army could possibly be strong enough to capture the village. On the top they had room to sow and store a large amount of corn, and cisterns to collect snow and water... They made a present [for the Spaniards] of a large number of [turkey] cocks with very big wattles, much bread, tanned deerskins, pine nuts, flour, and corn.
>
> ...the natives, who were peaceful, entertained our men well, giving them provisions and birds. Many of the gentlemen went up to the top to see it, and they had great difficulty in going up the steps in the rock, because they were not used to them, for the natives go up and down so easily that they carry loads and the

women carry water, and they do not seem even to touch their hands, although our men had to pass their weapons up from one to another.

When Juan de Zaldivar reached Acoma Pueblo towering 350 feet above the plain on December 1st, his men and horses desperately needed water and food. When seven of his soldiers trekked up to the mesa-top pueblo, the Acoma provided what they could. In exchange for maize and tortillas, the Spaniards gave the Acoma hatchets.

The path to Acoma Pueblo ca. 1905

The Indians said they would need time to grind sufficient flour to meet the needs of Zaldivar's force. The Spaniards descended the mesa with two "chiefs" of Acoma in tow. They advised Zaldivar to hold hostage the two men from Acoma that night to ensure that the pueblo would provide the flour they had asked for, saying they thought the maize and tortillas had been given grudgingly. Zaldivar released the Acoma men in an attempt to show good faith, but perhaps it was too late to expunge the insult his men had given the Acoma.

That day the Spaniards camped about five miles from Acoma where they found water for their horses. The next day the Acoma sent more tortillas and three fanegas (about six bushels) of maize. On December 4th, Zaldivar and eighteen of his men returned to Acoma with more hatchets to trade for the flour the Indians said (or so he believed) they would have ready. While in the pueblo, a soldier named Vivero stole two turkeys from an Indian and the Indian killed him. The Indians of the pueblo—men and women—then mobbed the Spaniards and killed eleven of them including Juan de Zaldivar—at least one of the Spaniards leaped to his death from the rim of the mesa. The remaining seven soldiers fled down the treacherous, narrow defile that provided the only path to the plain. They mounted their horses and, joined by the other twelve soldiers who had remained on the plain, rode back to San Juan Pueblo with Captain Gerónimo Márquez in the lead, enduring verbal abuse and flights of arrows from the Acoma who pursued them for a few miles.

When the reinforcements ordered by Oñate didn't arrive at Zuni, he abandoned his expedition to the South Sea and returned to San Juan Pueblo. When the Adelantado learned what had happened to his nephew, Juan, at Acoma Pueblo, he consulted with the priests and his officers on how to respond. On December 22, 1598, a formal hearing lasting several days began. At the end, after the survivors from the engagement at Acoma had told their story, Oñate asked the Franciscans what they thought the correct response should be. The clerics advised that if the Indians of Acoma would not submit to Spanish rule, then military force to make them submit was justified.

The Adelantado assigned the mission of bringing the Acoma to heel to his other nephew, Vicente de Zaldivar. Vicente set out after receiving detailed orders from the Adelantado on January 11th. He arrived at Acoma on January 21, 1599, with seventy-two men to call for peace and surrender of the perpetrators of the attack on his brother and the other Spaniards. Zaldivar had Indian interpreters convey this message to the people of Acoma, but they showed no sign that they intended to comply. Plan B was to attack Acoma Pueblo. The Acoma had planned on Spanish reprisal and had further fortified their nearly impregnable mesa by digging pitfalls at the base of the cliffs to trap the Spaniards' horses. They had also barricaded the pueblo and removed ladders providing access into the buildings.

Zaldivar deployed his men on two fronts—one a diversion. When the Indians atop the mesa responded to the diversion, Zaldivar sent eight men up the other side where they held onto their position in the pueblo all night in spite of continued attack, allowing the rest of Zaldivars forces to scale the mesa.

View from the heights of Acoma Pueblo

Three hundred Indians died in the first assault, and on the next two days, two hundred more died. Then the Spaniards set fire to the town, forcing the remaining population (estimated to be about 1,800) to seek refuge in their kivas (assembly lodges). Zaldivar's men had somehow managed to bring two pieces of artillery up the sheer cliffs of the mesa and they trained them on the Acoma people. The battle raged on with the Spaniards winning then losing ground. Finally, another 800 Indians had died and the rest of the people of Acoma surrendered; the record says 500 women and children and eighty men were captured alive.

By February 9, 1599, Zaldivar, his men, and the 580 prisoners from Acoma were at San Juan Pueblo. All of the prisoners would be tried in a Spanish tribunal at Santo Domingo Pueblo. The Adelantado appointed Captain Alonso Gómez Montesinos to represent the Indians as their guardian and defense attorney in the upcoming trial. Oñate, as governor of New Mexico, would sit in judgment.

Twenty-seven soldiers testified against the Acoma, insisting that the Indians had not been molested in any way before the attack on the Spaniards. The maintained that the attack appeared premeditated as the men with Juan de Zaldivar were led through the pueblo and separated into two groups, at which time a loud shout appeared to initiate the attack simultaneously on both groups. This testimony doesn't totally square with a letter written by one of the soldiers to another Spaniard. The letter by Alonso Sanchez, Treasurer of New Mexico, to Rodrigo del Rio, dated February 28, 1599, just two weeks after the trial of the Acoma, contains this statement of the insult that initiated the attack:

> *At this time there arose a minor incident when a soldier named Vivero took two turkeys from the Indians, and they killed him from one of the terraces. The entire pueblo then rose in arms and killed the maese de campo, Don Juan de Zaldivar, and ten other soldiers and captains, among whom was my son, Diego Núñez de Chaves, and Captain Escalante and Marcos Pereira.*

It seems likely that the theft of the turkeys occurred as described since this father would hardly want to justify the action that led to the death of his son at Acoma. According to the Indians' testimony, there may have been a stronger motivation for the action taken by the Acoma.

Six Acoma men named Caoma, Cat-Ticati, Taxio, Xunusta, Excasi, and Caucachi gave testimony and submitted to interrogation through an interpreter. Some of these men testified that they were not at Acoma when the attack occurred, and they therefore testified to what they had heard the cause of the attack was. They gave varying reasons for the attack on Juan de Zaldivar and his men: the Spaniards demanded flour and blankets in excess; they stole a turkey; they injured an Acoma; they killed an Acoma. As in many mob actions, the spark that ignited the hostilities would never be determined. Since a Spaniard testified in writing that Vivero stole two turkeys from an Acoma woman and that led to the violence, we might conclude that the theft caused the Acoma reaction. Once the first strike occurred, the Acoma and the Spaniards responded in the usual way.

Montesinos entered a petition for the Indians stating that "they had no witnesses or defense pleas to offer for having killed the Spaniards." Their only defense, according to Montesinos, was that "many of them were not guilty as they were absent when the Spaniards were killed, and they were unaware of the crime the others had committed." Montesinos asked the Governor to acquit the Indians, set them free, and allow them to go wherever they wished. Montesinos summed up his plea with a request for clemency, "... in view of the fact that they are *bárbaros* (uncivilized).

The record of the legal proceedings against the Acoma includes testimony by four Spanish soldiers who took part in the punitive raid that resulted in the capture of the prisoners before the bar. None of the surviving Spanish soldiers who took part in the melee in which Juan de Zaldivar died testified—thus no one contradicted the Indian defendants' testimony. Nonetheless, the verdict could have been predicted.

All the Indians of the Acoma Pueblo stood convicted of the crime of murdering Juan de Zaldivar and his men. On February 12, 1599, Governor Oñate sentenced the people of Acoma as follows:

- "The males who are over twenty-five years of age I sentence to have one foot cut off and to twenty years of personal servitude."
- "The males between the ages of twelve and twenty-five I sentence likewise to twenty years of personal servitude."
- "The women over twelve years of age I sentence likewise to twenty years of personal servitude."
- "Two Indians from the province of Moqui (Hopi) who were present at the pueblo of Acoma and who fought and were apprehended, I sentence to have the right hand cut off and to be set free in order that they may convey to their land news of this punishment."
- "All the children under twelve years of age I declare free and innocent of the grave offense for which I punish their parents."

The "freed" girls were consigned to the care of the Franciscans who were allowed to "distribute" them anywhere within New Mexico or elsewhere as they saw fit. Sixty young Acoma girls ended up in Mexico City convents and never returned to their homeland. The governor gave the boys under twelve to Vicente de Zaldivar to raise them in the Christian faith. Old and disabled Acoma became the wards of the Querechos (Apaches) to be confined to their pueblos. No one was to return to Acoma until 1640. Some historians doubt that the sentence of cutting off the feet of the men occurred, but the Spanish record seems clear. In 1601, Captain Velasco, one of Oñate's officers, wrote to the Viceroy of New Spain that "Twenty-four Indians had their feet cut off as punishment; all those more than twenty years of age were taken as slaves ...."

Unfortunately, we don't have a contemporary Acoma account of this incident to present the Indian side of the hostilities. A recent posting on a Native American web site gives a current view of what occurred at Acoma and in the aftermath:

Native News Online--*De Oñate had little trouble with convincing the Pueblo and other nations to agree to render their submission, just as long as de Oñate agreed to leave quickly, once they had done so. As with other towns, the residents of Acoma did submit, but, at Acoma, de Oñate did not totally withdraw. Acoma was an impressive site, a larger settlement, and de Oñate decided to leave a nephew with a party of 12 soldiers at Acoma, after the ceremony. The cause has been lost in the mists of time, but the Pueblo killed this party. De Oñate quickly returned and took vengeance on the community. Over 100 Acoma warriors died, and sixty maidens were seized from the town and transported back to Mexico, where they served as slaves.*

The above statement, though clearly incorrect on the details of the sequence of events, and even on the magnitude of the carnage, reflects a sense of the Indian viewpoint more than 400 years later. The Acoma "submitted" ceremonially in the belief that it would lead to the Spaniards leaving more quickly. The killing, by inference, was a conscious act by the Acoma provoked by the Spanish occupation of their pueblo.

Modern-day Acoma Pueblo

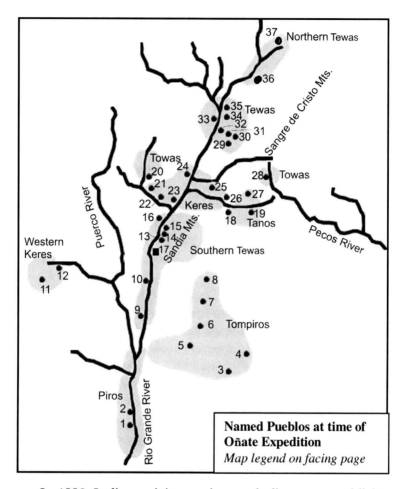

37 Northern Tewas

36

Sangre de Cristo Mts.

35 Tewas
34
33 • 32
32 • 31
29 •
30

Towas
24
20
21 23
22 25
Keres 26 • 27
16 18 • 19
15 Tanos
13 14

28 • Towas

Pecos River

Western
Keres

Puerco River

17 Southern Tewas

Sandia Mts.

12
11

10 • 8

9 • 7

6 Tompiros

5 •
4 •
3 •

Piros
2
1

Rio Grande River

**Named Pueblos at time of
Oñate Expedition**
Map legend on facing page

In 1998, Indian activists took a symbolic step to publicize their outrage over a twelve-foot high equestrian statue of the conquistador Oñate. Under the cover of darkness, Indians sawed off the right foot from the bronze statue, spurs, stirrup and all. They issued a press release saying, "We took the liberty of removing Oñate's right foot on behalf of our brothers and sisters of Acoma Pueblo. We see no glory in celebrating Oñate's fourth centennial, and we do not want our faces rubbed in it." From the Indian perspective, their ancestors submitted to Spanish aggression and oppression because they had no choice. In fact, in the seventeenth century, the pueblos would revolt against their Spanish overlords.

The map (page 266) showing the Pueblo Indian language groups at the time of the Oñate expedition gives a sense of the rich diversity and the extent of the population of the Rio Grande and tributary river valleys in the late sixteenth century. The individual pueblos keyed to this map are shown below. These named pueblos represent only a fraction of the cities, towns, and villages inhabited in the American Southwest at the time Oñate came to "conquer" Nuevo México.

1-Senecú	20-Jemez
2-Socorro	21-Zia
3-Jumano	22-Santa Ana
4-Tabira	23-San Felipe
5-Abo	24- Santo Domingo
6-Quarai	25-Cochiti
7-Tajique	26-San Marcos
8-Chililí	27-Galisteo
9-Belen	28-Cicuyé (Pecos)
10-Isleta	29-Tesuque
11-Acoma	30-Nambé
12-Laguna	31-Pojoaque
13-Alameda	32--San Ildefonso
14-Sandia	33- Santa Clara
15-Puaray	34- San Gabriel
16-Bernalillo	35- San Juan
17- City of Albuquerque, NM	36-Picuris
18-San Lazaro	37-Taos
19-San Cristobal	

Pueblos shown on Map

Oñate and his large expedition moved into the pueblo of Santo Domingo and then San Juan, displacing the Indians from their dwellings and seizing the foodstuffs stored in the pueblos. Spaniards and their servants took over many of the dwellings, forcing the Indians to seek shelter elsewhere. The Spaniards saw this as their god-given right as Christian overlords of those "bárbaros." The Indians saw the Spaniards as invaders, interlopers, occupiers of the land that was their heritage for as long as the people could remember. Spanish cattle roamed the countryside, altering the landscape and placing greatly increased demands for the maize that was their staple crop. No wonder the Indians resented the Spanish invasion. It is surprising that, in most cases, the Pueblo Indians resorted to passive resistance instead of outright warfare.

In 1601, one of Oñate's officers, Captain Velasco, wrote to the Viceroy of New Spain reporting on the state of affairs in New Mexico. He captured several key points that relate to the treatment of the Indians:

> *The system employed during this time to feed more than five hundred persons, men, women, and children, has been to send people out every month in various directions to bring maize from the pueblos. The feelings of the natives against supplying it cannot be exaggerated, for I give your lordship my word that they weep and cry out as if they and all their descendants were being killed. But in the end, necessity has compelled us to do this to keep from starving to death.*

At this point, the Spaniards had been unable to grow any crops of their own. On the other hand, Oñate saw no harm in allowing his large herd of horses to graze in the Indian's maize fields.

Captain Velasco also described an assault against the Jumano Pueblo about forty miles to the east of the Rio Grande resulting from the Indian's resistance to the Spanish demand for maize and blankets. Vicente de Zaldivar went to the Jumano Pueblo with seventy men to punish them for hiding their food. The Spaniards killed 900 Indians, burned and leveled their city, and took 200 away as prisoners.

Velasco wrote about the lack of honor in subduing the Pueblo Indians:

> *Even if thirty Spaniards should conquer all of the Indians that have been discovered, they would perform no great deed, for the Pueblo Indians are the most meek, humble, and timid people ever seen …. They are so simple that they tried to protect*

268

themselves against firearms by making shields from mats and from the little willow doors of their estufas and windows. Your lordship may well imagine how this treatment, entering their houses, taking their women, and causing them a thousand such annoyances and vexations, will incline them toward us and toward accepting baptisms and our holy Catholic faith.

We can see how the high-handed treatment of the Pueblo Indians, "meek and humble" though they might have been, would eventually lead to rebellion.

The governor had to deal first with rebellion among his own Spanish settlers. While he was away in 1601 living among the Plains Indians and searching for Quivira, a large number of the settlers deserted San Juan Pueblo and returned to Santa Bárbara in New Spain. When Oñate and Zaldivar returned from Quivira they found San Juan in an uproar. He sent Zaldivar in pursuit of the defectors, but they had too great a head start. The Viceroy sent reinforcements for Oñate's settlement so that it would endure.

Juan de Oñate accomplished more in the American Southwest than Pedro Menéndez de Avilés did in Florida. Oñate established the second permanent Spanish colony in North America, initially at San Juan Pueblo, then later in 1598 at the adjacent San Gabriel Pueblo.

Santa Fe, New Mexico
In 1608, the third Governor of New Mexico moved the Spanish capital twenty-five miles to a spot on the Santa Fe River. Governor Pedro de Peralta named the new capital La Villa Real de la Santa Fé de San Francisco de Asís, now Santa Fe, New Mexico.

Thus, New Mexico predates the first permanent English settlement in North America (Jamestown, Virginia) by nine years.

Oñate had other accomplishments in the southwest. At Zuni Pueblo in December, 1598, he sent Captain Marcos Farfán de los Godos and eight men on horseback to the Hopi to examine mines he had heard about. The Indians used the unprocessed minerals from the mines to paint their bodies in various colors. Farfán reported finding significant veins of ore, presumed to be silver based on its similar appearance to ore mined in Zacatecas. In February, Oñate had assays performed on the ore samples and found, "...this ore to be very rich for smelting." The assay produced a significant quantity of silver according to the official report.

As mentioned above, in 1601 Oñate traveled to Quivira in Kansas, inspecting the extensive Plains Indian settlement along the Arkansas River and confirming the death of Gutiérrez, the murderer of Bonilla; that accomplished one of the tasks given him by the viceroy. He made three attempts to reach the South Sea, finally succeeding in 1605 after traveling back to the Hopi territory and then following the Colorado River down to the Gulf of California. He had reached the Sea of Cortés, technically part of the "South Sea."

By 1606, defectors from New Mexico had told many tales of abuse, not only of the Indians but of the soldiers and settlers, attributed to Adelantado Oñate. The Viceroy, under orders from the king, recalled Juan de Oñate to Mexico City to answer charges of abuse and mismanagement. Cristóbal de Oñate assumed command as acting Governor of New Mexico in his father's absence. His father resigned in late 1607, and Cristóbal became the second Governor, but for only one year. Pedro de Peralta, the third Spanish governor of New Mexico, appointed by the Viceroy of New Spain, arrived at Santa Fe.

In 1613, Juan de Oñate was convicted: of using excessive force against the Acoma people; the unlawful hanging of two Indians, Spanish mutineers, and deserters; and adultery. His punishment included fines and banishment from New Mexico. He received some restitution of honor in Spain, being appointed as the King's mining inspector. He died in Spain thirteen years after his conviction for crimes committed in New Mexico.

Spanish rule would continue in New Mexico until the Louisiana Purchase ceded about half of the state to the United States in 1803. During the rest of the nineteenth century, Spanish control of the American southwest would dwindle. Texas fell to US control in 1836, and New Mexico, Arizona, and California fell even more easily. By the end of the nineteenth century, the US victory in the Spanish-American War sealed the present border and the southwest was politically part of the United States of America, although the culture remained Spanish in many respects.

Descendants of the original Spanish settlers who followed Oñate into New Mexico still retain their pride in Spanish conquest of the region. Native Americans still harbor less positive feelings about the "conquest" of a land that their ancestors had occupied for millennia. Hopefully, this history of La Florida honors both cultures.

Sources

The following books will provide the interested reader with the source of quotations in this book and additional reading on the subject of Spanish exploration and settlement attempts in North America in the sixteenth century.

The Spanish Settlements Within the Present Limits of the United States, 1513-1561, Woodbury Lowery, replica edition by Elibron Classics, 2006

The Spanish Settlements Within the Present Limits of the United States, Florida 1562-1574, Woodbury Lowery, replica edition by Elibron Classics, 2006

Pioneers of France in the New World, Francis Parkman, University of Nebraska Press, reprinted by Bison Books, 1996

The Journey and Ordeal of Cabeza de Vaca: His Account of the Disastrous First European Exploration of the American Southwest, Álvar Núñez Cabeza de Vaca, Dover Books Edition, translated and edited by Cyclone Covey, 2003

The De Soto Chronicles: De Soto to North America in 1539-1543, two volumes, Edited by Lawrence A. Clayton, Vernon James Knight, Jr., Edward C. Moore, University of Alabama Press, Tuscaloosa, 1993

Knights of Spain, Warriors of the Sun: Hernando de Soto and the South's Ancient Chiefdoms, Charles Hudson, University of Georgia Press, Athens, 1997

The Spanish Frontier in North America, David J. Weber, Yale University Press, New Haven, 1992

Cities of Gold, Douglas Preston, University of New Press, Albuquerque, 1992

"The Rediscovery of New Mexico," *Coronado Cuarto Centennial Publications, 1540-1940*, Volume III, Edited by George P. Hammond, University of New Mexico Press, Albuquerque, 1966

"Don Juan de Oñate: Colonizer of New Mexico 1595-1628," *Coronado Cuarto Centennial Publications, 1540-1940*, Volume V and VI, Edited by George P. Hammond, University of New Mexico Press, Albuquerque, 1953

A Voyage Long and Strange: Rediscovering the New World, Tony Horwitz, Henry Holt Company, New York, 2008

The Spanish Pioneers in United States History: Santa Elena, Spanish Settlements on the Atlantic Seaboard from Florida to Virginia, 1513 to 1607, Eloy J. Gallegos, Villagra Press, Knoxville, 1998

The Melungeons: The Resurrection of a Proud People, An Untold Story of Ethnic Cleansing in America, N. Brent Kennedy with Robyn Vaughan Kennedy, Mercer University Press, Macon, 1997

Malungu: The African Origin of the American Melungeons, Tim Hashaw, Electra Magazine, Volume 5, No. 3, July/August 2001

Image Credits

P. 4   Indian village in North Carolina in 1586, engraving by Theodore de Bry after painting by John White, *Das sechste Theil Americae oder Der Historien Hieron. Benzo das dritte Buch. Darinnen erzehlet wirt, wie die Spanier die ... Landschafften dess peruauischen [sic] Königreichs eingenommen ... Sampt einem kurtzen ... Tractätein von den glückhafftigen Inseln. Mit ... Erklärungen ... Auch einer Landtaffel dess peruanischen Königreichs. Alles mit Kupfferstücken vorgebildet vnd an Tag geben durch Dieterich von Bry,* 1619, Library of Congress, the Kraus Collection of Sir Francis Drake, Digital ID rdbk d0321_0844.

P. 5   Zuni Pueblo ca. 1903, photograph by Edward S. Curtis, Curtis Collection, Library of Congress Prints and Photographs Division, Digital ID 3c02038.

P. 6   Baskets in the Painted Cave-Yokuts, by Edward S. Curtis, Curtis Collection, Library of Congress Prints and Photographs Division, Digital ID 3c18769.

P. 8   Scalps and other trophies of war, *Das sechste Theil Americae oder Der Historien Hieron, etc.,* Library of Congress, the Kraus Collection of Sir Francis Drake, Digital ID rdbk d0321_0844.

P. 11   A barbacoa in Florida, ibid.

P. 12   Women captives, ibid.

P. 16   Christopher Columbus Portrait, ibid.

P. 19   Map of La Florida and New Spain, by author.

P. 21   Ponce de León Portrait, from *Die illustrierte neue welt,* by John Ledyard Denison, 1858, Library of Congress, Prints and Photographs Division, Digital ID 3a06688.

P. 23   Map of Ponce de León's first voyage to La Florida, by author.

P. 26   Ponce de León Memorial at Catedral de San Juan Bautista, photograph by author.

P. 28   Vasco Núñez de Balboa Portrait, Wikipedia, from *Vasco Núñez de Balboa,* by Frederick A Ober, 1906.

P. 29   Balboa's war dogs attack the Quarequa, *Das sechste Theil Americae oder Der Historien Hieron, etc.*, Library of Congress, the Kraus Collection of Sir Francis Drake, Digital ID rdbk d0321_0844.

P. 30   Balboa claims the South Sea, lithograph by Gebbie & Co., 1893, Library of Congress, Prints and Photographs Division, Digital ID 3a06600.

P. 31   Hernán Cortés, engraving by W. Holl, Library of Congress, Prints and Photographs Division, Digital ID 3a34023.

P. 34   Map of Pineda's Settlement at Río Pánuco, by author.

P. 35   Map of the United States showing Winyah Bay and Sapelo Sound, by author.

P. 39   Pánfilo de Narváez Portrait, artist unknown, Wikipedia Commons, public domain.

P. 41   Map of Narváez route, by author.

P. 45   Timucuan Indian village in Florida, *Das sechste Theil Americae oder Der Historien Hieron, etc.*, Library of Congress, the Kraus Collection of Sir Francis Drake, Digital ID rdbk d0321_0844.

P. 53   Map of Cabeza de Vaca's route, by author.

P. 68   Map of Fray Marcos's route to Cibola, by author.

P. 71   Zuni Pueblo ca. 1903, Zuni Pueblo ca. 1903, photograph by Edward S. Curtis, Curtis Collection, Library of Congress Prints and Photographs Division, Digital ID 3c02037.

P. 72   Hernando de Soto Portrait, engraving by J. Maca, Library of Congress Prints and Photographs Division, Digital ID 3a04299.

P. 79   Map of De Soto's route from Havana to Anhayca, by author.

P. 97   Map of De Soto's route from Anhayca to Mabila, by author.

P. 99   Queen on a canopied litter, *Das sechste Theil Americae oder Der Historien Hieron, etc.*, Library of Congress, the Kraus Collection of Sir Francis Drake, Digital ID rdbk d0321_0844.

P. 113 Map of De Soto's route from Mabila to Guachoya, by author.

P. 121 Romantic but highly inaccurate depiction of De Soto at the Mississippi, from *The American Continent and its inhabitants before its discovery by Columbus,* by Annie C. Cady, Gebbie & Co., 1893, Library of Congress Prints and Photographs Division, Digital ID 3a06597.

P. 128 Map of Moscoso's route into the Southwest, by author.

P. 132 Map of Moscoso's voyage to New Spain, by author.

P. 140 Map of Coronado's route to Cibola, by author.

P. 142 Coronado leading his detachment to Cibola, by Frederic Remington, 1897, Library of Congress Prints and Photographs Division, Digital ID 3a38351.

P. 147 Hopi Pueblo ca. 1906, photograph by Edward S. Curtis, Curtis Collection, Library of Congress Prints and Photographs Division, Digital ID 3a47119.

P. 149 Map of Coronado's route from Hawikuh (Cibola) to Pecos (Cicuyé), by author.

P. 153 Map of Coronado's route from Pecos (Cicuyé) to Quivira, by author.

P. 155 Apache Man ca. 1905, photograph by Edward S. Curtis, Curtis Collection, Library of Congress Prints and Photographs Division, Digital ID 3c12206.

P. 156 Plains Indian wickiup dwelling ca. 1903, photograph by Edward S. Curtis, Curtis Collection, Library of Congress Prints and Photographs Division, Digital ID 3c01173.

P. 157 Coronado's and De Soto's men came within 300 miles of each other, map by author.

P. 160 Map of New Spain ca. 1539, by author.

P. 165 Pedro de Alvarado Portrait, artist unknown, Wikipedia Commons.

P. 165 Juan Rodríguez Cabrillo Portrait, from a sixteenth-century oil painting, Wikipedia Commons.

P. 167 Map of Cabrillo/Ferrelo voyage, by author.

P. 170 Viceroy Luís de Velasco Portrait, artist unknown, Wikipedia Commons.

P. 171 Map of Bazares route, by author.

P. 173 Map of Arellano's city of Puerto de Santa Maria, by author.

P. 180 Map of Villafane's voyage, by author.

P. 186 Map of Jesuit Mission at Ajacán (Chesapeake Bay area), by author.

P. 187 Murder of Father Segura, *Das sechste Theil Americae oder Der Historien Hieron, etc.*, Library of Congress, the Kraus Collection of Sir Francis Drake, Digital ID rdbk d0321_0844.

P. 190 First landing of the French in Florida, ibid.

P. 191 Timucuan Indian shows Laudonniere the column erected by Ribault, ibid.

P. 192 Map showing the route of the Spanish treasure fleet through the Bahama Channel, by author.

P. 194 Fort Caroline, *Das sechste Theil Americae oder Der Historien Hieron, etc.*, Library of Congress, the Kraus Collection of Sir Francis Drake, Digital ID rdbk d0321_0844.

P. 195 Pedro Menéndez de Aviles Portrait, by Francisco de Paula Martí, 1791, Library of Congress Prints and Photographs Division, Digital ID 3c02263.

P. 197 Saint Augustine with fortifications, derived from St. Augustine map, Wikipedia Commons.

P. 198 Map of Florida, Georgia, and South Carolina showing settlements by Menéndez, by author.

P. 207 Illustration of planting the cross, derived from an illustration in *Das sechste Theil Americae oder Der Historien Hieron, etc.*, Library of Congress, the Kraus Collection of Sir Francis Drake, Digital ID rdbk d0321_0844.

P. 213 Indians murder priest, ibid.

P. 221 Map of the Juan Pardo expedition, by author.

P. 229 Map of early Melungeon lands, by author.

P. 233 Sir Francis Drake Portrait, engraving by W. Hall, Library of Congress Prints and Photographs Division, Digital ID 3a38830.

P. 234 Sir Francis Drake's Landing in New Albion, author unknown, 1590, Wikipedia Commons.

P. 238 Map of Chamuscado/Rodríguez route, by author.

Index

A

Abo Pueblo, 267
Acoma Pueblo, 149, 240, 243, 244, 258, 259, 260, 261, 262, 263, 264, 265, 266, 267, 270, 278
Act of Obedience and Vassalage, 254, 256
Adelantado, 39, 40, 64, 66, 74, 76, 77, 78, 110, 126, 171, 195, 201, 202, 204, 205, 206, 207, 209, 210, 211, 212, 213, 214, 215, 217, 219, 251, 253, 254, 256, 257, 258, 260, 262, 270
Africa, 3, 15, 17, 59, 67, 217
Aguacay, 128, 129
Ajacán, 184, 186, 187, 189, 225, 277
Alabama, 10, 55, 107, 108, 175, 215, 272
Alabama River, 55, 107, 175, 215
Alameda Pueblo, 267
Alaminos, Antonio de, 23, 33
Alarcón, Hernando de, 161, 162, 163
Albuquerque, New Mexico, 149, 240, 241, 242, 258, 267, 273
Alcaraz, Diego de, 63
Alibamo, 115, 118, 119, 120
Allegheny Mountains, 227
Almadén, Mexico, 245
Almanza, Martín Enríquez de, 238
Altamaha, 96
Alvarado, Pedro de, 74, 134, 149, 150, 164, 165, 166, 276
Amazons, 161
American Historical Society, i
Aminoya, 130, 131
Añasco, Juan de, 74, 77, 79, 80, 81, 90, 91, 98, 118, 119, 124, 125, 127, 133, 134
Angola, 230
Anhayca, 88, 89, 90, 91, 92, 95, 96, 98, 275

Anilco, 123, 124
Anna Maria Island, Florida, 80
Antelope Mesa, 146
Antillia, see Seven Cities, 135, 136
Anunciacion, Fray, 177, 179
Apache, 141, 154, 249, 257, 264, 276
Apafalaya, 114
Apalachee, 44, 46, 48, 49, 50, 86, 87, 88, 90, 91, 92, 93, 94, 95, 96, 101, 106, 126, 134, 171, 173, 189, 216
Apalachee Bay, 90, 171, 173, 189
Apalachicola Bay, 51, 52, 90, 95
Apalachicola River, 48, 49, 51, 52, 90, 95
Appalachian Mountains, 226
Appomatock, 228
Arabic, 135, 229, 231
Aragon, 16, 27
Arawak, 18
Archaeologist, 13, 89, 156, 174, 232
Arellano, Tristán de Luna y, 155, 157, 172, 173, 174, 175, 176, 177, 178, 179, 181, 182, 183, 221, 224, 277
Argentina, 66
Aristotle, 14
Arizona, 61, 68, 140, 146, 162, 163, 243, 251, 271, 278
Arkansas, 122, 123, 124, 128, 155, 270
Arkansas River, 122, 123, 124, 155, 270
Armor, iv, 49, 51, 82, 104, 110, 112, 117, 130, 138, 144, 175, 178, 206
Arthur, Gabriel, 227
Ashiwi, 146, 148
Asia, 2, 3, 15, 16, 17, 18, 169
Astrolabe, 133
Asturias, Spain, 220, 225
Asunción, Paraguay, 66
Atahachi, 107, 108

Felipe, King of Spain, 184, 190, 242

Ferdinand II, King of Aragon, 16, 17, 22, 27

Feria, Fray Pedro de, 173, 179

Fernández, Beníto, 97

Ferrelo (Ferrer), Bartolomé, 168, 169, 276

Figucroa, Gómez Suárez de aka Garcilaso de la Vega, the Inca, 75

Flores, Pedro, 225

Florida, i, ii, iii, 10, 11, 23, 24, 25, 26, 33, 34, 35, 39, 41, 42, 43, 45, 46, 47, 50, 54, 65, 66, 74, 77, 78, 79, 80, 81, 83, 84, 95, 111, 125, 169, 171, 172, 174, 181, 184, 187, 189, 190, 193, 195, 196, 197, 199, 200, 201, 202, 203, 204, 207, 208, 212, 213, 215, 216, 217, 218, 219, 269, 272, 273, 274, 275, 277

Florida Keys, 24, 33, 79

Flota, annual treasure fleet, 216

Fort Caroline, 193, 194, 195, 196, 197, 202, 216, 217, 277

Fort Coligny, 189

Fort San Marcos, see Fort San Felipe, 225, 235

Fort San Mateo, 198, 202, 203, 207, 217

Fort San Pablo, 224, 225

Fort San Pedro, see Chiaha, 224

Fort Santiago, see Guatari, 222

Fort Smith, Arkansas, 122

Fort Yuma, Arizona, 162, 163

France, 28, 183, 184, 189, 190, 192, 193, 196, 198, 199, 203, 216, 217, 218, 272

Franciscans, 40, 67, 137, 159, 239, 241, 243, 251, 254, 257, 260, 264

French, ii, 37, 40, 47, 64, 67, 71, 181, 183, 189, 191, 192, 193, 195, 196, 197, 198, 199, 200, 202, 203, 208, 215, 216, 217, 222, 223, 228, 229, 232, 233, 234, 277

French Broad River, 103, 223

Frobisher, Martin, 234

G

Galicia, Spain, 220, 225

Galisteo Pueblo, 267

Galiuro Mountains, 141

Gallegos, Juan, 145, 158

Gallegos, Baltasar de, 74, 82, 83, 84, 98, 109, 110, 114, 116, 126, 273

Gallegos, Hernán, 241

Gallinas River, 246

Gallinas, New Mexico, 246

Galveston, Texas, 56, 59

Galway, Ireland, 17

Garay, Francisco de, 33, 34

Garcilaso de la Vega, the Inca aka Gómez Suárez de Figueroa, 75, 85, 93, 96, 101, 111, 112, 114, 119, 120, 134, 215

Genoa, 15, 18

Georgia, 38, 97, 172, 183, 208, 227, 272, 277

Ghana, Africa, 17

Gila River, 141

Gilbert, Sir Humphrey, 234

Glorieta Pass, 249

Gold, v, vi, 3, 7, 14, 20, 21, 29, 30, 31, 44, 45, 46, 49, 50, 63, 65, 66, 67, 68, 69, 72, 73, 74, 78, 84, 85, 91, 95, 100, 103, 112, 122, 125, 128, 134, 135, 137, 144, 145, 147, 148, 150, 152, 153, 155, 161, 164, 181, 185, 193, 201, 205, 216, 233, 234, 241, 247, 248, 249, 251, 253, 255

Gomes, Estevâo, 37

Gordilla, Francisco, 35, 36

Gorget, 7, 102, 155

Gourges, Dominique de, 217, 218

Granada, Spain, 21

Grand Canyon, 148

Great Abaco Island, 23

Great Plains, 4, 154, 257

Great Smoky Mountains, 223

288

CPSIA information can be obtained at www.ICGtesting.com
Printed in the USA
BVOW071710200812

298293BV00001B/7/P